The Role of Media in Promoting Regional Understanding in South Asia

The Role of Media in Promoting Regional Understanding in South Asia

Editor

Priyanka Singh

idsa

INSTITUTE FOR DEFENCE STUDIES & ANALYSES
NEW DELHI

PENTAGON PRESS

The Role of Media in Promoting Regional Understanding in South Asia
Editor: Priyanka Singh

First Published in 2016

ISBN 978-81-8274-868-2

Disclaimer: The views expressed in this book are those of the authors and do not necessarily reflect those of the Institute for Defence Studies and Analyses, or the Government of India.

Published by
PENTAGON PRESS
206, Peacock Lane, Shahpur Jat,
New Delhi-110049
Phones: 011-64706243, 26491568
Telefax: 011-26490600
email: rajan@pentagonpress.in
website: www.pentagonpress.in

Branch
Flat No.213, Athena-2,
Clover Acropolis,
Viman Nagar,
Pune-411014
Email: pentagonpresspune@gmail.com

In association with
Institute for Defence Studies and Analyses
No. 1, Development Enclave,
New Delhi-110010
Phone: +91-11-26717983
Website: www.idsa.in

Printed at Aegean Offset Printers, Greater Noida, U.P.

Contents

PART II
THE STATE OF MEDIA IN SOUTH ASIA: COUNTRY PERSPECTIVES

PART III
INFLUENCE OF MEDIA ON FOREIGN AND SECURITY POLICIES OF STATES

Foreword

The Institute for Defence Studies and Analyses has been hosting South Asia Conference aimed at strengthening regional cooperation and understanding, for the last eight years. The conference (also called dialogue) has received overwhelming response over the years and has evolved into an effective platform for healthy exchange of ideas and alternatives at the Track II level. The last seven dialogues focussed on issues such as *economic integration, regional understanding on terrorism, evolving a framework of cooperative security, stability and growth, perceptions on India's role*, etc.

The 8th South Asia Dialogue was held on October 28-29, 2014 on the theme: *"The Role of Media in Promoting Regional Understanding in South Asia"*. Eminent experts and scholars from the South Asian countries including Myanmar participated in this Dialogue. The Dialogue provided an opportunity to deliberate on the significant role played by the media in shaping public opinion in different countries of South Asia and explored the ways in which it can strengthen regional integration efforts.

The present book edited by Dr. Priyanka Singh, Associate Fellow at IDSA, is a collection of papers presented at the 8th South Asia Dialogue. It draws upon in-depth understanding and well-researched narratives from a cross-section of policy makers, academics, civil society actors and young media professionals from the whole of South Asian Region and Myanmar. The book endeavours to put across a confluence of ideas and shared reflection on issues of common interest.

Today, the media has a crucial role to play in shaping as well as influencing national and international affairs. It has the power to create disharmony as well as dispel disharmony. Through balanced reporting, media has the ability to impact interstate relations to a great extent. In the South Asian context, where interstate relations have been a hostage of historical prejudices, media has even greater role to play in creating an atmosphere of trust and understanding among people and governments across the frontiers of the state. In this context, it is timely to explore the role media can play in enabling the process of regional cooperation, which has not been exploited for common good. The deliberations in the conference opened up a new vista of understanding pertaining to the way media is operating in different countries of the region, and the way it can be harnessed for promoting trust and understanding at the regional level.

It is hoped that besides serving the academia and policy makers, the book will be of immense interest to media community. It would help policy makers to understand the positive role media can play in strengthening inter-state relationship given its reach and power to shape public discourse. At the same time, it will also be useful to the media persons in the region to analyse and introspect their role in creating positive or negative impact on interstate relations. The final message that the book conveys is unexceptionable—the media can, and must, play its due role in enhancing interstate trust and creating the conditions for enhanced regional cooperation in South Asia.

I commend Dr. Priyanka Singh for bringing out a timely and useful account based on regional perspectives regarding media and its prospective contribution towards better integration and enhanced cooperation.

New Delhi

Brig. Rumel Dahiya, SM (Retd.)
Deputy Director General
Institute for Defence Studies and Analyses

Acknowledgements

The present book emanates from the proceedings of the 8th South Asia Dialogue (October 28-29, 2014) held at the Institute for Defence Studies and Analyses, New Delhi. Events and conferences at IDSA have always been a team effort. The South Asia Dialogue 2014 was no exception. Therefore, it is a pleasant duty to express my sincere thanks to each and every one involved in the seamless and successful organization of the Dialogue.

I wish to register immense gratitude to Brigadier Rumel Dahiya (Retd.), Deputy Director General, IDSA, for having reposed faith and entrusting me with this huge responsibility. During the entire process, thick and thin, his unstinted support and guidance inspired and enabled me to put together one of IDSA's major calendar events. I also wish to thank Dr. Arvind Gupta, formerly Director General, IDSA, and presently, Deputy National Security Advisor, Government of India, who was keenly involved in the process till a certain stage. My Centre Coordinator, Dr. Ashok K. Behuria has been the driving force behind this whole effort. I am indebted to him not only for his unwavering support in organizing the Dialogue, but also, for his out of the way help in bringing out this edited volume. My senior colleague, Dr. Smruti S. Pattanaik, offered invaluable help since the early stage of coordination. She generously facilitated finding suitable resource persons including few eminent chairpersons and was by my side in every moment of anxiety. I must acknowledge the guidance and support from Dr. Ajey Lele, Assistant Director, IDSA, in organizing the Dialogue.

I am grateful to the eminent set of chairpersons—Professor S.D. Muni, Mr. Prem Shankar Jha, Mr. Vinod Sharma, Commodore (Retd.) C. Uday Bhaskar and Dr. Chandan Mitra who moderated various sessions of the dialogue smoothly. My heartfelt thanks to participants from all the South Asian countries including India, and Myanmar for having being able to come and participate in the Dialogue and render it much meaning and significance.

I wish to extend special gratitude to my colleagues at IDSA's South Asia Centre: Ms. Sumita Kumar, Dr. Anand Kumar, Dr. Nihar Nayak, Ms. Gulbin Sultana, Dr. Yaqoob ul Hassan and Mr. Hrishabh Sandilya for lending precious help in coordination and rapporteuring during the Dialogue. I want to sincerely thank my friends and colleagues involved with the event in various capacities: Dr. Prasanta K. Pradhan, Dr. Saurabh Mishra, Mr. Avinash A. Godbole, Mr. Rajorshi Roy, Dr. Saroj Bishoyi, Mr. Nachiket Khadkiwala, Mr. Amit Kumar, Mr. Sanjeev Shrivastava, Mr. Sanket Sudhir Kulkarni, Mr. Satyam Malviya, Dr. Titli Basu, Dr. Sampa Kundu, Dr. Pranamita Baruah, Ms. Rajbala Rana and Ms. Kuhoo Saxena. I am thankful to the Conference Cell, especially Ms. Ameeta Narang for her kind help and cooperation, the staff in the office of the Director General, Deputy Director General, the Systems Cell, the Establishment Cell and the Estate Cell. Last but not least, I wish to thank all IDSA colleagues for their best wishes in this endeavour.

Mr. Vivek Kaushik, Associate Editor, *Strategic Analysis*, deftly coordinated the publication process and offered valuable advice in the preparation of the manuscript. Mr. Ram Mohan did an excellent job in transcribing the various sessions of the Dialogue. I am grateful to Mr. Rajan Arya, his staff at the Pentagon Press and Mr. Virender Negi who invested great deal of hard work and initiative in ensuring timely publication of the book.

New Delhi **Priyanka Singh**

Abbreviations

AJSC	Afghan Journalists' Safety Committee
AM	Amplitude Modulation
ASEAN	Association of Southeast Asian Nations
BBC	British Broadcasting Corporation
BIMSTEC	Bengal Initiative for Multi-sectorial Technical and Economic Cooperation
BJP	Bharatiya Janata Party
BTV	Bangladesh Television
CASA 1000	Central Asia South Asia Electricity and Trade Projects
CNN-IBN	Cable News Network–Indian Broadcasting Network
DW	Deutsche Welle
EU	European Union
FES	Freidrich Ebert Stiftung
FM	Frequency Modulation
GDP	Gross Domestic Product
GNP	Gross National Product
IMS	International Media Support
ISAF	International Security Assistance Force
MEA	Ministry of External Affairs
MGC	Mekong-Ganga Cooperation
NATO	North Atlantic Treaty Organization

NDTV	New Delhi Television
PMO	Prime Minister's Office
RFA	Radio Free Asia
RSF	Reporters Sans Frontières
SAARC	South Asian Association for Regional Cooperation
SAFMA	South Asian Free Media Association
SIC	SAARC Information Centre
TAPI	Turkmenistan-Afghanistan-Pakistan-India
TRP	Television Rating Point
TV	Television
UK	United Kingdom
UPA	United Progressive Alliance
US	United States
USAID	United States Agency for International Development
VOA	Voice of America

About the Contributors

Smruti S. Pattanaik at present is Research Fellow at the IDSA. She joined IDSA in 1998. Her area of specialisation is South Asia. Her current research project focuses on "Federalising India's Neighbourhood Policy: Role of States". She has been a recipient of many international fellowships. She was a visiting Asia fellow (Asian Scholarship Foundation, Bangkok) at the Department of International Relations, Dhaka University in 2004. In 2007, she was also selected for a follow up study grant by the Asian Scholarship Foundation to research on politics of identity in Bangladesh She was also awarded the Kodikara fellowship in 1999 (RCSS, Colombo). As a Postdoctoral Fellow at MSH (Fondation Maison des Science de l'Homme), and the Centre for International Relations and Research (CERI, Science Po), Paris, she conducted research on "Broadening Consensus in Fighting Religious Militancy, Terrorism: Can Democracy in Pakistan Ensure Regional Stability". In addition, she was a Visiting Fellow (September-October 2011) at the International Peace Research Institute, Oslo (PRIO) and worked on "Afghanistan: Need for a Regional Approach". She was a Visiting Professor on ICCR's India Chair at the University of Colombo for a semester in 2013.

Ashok K. Behuria is Research Fellow and Coordinator of South Asia Centre at the Institute for Defence Studies and Analyses (IDSA). He is a Ph.D. in International Relations from Jawaharlal Nehru University, New Delhi, India. He has published many research articles on strategic issues related to South Asian security situation in Indian and foreign journals. He has edited books on South Asia and continues with his research on the need for regional and inter-state cooperation to unleash the collective potential for growth and prosperity for states in the region.

Rasul Bakhsh Rais has a Ph.D. in Political Science from the University of California, Santa Barbara. Before joining LUMS (Lahore University of Management Sciences), he served as Professor/Director, Area Study Centre and prior to that as Associate Professor in the Department of International Relations, Quaid-i-Azam University, Islamabad for nearly 22 years. He was a Professor of Pakistan Studies at Columbia University, New York for 3 years, 1991-94. He was awarded the Fulbright fellowship at Wake Forest University, 1997-98, Social Science Research Fellowship at Harvard, 1989-90, Rockefeller Foundation fellowship in International Relations at the University of California, Berkeley, 1985-85. He is author of *Recovering the Frontier State: War, Ethnicity and State in Afghanistan* (Lanham: Lexington Books, and Oxford University Press, 2008), *War without Winners: Afghanistan's Uncertain Transition after the Cold War* (Oxford University Press, 1996), *Indian Ocean and the Superpowers: Economic, Political and Strategic Perspectives* (Croom Helm, London, 1986) and editor of *State, Society and Democratic Change in Pakistan* (Oxford University Press, 1997).

Syed Badrul Ahsan is currently Associate Editor, *The Daily Observer*. Ahsan's career began with teaching English language and literature at various schools, notably Greenherald and Scholastica, in Dhaka between the late 1970s and early 1980s. He then joined Notre Dame College as lecturer in English and while engaged there began to write articles on international affairs for newspapers in Bangladesh. Ahsan's entry into journalism came through the *New Nation* newspaper, which he joined as assistant editor in 1983. In subsequent years, he moved on to such newspapers as the *Morning Sun*, the *Bangladesh Observer*, *The Independent*, *News Today* and *New Age*. He was also associated with the weekly *Dhaka Courier*. At all these organisations, Ahsan contributed editorials, post-editorials on national, regional and global issues, articles on the arts and book reviews. He joined the *Daily Star* as editor, current affairs, in January 2007. He was appointed executive editor of the newspaper in October 2011. His responsibilities at the *Daily Star* include writing editorials and a weekly column. Ahsan has had a stint in diplomacy as minister press at the Bangladesh High Commission, London, from 1997 to 2000. He has been associated with the South Asian Free Media Association (SAFMA).

Amrullah Saleh was born in the Panjshir Province of Afghanistan in 1972. He is an ethnic Tajik. In the late 1990s, in his early 20s, Amrullah Saleh resisted the Taliban regime along with the United Front under the command of Ahmad Shah Massoud. In 1997, Saleh was appointed by Ahmad Shah Massoud to lead the United Front's international liaison office at the Embassy of Afghanistan in Dushanbe, Tajikistan, where he served as a coordinator for non-governmental (humanitarian) organizations and as a liaison partner for foreign intelligence agencies. After the September 11, 2001 attacks against the United States, Amrullah Saleh participated in leading intelligence operations of the United Front on the ground during the War in Afghanistan (2001–present) toppling the Taliban regime. After the creation of the Islamic Republic of Afghanistan, Saleh was appointed to head Department One of Afghanistan's main intelligence agency, the National Directorate of Security (NDS). The duties of Department One included liaison with foreign military, diplomatic, and intelligence organizations. In 2004, Amrullah Saleh was appointed as the head of the NDS by the then President Hamid Karzai. In June 2010, Saleh resigned from his position and subsequently founded the Baseej-i-Milli (National Mobilization) and Green Trend as a pro-democracy and anti-Taliban movement and is running it until now.

Kunda Dixit is Editor/Publisher of the *Nepali Times*. He has a Master's degree from Columbia Journalism School, New York (1985) in Journalism. He is also a Visiting Faculty at the Department of Media and Communications in Kathmandu University 2006-present. He is the co-publisher of Himalmedia from 1995-present where he is overseeing management, marketing, and planning for the group's four publications including *Himal Khabarpatrika*, Nepal's most widely-read Nepali language magazine and *Nepali Times*, the country's foremost English publication. Earlier, he was Director, Panos Institute South Asia, Kathmandu (1996-99), Regional Director, Inter Press Service, Asia-Pacific (1990-95), Regional Editor for Inter Press Service (1986-89) and BBC News Reporter at the United Nations, New York (1984-86). His publications include: *Bikas-Binas* (Development-Destruction), co-edited with Ludmilla Tuting Geo-Buch Verlag, Munich 1985, *Funny Side Up*, Frying Pan Publications Kathmandu 1985 (collection of satire columns) and *A People War* (pictorial retrospective of the ten years of conflict in Nepal) Nepalaya, Kathmandu 2006.

Dilrukshi Handunnetti is a multiple award-winning journalist who counts over two decades of mainstream journalism. A lawyer by training, she has specialized in investigative reporting, in addition to international affairs, parliamentary/political reporting and column writing. In the recent years, she has tabled in reporting and analysing South Asian affairs with strong focus falling on Indo-Sri Lanka relations. In addition to holding a senior position with the *Ceylon Today* newspaper, she contributes to a number of international outlets including Integrated Regional Information Network (IRIN), Reuters Alertnet, SciDevNet, Himal Southasian and Down to Earth. She won the Mervyn de Silva Journalist of the Year – 2012 Award for excellence in journalism. Besides writing, Handunnetti continues to find time to lecture and train journalists, here and abroad.

Ibrahim Waheed has worked with the Maldivian Government and as a statesman for 32 years in jobs and assignments including functioning as: Teacher, Majeediyya School, Maldives, Educational Director as Non-Formal Head (and Founder) of Department of Public Examinations and Director/ Director General, Ministry of Information. He has a degree in English Language/Linguistics, from the American University of Beirut, Lebanon, and has a Certificate in Educational Assessment and Certificate in Information Technology, Cambridge, UK. Amongst his political and state assignments, Ibrahim Waheed has been Member, Advisory Council to the President of the Republic, Official Government Spokesperson (first ever), Deputy Minister of Finance and Treasury and Commissioner of Elections. He has been a presenter at Television Maldives on part-time basis and also Member of National Center for Linguistics and Historical Research. He has been Government/Country Representative at various international conferences, meetings and workshops. He is the co-Founder and Executive of 'Ecocare Maldives', one of the largest environmental NGO's in the Maldives. He has been regularly contributing to many dailies/periodicals in the Maldives and won various national and international awards including India's Sahitya Akademi Munshi Premchand Fellowship Award in 2008 and the SAARC Literary Award in 2011 (in the area of Creative Writing).

Kaberi Gayen is a Professor of Mass Communication and Journalism in the University of Dhaka, Bangladesh. She graduated from the University of Dhaka, and obtained her PhD from Edinburgh Napier University, UK in 2004. Her areas of interest include: Critical Theory of Media; Analysis of Social Network and Social Capital; Gender; and Film Theory. She has written extensively in scholarly academic journals, and has delivered lectures in numerous academic seminars and conferences worldwide. She has visited many countries as visiting research fellow and visiting professor. She is the author of two books: *Modelling Influences of Communication* (2009), and *Construction of Women in the War Films of Bangladesh* (2013).

Tenzing Lamsang is the Editor-in-Chief of the *The Bhutanese*—a newspaper committed to serious journalism and aims to influence public opinion and government policy. After graduating from St. Stephen's College (Delhi University) with History Honours in 2006, he worked as a reporter in *The Indian Express* newspaper in New Delhi from 2006-2008. Between 2008 and 2010, Tenzing joined Bhutan's national newspaper *Kuensel* as the Chief Reporter. From 2010 to mid-2011, he was the News Editor of Bhutan's first Business Paper *Business Bhutan* which he left afterwards to launch *The Bhutanese*. He won Bhutan's best investigative journalist award in 2010. *The Bhutanese* has been at the forefront of the Bhutanese media breaking not only some of the biggest stories but also delving into several sensitive issues. Tenzing Lamsang is interested in issues of corruption, good governance, economy and business, and strategic issues. As a journalist, he has done several in-depth stories strengthening the democratic and intellectual discourse in Bhutan. He is also a member of the SAARC think tank on Right to Information.

Myo Lwin has a career spanning 13 years as a journalist at the *Myanmar Times* weekly business journal. His duties include: making yearly plan and production of special publications such as sector surveys/special report and country features of embassy anniversaries. His work profile requires multi-tasking involving story writing, translating, editing, page layouts, etc. He has additional 11 years' experience as a reporter cum assistant editor with the state newspaper *The Working People's Daily* (now the *New Light of Myanmar*) where his duties include feature writing, translation and page layouts for international news.

Danish Karokhel is the founding Director of *Pajhwok Afghan News*. In his eight year stint, he has been responsible for the agency's vision and direction; daily production of high quality news stories, photos, and multimedia in three languages for a wide Afghan audience, international media, wire services, diplomats, researchers and government ministries; the creation of a sustainable revenue stream; and the professional development of *Pajhwok* journalists. *Pajhwok* is committed to promoting human rights, holding government officials and elite accountable to the Afghan people, and fostering greater participation in national life. Danish Karokhel's career as a journalist began in 1997 when he reported for a series of newspapers published in Pakistan. With a deep understanding of the significance of independent media to Afghanistan's future, he returned to his country after the fall of the Taliban to report on the war for local and international media organizations. In addition to leading *Pajhwok*, Danish is a member of several regional leadership initiatives and a regular speaker at conferences on behalf of the Afghan media especially regarding development of journalistic capacity. He won the International Press Freedom Award of the Committee to Protect Journalists (CPJ) in 2008 and the Press Freedom Whiting Award (2012) from South Asian Free Media Association (SAFMA). In May 2014, Danish Karokhel has been included in the first-ever list of 100 information heroes by Reporters without Borders—also known as RSF.

Shruti Pandalai is a media professional understanding India's policy challenges at IDSA. She has been a Television Journalist—a News Anchor and Senior Correspondent—with TIMES NOW, a 24 hour English News network by the Times of India group, since its inception till 2009. Part of the core editorial team, she tracked both national politics and international affairs. An academic sabbatical led to her pursuing an MA in International Studies and Diplomacy at SOAS, University of London. Here International Security, Diplomacy, South Asian area studies were key research interests. Her research paper at SOAS investigated the role of the media as an "agenda setter" in the process of policy formulation and has evolved into a larger project at IDSA. This project looks at the Role of Media and Perceptions in India's Strategic Thought and Practice. "Who Sets the Agenda? Does Prime Time Really Pace Policy? The Indian Experience", IDSA Monograph Series (2013) was the first culmination of this project. The Rise of New Media and its Impact on National Security is also a theme she works on currently and is working on project for the Ministry of Home Affairs. Great power politics, India's neighbourhood relations and scenario forecasting are her other key research interests.

Lakshman F.B. Gunasekara is a professional journalist, political analyst, social activist and, communications consultant in a range of social action areas including gender issues advocacy, environment and disaster management, and, ethnic conflict resolution. Formerly Chief Editor of the *Sunday Observer* newspaper (1999-2004), he now free-lances while serving as the Sri Lanka Correspondent for *The Yomiuri Shimbun* newspaper of Japan (since 1992).

Beginning his journalism career in 1978 in the *Sun/Weekend* newspapers, Sri Lanka, he later served as News Editor in *The Island* and *Sunday Island* newspapers before joining the founding team of *The Sunday Leader* newspaper as its first news editor. In the early stages of the ethnic war, Lakshman Gunasekara studied ethnic bias in the Sri Lankan news media in a research project with the Marga Institute (1981-84). More recently, he was coordinator/ editor of *Vimarsanam-Vimansaa*, a website monitoring the post-war reconciliation process in Sri Lanka run by Young Asia Television, Sri Lanka.

A founder-member of the Free Media Movement and one-time FFM secretary and trustee, he is a founder-member and past President of the South Asian Free Media Association (SAFMA, affiliated to SAARC) and remains President of the SAFMA Sri Lanka Chapter. He has taught journalism at the University of Colombo, Sri Lanka College of Journalism and other institutions and, lectured at the Asian College of Journalism, Chennai. As a social activist on media rights, ethnic and gender issues, he has studied media in relation to Sri Lankan ethnicity and conflict, while serving as an adviser to various governmental and non-governmental organisations, as well as international organisations, on Sri Lankan affairs, particularly in the area of media and society, and media rights.

Khin Maung Soe is senior lecturer responsible for teaching Rhetoric (Presentation, Public Speaking and Project Report Writing) for both the IFC and HND courses at Chindwin College Mandalay and Yangon, which has affiliation with University of Sunderland and University of Volverhampton in the UK through the Tyndale Group in Singapore. He has done a Certificate course in Book-keeping and Accounting (LCCI) and Journalism and has undergone training in AEC (ASEAN Economic Community), School of Administrative Studies, Thailand. Under the Australian Department of Foreign Affairs and Trade (DFATA) Business Development Exchange Project, ODI, he has been carrying out research on the potential for business engagement in skill development. Khin Maung Soe has also contributed news stories and articles to the weekly News and Business Periodical *The Myanmar Times.*

Dawa Penjor is the Executive Director of Bhutan Media Foundation (BMF). BMF is a non-profit, independent organization established under a Royal Charter in February 2010 with the aim to sustain democracy by developing the Bhutanese media, through initiatives to build Journalistic Excellence, promote Media Innovation, support promotion of Freedom of Expression, Freedom of Information, and Freedom of Press. Prior to joining BMF, he worked for over ten years with the Department of Information and Media, Royal Government of Bhutan as a research officer, Senior Information and Media Officer and Head of the Media Relations Division. He worked as a core member on the drafting committee for the Bhutan Infocomm and Media Act (2006), Policy Guideline on Information Sharing (2006), the Bhutan Government Web Portal (www.bhutan.gov.bt), the Position Classification System of the RGoB (2007), Right to Information Bill (2012) and Bhutan eGov Master plan (2013). Dawa has a Master's in Public Administration (Honors and Outstanding Student Award) from the University of Texas at El Paso, USA and also a Diploma in Development Journalism from Indian Institute of Mass Communication (IIMC), New Delhi (Recipient of United News of India Award, 2007).

Deepak Adhikari is a Kathmandu-based journalist. In a career spanning over a decade and half, he has covered socio-political issues of Nepal including the peace process following the end of decade-long Maoist insurgency, human rights, environment, mountaineering and geopolitics. His work has appeared in the *Time* magazine, *The Caravan* magazine, *Himal Southasian* magazine, Al Jazeera English, *Nikkei Asian Review* magazine, among others. In between November 2010 to February 2014, he served as Nepal correspondent for Agence France-Presse (AFP), the global news agency. Prior to joining AFP, he worked for *Kantipur*, Nepal's largest-selling newspaper as a reporter and editor. From 2004 till 2008, he worked as reporter at *Weekly Nepal* magazine, producing investigative reportages on human trafficking, organ trade and sex trafficking, thus, highlighting socio-economic issues of Nepal. He was an Alfred Friendly Press Fellow in 2008. He has translated a biography of Nepal's pioneering conservationist from English to Nepali.

SOUTH ASIA
TURKMENISTAN
TAJIKISTAN
CHINA
AFGHANISTAN
IRAN
PAKISTAN
NEPAL
BHUTAN
INDIA
BANGLADESH
MYANMAR
LAOS
THAILAND
OMAN
SRI LANKA
MALDIVES
INDONESIA
Herat
Kabul
Kandahar
Islamabad
Srinagar
Leh
Lahore
New Delhi
Kathmandu
Thimphu
Guwahati
Imphal
Kanpur
Varanasi
Patna
Karachi
Ahmadabad
Dhaka
Kolkata
Chittagong
Nagpur
Mumbai
Naypyitaw
Vishakhapatnam
Chennai
Bengaluru
Jaffna
Colombo
Male
Gulf of Oman
Arabian Sea
Bay of Bengal
Andaman Sea
Laccadive Sea
INDIAN OCEAN
© Institute for Defense Studies & Analyses
New Delhi, GIS Lab.
Map not to scale

Opening Remarks by Brigadier Rumel Dahiya (Retd.)
Deputy Director General, IDSA at the 8th South Asia Dialogue

Members of the Executive Council of the Institute for Defence Studies and Analyses (IDSA), distinguished diplomats, delegates to the conference, members of the strategic community, friends from the media, IDSA colleagues, ladies and gentlemen, it gives me great pleasure to welcome you all to the 8th South Asia Dialogue being organized by IDSA on the theme: "The Role of Media in Promoting Regional Understanding in South Asia". The Honourable Minister of State for Information and Broadcasting, Shri Prakash Javadekar, was to inaugurate this conference but he had to participate in another, perhaps even more important, programme which came up only last evening. Therefore, he recorded his message late at night yesterday and sent it which would be played after I finish. He has conveyed his sincere regrets for not being able to participate in person.

In the last eight years the conference has emerged as a platform for scholars and experts from India and other countries of South Asian Association for Regional Cooperation (SAARC) for exchange of views on a variety of issues concerning South Asia. In addition, scholars and experts from Myanmar have been joining us since 2012. In the last seven conferences, we discussed themes such as: *Economic Cooperation for Security and Development in South Asia; Changing Political Context in India's Neighbourhood and Prospects of Security and Regional Cooperation; South Asia 2020: Towards Cooperation or Conflict;*

The Common Challenge of Terrorism in South Asia and Prospects of Regional Cooperation; Cooperative Security Framework for South Asia and *Prospects for Stability and Growth in South Asia.*

The 7th South Asia conference held in IDSA last year was on the issue of *India and South Asia: Exploring Regional Perceptions.* It discussed the importance of the media in shaping perceptions which can foster a more cooperative image of the neighbourhood. We take this idea forward through the 8th South Asia Dialogue and deliberate on how the neighbourhood as a whole could make media a force multiplier for improving regional cooperation. This dialogue is informed by the assumption that media plays a significant role in South Asian politics and in shaping perceptions. Adversarial and negative reporting comes in the way of regional cooperation and integration; hyper active 24x7 media sometimes plays a role in perpetuating cynicism and making it more difficult to resolve conflicts. There is a famous saying *to give peace a chance sometimes peace has to become the story.* The role of media in South Asia assumes great significance in this context.

Leaps in technology have made mass media an important actor in framing perceptions and impacting inter-state relations. The average person relies solely on this information believing it to be the full story and the true story on any issue. The ability to convey or withhold information represents the media's greatest power. However, this freedom can be dangerous, particularly at a time of troubled relations. Media's power can be used negatively, particularly when unbalanced, misleading or inaccurate information promotes stereotypes. The key question regarding the promotion of accurate information and informed dialogue is how to balance the need to limit the power of media to shape opinions while protecting the freedom of expression that allows for a healthy exchange of views and ideas.

There is a trend in certain sections of the news media, particularly the broadcast media, towards fragmenting of issues and focus on the spectacular. The intense competition and the pressure to constantly produce breaking news results in a construction of events as spectacle, lacking in any analysis or background information and failing to grapple with complexity and raising several ethical questions. This influence of sound-byte journalism and the constant need for polarization and political theatre in television journalism to make news and current affairs into drama, that will grab the eyeballs and enhance TRPs, sets the norm for what constitutes news as well as viewers' expectations of the medium and the views of world around them. The media shows a tendency to stick to simplistic categorizations based on common sense and a black and white interpretation of events leaving out the shades of grey and the complexities in the process. The representation of conflict as a struggle between good and evil is found across South Asia particularly when reporting events from zones of conflict. The danger of simplistic narratives and other stereotype views is that when promulgated through the media they can become the dominant prism through which people perceive the other country. The news media, in particular, should work to provide a more accurate depiction of the neighbourhood.

There is a need to strengthen ongoing efforts towards developing a more layered representation of both cases of cooperation and conflict in South Asia. We need to develop a better understanding of the nature of state, media and civil society interactions and dynamics in the region. It will have such a significant impact on public diplomacy, public discourse and policy. We need to enable consideration of working towards a plural media that reflects diverse opinions beyond the ultra-nationalistic constructs. The idea must be to break negative assumptions and not to reinforce prejudice. Commercial considerations of news media cannot come at the cost of peace in the neighbourhood. There is evidence of media being a constructive player for an exchange of healthy ideas on cooperation in the region and here I am reminded of the idea of Lahore bus service which was mooted by Mr. Nawaz Sharif, the then and present Prime Minister of Pakistan, in an interview to an Indian newspaper. Instead of amplifying the cleavages and negativity, the impetus on informed, objective and verified reportage which goes beyond statistics and also focuses on people, is need of the hour.

While the governments in the region need to look at their abilities to strategically communicate with the media, they also need to solve core issues of access in terms of granting visas, access to channels from the region, etc. There should be uninterrupted access to media and entertainment sources among countries in the neighbourhood which would go a long way in shaping perceptions on either side. Social media and digital journalism bring with it new opportunities that can shed light on the constituencies of peace and improve perceptions across the region. These must be maximized.

These and other questions mentioned in the concept note of the conference will inform the discussions over the next two days. I am grateful to the delegates from Afghanistan, Bangladesh, Bhutan, Maldives, Myanmar, Nepal, Pakistan and Sri Lanka for travelling to New Delhi for this conference. I wish you a pleasant stay in India. I am also grateful to our young scholar, Dr. Priyanka Singh, for organizing this dialogue and the scholars and staff of the Institute for enthusiastically cooperating in this endeavour.

Thank you!

Inaugural Address by Shri Prakash Javadekar*

Hon'ble Minister of State (Independent Charge), Ministry of Environment, Forest and Climate Change, Government of India at the 8th South Asia Dialogue

The Institute for Defence Studies and Analyses has organized the South Asia Dialogue on: "The Role of Media in Promoting Regional Understanding in South Asia". I welcome all the delegates from our neighbouring countries who have made it convenient to participate in the dialogue.

The 21st century's requirement and the expectations of society are much different from those of the earlier one because it is a fast changing society and it is the aspirations of the poor which is dominating the discourse. India, the world's largest democracy, elected a new government just five months ago with a clear mandate in which the youth and the poor participated enthusiastically and voted for a predictable policy regime for good governance with aspirations to progress rapidly. And therefore Mr. Narendra Modi, the Prime Minister, was chosen by people in a referendum-like voting because he emerged as a credible leader. What did the outcome of elections reveal? The outcome reflected the aspirations of people; that not only the middle class but also the poor have aspirations—aspiration to get educated, aspiration to get opportunity and aspiration to get jobs and stand on their own feet and live with dignity. These are the aspirations of the common man. Please note

*At the time of the conference in October 2014, Shri Prakash Javadekar was Minister of State (Independent Charge), Ministry of Information and Broadcasting, Government of India.

that many a time, media misses the bus of the public sentiments and this is a universal phenomenon. The headlines which appear in various print and broadcast media, which continue with controversial stories—actually matters very little to the voters. The verdict the people deliver is sometimes entirely different from what media forecasts. Sometimes, media finds sync with the public opinion and gets it right. But that is the strength and weakness of the media. Strength is that it can shape public opinion and weakness is that it falls prey to its own convictions and they become views—not the newspapers but views papers.

In print media, even in broadcast media, there is a role for news and views. People see all but they have their own intelligence. Our eminent jurist, late Nani Palkiwala, used to say that Indian illiterate intelligence is more powerful than the educated in capacity. So many times it has become more effective and delivered the verdict which the intellectual debate does not produce. These are the realities of the society. I think the media has, firstly, the challenge to really understand whether it is in sync with the societal thinking. Secondly, their role to proactively change the society for the better and to that end, it will not be in sync with the society. But you have to shape the minds of the people and, therefore, media should work in a mission mode.

When the South Asian countries are meeting, every country has different abilities, strengths, weaknesses, opportunities and to that end media has a very important role to play in bringing these issues for public debate. There are sensibilities each country has. Sometimes we see something published in some country, it flares up sentiments in another country. I call these as sensibility issues. One must recognize that these sensibilities matter. We have a role to play and our role is to arrive at a better understanding. We should not create sensationalism. Social media can be viral but the main media cannot be. I think freedom of press has not come for free and, therefore, freedom entails responsibility. I would have been really happy to be with you for this dialogue among the policymakers, academicians and media persons. Media has a definite role in promoting regional understanding because ultimately we have to grow together. It is not only TRPs which matter, it is not that only your advertisement revenues and circulation matter. What matters is your commitment for the betterment of the society and your readiness to fight for a cause.

Journalism to me is a big mission and people have suffered—they have paid price for standing by truth and, therefore, our mission should be to continue with that. Many journalists are killed in war torn countries like Syria and elsewhere. This is the price people are paying even today. Fortunately in South Asia, there is no such tension but still it matters and, therefore, the role of media in the total renaissance is important and it can work as a catalyst. Therefore, I wish this dialogue the very best. I had committed to come but could not make it because of an urgent meeting. I think this dialogue will definitely come out with good suggestions and I would welcome all those suggestions. India will do its bit to promote regional understanding more effectively. Media is playing an important role at the bilateral and multilateral platforms. This is likely to continue in order to arrive at a better understanding among the countries. With this, I once again wish you all the best and thank you.

Introduction

Priyanka Singh

Media plays a very significant role in generating public awareness, shaping public opinion and forming popular perceptions. It is regarded as the fourth estate and an important pillar of democracy. With the mushrooming of media around the world—print, audio-visual and social—this role has been enhanced and has become even more significant. The manner in which reports are filed and news is disseminated have considerable impact on public opinion. In an interconnected world, the role of media in influencing foreign policy of states can hardly be ignored.

In South Asia, a region where inter-state relations are held hostage to zero-sum politics, media has a big responsibility in creating an environment of trust and understanding. Since the states of the region are socially, historically, culturally and economically interconnected, the role of media assumes even more significance. However, unfortunately, the media in different states of South Asia is yet to show essential maturity and wisdom in enabling an environment of mutual trust and confidence. The discourses in media are often mired in narrowly conceived nationalist templates which far from bridging differences, escalate them, causing irreparable harm to regional understanding. While tension and conflict among states and communities find more news space, shared history and culture are conveniently ignored. All this results in media adding to interstate conflicts and increasing the political temperature rather than acting as an agent of change and reconciliation. With the proliferation of audio-visual media in the region and the competition among channels for better TRP (Television Rating Point) ratings, there is often a temptation to sensationalise issues through select reporting.

This is not to say that there is a complete absence of responsible media in the region. Joint media initiatives like the one between the Jang group of Pakistan and the Times group in India to launch *Aman ki Asha* (Hope for Peace) did try to create an environment of trust to contribute to India-Pakistan peace process. Similarly, *The Statesman* from India and *Prathom Alo* from Bangladesh also tried to replicate this exercise to promote India-Bangladesh relationship. Groups like South Asia Free Media Association (SAFMA) have also endeavoured to bring together scholars, retired bureaucrats, politicians and media person together in South Asia to promote people to people contact.

Media cannot be looked at as a monolithic entity. There are several layers to it. Moreover, the media is facing several restrictions. There is the issue of media censorship and media freedom. There is also the issue of media ownership—by political parties, interest groups and business houses. With their vested interests, the owners sometimes dictate the line a media group would take at the expense of neutrality. The influence of certain institutions on media begs close scrutiny in view of their impact on foreign and security policies of some states. The differences in approach between vernacular and English media and their influence on society and politics is another area which has not received much critical attention. The social media is assuming importance in most of these countries with the penetration of internet and wider use of mobile phones, especially among the youth, who constitute a critical mass in South Asia.

Whether it was the case of showing doctored images about fictitious attack on Rohingyas as attack on Muslims in North East; the picture of Shivaji and Ambedkar, which led to violence in Pune in India; or the derogatory message against the Prophet, maliciously circulated in the social media attributing the act to a Buddhist, which led to violence in Ramu in Bangladesh—the social media is playing a disproportionate role in spawning insecurity and violence in the multicultural setting in South Asia.

Given the increasingly significant role played by the media, the 8th South Asia Dialogue organized by the Institute for Defence Studies and Analyses (IDSA) sought to explore the following issues and questions:

- What is the role that media plays in shaping public opinion in different countries in South Asia?

- How does media influence foreign and security policies of states? Is there any difference between the vernacular and English language media in this regard?
- What are the forces influencing media and its approach to regional issues?
- How does media ownership impact reporting by different media houses?
- Does media play a role in promoting jingoistic nationalism in the region? How does it interfere with the process of regional unity and integration?
- Can media play a role in promoting regional understanding and contribute to regional peace and amity?

This edited volume is a compilation of papers presented in the dialogue proceedings and presents a wide spectrum of perspectives from the entire South Asian region including Myanmar. Starting from the 6th South Asia Conference held in 2012 at IDSA, participants from Myanmar have shared their views on regional integration at this platform. Given Myanmar's geographical contiguity with the South Asian region as well as socio-historical linkages, its participation was deemed essential to include it as an important dialogue partner in the annual event at IDSA focussing on regional cooperation.

The South Asia Dialogue 2014 was inaugurated by a recorded address from the then Hon'ble Minister of State for Information and Broadcasting (Independent Charge), Shri Prakash Javadekar, who emphasised on the useful role media could play in enhancing regional understanding and cooperation. The dialogue proceedings were divided into five sessions based on issues related to the main theme. Session I dealt with media in South Asia providing an overall analysis of the role played by media in shaping public discourse in the region. Session II and III focussed on country perspectives on issues of ownership, making of news, media censorship and vernacular media. Session IV covered media's approach to security and foreign policy issues and its overall impact on society, politics and government policies in different countries. In the concluding session, the participants came out with suggestions regarding how the media can leverage its position and play a role in promoting regional peace and amity.

Broadly based on the structure of the dialogue, the book is divided into three parts corresponding to the thematic sessions.

Part I: The Role of Media in Shaping Public Discourse in South Asia

The first chapter in part I titled, "Media-scape in South Asia and the Issue of Regional Cooperation", by Smruti S. Pattanaik and Ashok K. Behuria is based on the premise that media's role in shaping public perception on regional cooperation is rather limited, because of the lack of focus on the issue in the regional media. Nevertheless, the authors recognise the influence and impact of the media and its growing penetration in the region. In addition to print media, the emerging role of the audio and visual media has provided a significant momentum to the dissemination of information on diverse issues. They also mention that the advent of private media has overshadowed the traditional state-owned entities which primarily presented statist view-point instead of providing alternate viewpoints, as expected from a free media. Added to this, they point out that the boom in social media has also proved to be a watershed in information sharing across the South Asian region. They deal with issues like what constitutes a media narrative, whether media flares up or soothes conflict between states and whether the media could engage in broader exercise of creating the condition for regional cooperation and goodwill.

Rasul Bakhsh Rais's paper, "The Media and Foreign Policy Discourses in Pakistan", discusses the media landscape in Pakistan—a country, which is undergoing unprecedented internal security crisis. He argues that the media scene in Pakistan is rather optimistic in view of the fact that the media has successfully reached out to a larger section of the population than what it could afford to do about a decade ago. The paper argues that media in Pakistan is still a powerful constituency. It generates public awareness and opinion, acts as a medium of exchange and it is accommodative of dissenting ideas and views. The paper employs three variables—Pakistan's relations with India, the United States, and other Muslim nations to conclude that media is indeed a powerful force in shaping the foreign policy of Pakistan.

Presenting a Bangladeshi perspective on the subject, Syed Badrul Ahsan's paper titled, "Impact of Media Ownership on Reporting: When Journalism is Prey to Predatory Instincts", gauges the impact of media ownership on the nature of reporting. He discusses ownership as a key factor that impinges the quality, nature and substance of news. It is observed that ownership drives the editorial policies of the media houses in Bangladesh, where there is serious financial crunch in the media sector. Thus, ownership becomes the virtual pivot in generation and dispersion of news and information.

Amrullah Saleh in his paper titled, "Media in Post 9/11 Afghanistan", juxtaposes the pre and post 9/11 media scenarios in a country ravaged by prolonged phase of civil strife and a long haul of external intervention. He posits that post 2001, the sphere of Afghan media has actually flourished and, today, there is greater diversity with considerable scope and space for divergence in views. In post-Taliban Afghanistan, media is playing an appreciable role in spreading awareness and acting as the crucial agent of change.

The last chapter in this section, "Media in the Age of Intolerance and Terrorism", by Kunda Dixit weighs the relative consequences when media is put under a tight leash in an authoritarian regime and when it is let rather loose under a democratic state structure. He argues, that while in a totalitarian structure, there is likelihood that flow of information is muzzled, media in free market societies have a tendency to get over-corporatized and produce biased opinions that steer far away from truth and facts.

Part II: Country Perspectives

This part of the book begins with the chapter, "Promotion of Jingoism in the Region by the Media: The Case of Sri Lanka", by Dilrukshi Handunnetti. The paper explores how the undercurrents of nationalism, pervasive in both state-owned and private sources of media have, sometimes, vitiated the regional atmospherics and harmed ties between neighbouring states of South Asia. While doing so, she takes up the case of post-war Sri Lanka when media across the board engaged in massive propagation of statist position in complete disregard of the acts of gross human rights violations and excesses committed during the war by Sri Lankan security forces.

The second paper titled, "Maldivian Media: Ownership, Orientation and Trends", by Ibrahim Waheed takes a comprehensive view of this island nation before dwelling upon the contours of traditional and non-traditional media there. There are several forces that influence the media trends in Maldives including ownership and nature and scope of political influence. Certain legislations instituted in Maldives to regulate media have been discussed to arrive at an understanding on how media operates in the country and gauge its impact at the regional and international level.

Kaberi Gayen's paper, "Regional Understanding: Does Media Ownership Really Matter?" hinges on the pivotal role media plays in the state and society with special focus on Bangladeshi media. She argues in the paper that there is a constant churning between several actors and factors—nature of state politics, ideology, etc.—that drive the politics of the state and, more importantly, source of finances that invest in the media sector. The paper examines whether the complex interplay of such forces actually influences the opinion of a state like Bangladesh; the pattern of media ownership in the country and how well media can be used to promote understanding and mutual trust in the region.

In recent times, a flourishing media landscape in Bhutan has complemented quite well the country's smooth transition from monarchy to a representative democracy. The phenomenal growth in the media sector of Bhutan has been ably captured in the chapter, "The Role of the Bhutanese Media in Bhutan's Democratic Evolution and Governance", by Tenzing Lamsang. The chapter brings forth the diversification of roles being played by the Bhutanese media and analyses its contributions towards democracy taking strong roots in the country. The author notes that the media industry in Bhutan is constantly striving to strengthen the foundations of democracy by keeping a close vigil against corruption and malpractices. The chapter also deals with challenges confronting the relatively nascent media in Bhutan and looks at the possibilities of Bhutanese media being sensitised about the issue of regional integration and playing a constructive role in it.

Myo Lwin in his paper titled, "The Role of Media in Myanmar", provides the reader with a useful narrative on the dramatic shift undergone by the media sector in Myanmar in the last few years. Parallel to democratic transition, media in Myanmar has witnessed unprecedented growth and expansion with regard to the circulation and readership of several weeklies and dailies. Initially concentrated in the main urban centres, media industry is gradually spreading out in different regions of the country dominated by different ethnic groups. The revocation of the pre-press censorship in 2012 has contributed towards unhindered sharing of information and news across the country. This kind of unobstructed flow of information has led to positive outcomes. There have been few shortfalls as well, where media was allegedly involved in sensationalizing developments merely for commercial gains.

Danish Karokhel in his paper titled, "Evolution of Afghan Media: Role in Promoting Regional Understanding", puts together a detailed account of the development of media in Afghanistan by making a fourfold classification of media scenario in Afghanistan—state media, private media, jihadi media and foreign media. Karokhel calls the evolution of media in Afghanistan a natural process that was, in post 9/11 period, characterized by huge influx of foreign funds being funnelled into the media industry. The media domain in Afghanistan is driven by the larger geo-politics of the Af-Pak region and is, sometimes, marred by lack of professionalism. Towards the end, Karokhel advocates meaningful initiatives that could enhance the level of media cooperation, networking and information sharing at the regional level.

Shruti Pandalai's paper, "Truth vs Hype: Media, Hyper-nationalism and Impact on Perceptions in India-South Asia Relations", explains the inherent dilemma regarding the role of media as an agent shaping public opinion and, its role as an 'agenda setter' in matters of foreign and security policy of state. While media has been at the forefront of debating issues concerning national interest and the country's security, most of the media professionals are not inclined to work towards bettering relationship between states. Pandalai's exposition is based on the argument that even as the media may appear to be influencing foreign policy of a country, such impact could be rather short-lived.

Part III: Influence of Media on Foreign and Security Policies of States

Lakshman Gunasekara's paper on "News Media Re-Presentation and Agenda-Setting in Public Discourse on Foreign Relations: The Case of Sri Lankan Popular Attitudes Towards India", examines the role of mass media in foreign policy making. The paper contends that media can play such a role because it can shape political and social attitudes, which is referred to as its social communication function. Representation of popular perception is at the core of media's functions and, through this paper, Gunasekara tries to evaluate the impact of such dynamics not only on Sri Lanka's overall ties with the South Asian region but also vis-a-vis its important neighbour, India.

Khin Maung Soe's paper titled, "The Role of Media in Shaping Foreign Policy Discourse in Myanmar", traverses through the political evolution of the country—from military dictatorship to democracy—and analyses the role played by Myanmar's media during this process. The paper also makes an attempt to take a broader view of media's role in shaping public opinion and perceptions in other countries, before looking at similar possibilities for media in Myanmar, especially in the wake of the much-anticipated political transition and change.

Dawa Penjor in his paper titled, "The Role of Bhutanese Media in Amalgamating South Asia: Quest for a Happy South Asian Society", draws upon the framework of Gross National Happiness (GNH) to look at possibilities of forging media-led regional cooperation in South Asia. The paper argues that there have been some discouraging trends in interstate affairs in South Asia in the past when media of one country, in order to be seen as fostering a sense of nationalism, has often ended up maligning the other country's image. This practice still continues with many media persons across nations not bothering to abide by factual data and ground realities. Such negative tendencies, inevitably, produce animosity between countries and dilute whatever little measure of goodwill exists amongst neighbouring states. The author hopes that the situation will change and media will play a positive role in future.

Deepak Adhikari in his paper titled, "The Role of Media in Shaping Foreign Policy Discourse in Nepal", spells out the political transition being witnessed in the Himalayan state. The paper comprehensively captures how the country is charting a new course towards democracy and popular representation especially in the wake of end of Maoist insurgency and Monarchy. Since then, Nepal has been constantly jostling through phases of extreme political uncertainty and turmoil to envisage and draft a unanimous and acceptable constitution for the country. Though the Nepalese media industry is still not very mature and needs to learn far more, Adhikari argues that there is a definite impact of media narratives on foreign policy and the India-Nepal relations feature on Nepal's media portrait in a major way.

The following key points emerge from the papers in this volume. There is a consensus that media has a crucial role to play in national security. It has, at the same time, the power to create harmonious ties between the states or vitiate the atmospherics. A balanced, neutral and unbiased reporting by the media has the potential to positively impact relations between the states. It is also acknowledged that media is constantly under pressure from several quarters. Sometimes, the governments exercise excessive pressure on the media to disseminate information based on a particular line. Similarly, ownership of media by business houses also impacts the reporting and content in a big way. Yet, media in every country has sections who stand up to such pressures and try their best to serve news in a rather balanced, unprejudiced and unbiased manner. The authors refer to the expansion of media in detail and note that with the advent of the visual media, with many media persons not having in-depth knowledge of subjects and issues, there is a need to promote greater understanding of issues amongst them. There should be efforts to provide comprehensive training of history, geopolitics, culture and economy, etc. to those involved in reporting and writing on such issues. There is need to train media persons in specialized institutions which would sharpen their understanding and analytical skills.

There is a concern expressed by some that large number of media houses are in a bad financial state, which makes them vulnerable to inducements from various quarters and obliges them to follow a certain line. This aspect needs particular attention.

In order to improve the quality of media reporting about regional politics, there is a need to make visa regulations more flexible-one which would allow unrestricted movement of journalists in the region. In this regard, multiple entry visa for journalists/newspersons is a good option. This would ensure more interaction between the media of all South Asian countries and, hence, promote greater understanding and goodwill. The agreement to allow better access for journalists to neighbouring countries can be worked out if not bilaterally, then multilaterally, for instance within the framework of the SAARC.

To conclude, there is a general consensus among the contributors that the media should give greater coverage to issues related to the neighbourhood in different countries. In fact, there is a suggestion that visual media should make it a point to telecast daily/weekly programmes on neighbourhood and that the print media should carry specific columns to cover news related to events in the neighbouring countries. In all, the media has a responsibility towards the larger South Asian region and must play its due role in enabling a culture of mutual trust and understanding, which will, in turn, prepare the grounds for effective regional cooperation and ensure peace, prosperity and sustainable growth in the region.

PART I

The Role of Media in Shaping Public Discourse in South Asia

1

Media-scape in South Asia and the Issue of Regional Cooperation

Smruti S. Pattanaik and Ashok K. Behuria

There has been a media explosion in South Asia in the last few decades with the advent of internet and audio-visual media. In fact, in the region, India tops with about 82,000 newspapers, over 800 television channels and 61.3 million internet users while other countries have a proportionate presence of print and audio visual media as well as penetration of internet.[1] This has resulted in media acquiring unprecedented gravitas in society and politics of different countries. Role of media is shaping and presenting public opinion on a variety of issues in South Asia has indeed been gargantuan. While the print media has traditionally played an important role, the impact of visual media has been far effective over the last few decades in bringing visuals to the drawing rooms of people. The television channels are no more restricted to the ones owned by the government. The private sector has emerged as an important player and corporatized the manner in which media reports. Success is not measured by the quality of the news but the sensationalism it is able to create which is geared towards TRPs. There has also been an explosion of the social media that has remained beyond the domain of both these players and controlled by international entities like the Facebook and the Twitter. Though at present this remains limited to the urban social space, it is slowly penetrating the non-urban locales and its impact has been phenomenal in terms of the space it provides to the people to interact and exchange views especially with controlled visa regimes that characterises the people-to-people contact in the region.

Nevertheless, there is a contrarian perspective, that the proliferation of media network has indeed made the media less effective and "[r]ather than creating the context for greater popular engagement with global issues, conflict and foreign policy, the panoply of contrasting voices may well have created less potential for people to mobilise opinion and effect political influence".[2] If one looks at it closely, such a view underscores a lament that the media has not been able to realise its potential because of various limitations—inability to pursue any particular agenda because of the diversity of opinion it has to have space for in the best of circumstances; compulsions of commercial viability that leads media to cater to public sentiments at the cost of objectivity; eternal search for popularity (the so called TRPs); tendency to defer to the governmental thinking and self-censor its coverage of issues pertaining to national security and foreign policy issues, etc. In the case of the media in South Asia, the socio-political and economic contexts in which it is embedded in different countries also determine its behaviour and its aspirations, constraining its capacity to play a greater role in shaping the discourse on regionalism.

Issues at Stake

Given the role media is now playing to shape public discourse and political climate in the region, the questions that become relevant here are: what determines the media narrative and how news space is allocated to incidents?; To what extent ownership and the corporate interests play a role in shaping the debates in the media? Is there a value in neutral news reporting? The chapter will also analyse to what extent media plays a role in foreign policy and helps the cause of regional cooperation.

Governmental Influence

The media has to contend more with the domestic context of their reportage than international ramification their reporting may have. Since they have to operate within the domestic political environment and subjected to domestic laws, the media often tries its best to play it safe and not to provoke government's wrath. The media reporting is also sometimes ideologically motivated and there are planted stories by the security agencies to project a particular point of view when it comes to analysing bilateral ties within the region. The governments with the enormous resources at their disposal have the ability to influence the content in this regard. For example as an analyst explains, "[r]eferred to variously as perception management, strategic communication, public diplomacy and, recently, global engagement, these activities involve the promotion of policy through carefully crafted PR campaigns, exploitation of links with journalists and media outlets and, most generally, taking advantage of the considerable resources at the disposal of governments in order to attempt to dominate the information environment".[3]

While the media has taken centre stage, the nation states are yet to learn how to strike a balance between the people's right to know and the foreign policy compulsion that focuses on improving relations with its neighbours. Adding to this dilemma is the mushrooming of social media over which the governments of the region have little control even as they contemplate measures to gag the media and stifle freedom of speech and expression. According to an expert, at the "initial stages of a foreign policy event, when elites have a substantial informational advantage, the public's perception of reality is very elastic"[4] and, therefore, they consider it useful to use media to shape public opinion in favour of the foreign policy direction they take.

The government control over newsprint and advertisement provides it with a handle through which it can really strangle a newspaper and force it to toe the government line while reporting on foreign policy and domestic issues. The media is also severely constrained by government laws promulgated from time to time to have a control over the media.[5] In Bangladesh, according to an analyst writing in the context of the problems faced by the visual media, "Media people used to get various directives and advices from the caretaker government (2006-2009) authorities on do's and don'ts of programming agendas".[6] In India, the Press Council plays the role of the regulatory body. But from time to time, the government has placed restrictions on issues that cannot report citing national security reasons—the main excuse under which press freedom can be curtailed without any question. In Sri Lanka, the previous government of Mahinda Rajapaksa had set up Media Centre for National Security in 2006 which regulated the reportage on the war with the LTTE (Liberation Tigers of Tamil Eelam). It was shut down in December 2013 after it was plagued with various controversies pertaining to the activities of its

Director General.[7] The situation is not too different in other countries of the region.

In spite of such tendency to control the media, in recent decades, the media in South Asia has undergone dramatic transformation. It has tried to probe and serve issues which were regarded sensitive from the governmental viewpoint such as corruption in high places, mal-governance, plight of the minorities, behaviour of the security agencies, etc. This is due to intense competition among the media houses to earn viewership and establish their credibility. Moreover, the rise of the social media[8] has made it imperative for the mainstream media to be even more investigative and objective in its coverage of issues of public interest.

Content and Narrative: Promoting Hatred by Design or Default?

The print and visual media have different ways of influencing public opinion, and thereby, influencing foreign and security policy. The print media caters to those who are literate and can read and have access to newspaper. In many of the rural areas, the visual media has a greater impact given the penetration of satellite television. The impact of visual media is direct and effective—as it is said, "a picture conveys thousand words". In the case of both print and audio-visual media, they tend to emphasise on some issues while ignoring others. In most cases, ownership determines the editorial policy and the content to a very large extent, while the editors play a secondary role. Since it is the business and political interests that drives the editorial policy, the editors are careful about the content of the newspaper at the cost of objectivity and social responsibility.

Let us take the case of print media and its impact. In case of the print media, the headlines are chosen carefully to draw the attention of the reader and the selection of which news would hit the headlines is done according to the editorial policy of the newspaper as well as the dominant public sentiment. The same is true of the visual media. There are several instances of politically motivated news items that are given primacy by particular media houses that affect bilateral relations between countries. In the past, for example, the Nepali media Channel *Nepal Television* owned by a media baron of Kashmiri origin, Jamim Shah, attributed a statement to one of the Indian actors, Hrithik Roshan, that inflamed Nepali nationalism and led to riots in Kathmandu in 2001 with a motive to spark violence in which business owned by people of Indian origin were attacked.[9]

This incident fed into simmering anti-Indian public sentiment in Nepal and political parties took full advantage of the public anger and channelized riots in a particular manner to make political mileage out of it.[10] Later, it was reported that vested interest groups spread rumours to inflame anti-India sentiments and India was forced to request Nepal to protect its citizens. In 2004, the newspaper *Space Time* owned by his group was behind yet another spate of inflaming popular sentiments against India. In recent past, certain media houses in Nepal portrayed the Indian aid and evacuation effort in Nepal in the aftermath of earthquake and Chinese rescue operation differently interpreting Indian aid as an attempt to influence Nepalese politics and Chinese aid as benign devoid of any foreign policy motive.[11] In October 1990, the *Daily Inquilab* published in Bangladesh (known for its leaning towards Jamaat-e-Islami Bangladesh) carried a story titled, 'Babri mosque was demolished' leading to large scale politically instigated violence against the Hindu minorities condoned by the then General Ershad's regime. In the past, the weekly magazine *Holiday* in Bangladesh launched a scathing attack on India and ran a series of news items targeting Mujib and India and contributed to anti-India sentiment that largely flew from the governance problem. *Holiday* was motivated both by political and ideological reasons given the affiliation of its publisher Enayetullah Khan to Bangladesh Nationalist Party (BNP) known for its reservations against India.

All these instances only confirm the potential role that the media can play in instigating politically and ideologically motivated violence, sometimes blatantly pursuing the political interests of particular political parties. While one sees media propelled anti-India sentiment being one sided as far as India's national media is concerned in these two instances, in the context of India-Pakistan relations, such reporting is noticed on both sides of the border. This is not to deny that the media houses in India and Pakistan have also played a commendable role in at least trying to bring these two countries together through their initiative of *Aman ki Asha*. The joint editorial statement of the Jang group in Pakistan and the Times group in India on the *Aman ki Asha* website reads: "This vast subcontinent senses the bounties a peace dividend can deliver to its people yet it recoils from claiming a share. The natural impulse would be to break out of the straitjacket of stated positions and embrace an ideal that promises sustained prosperity to the region…"[12]

It is ironical, however, that the television channel run by the same Times group in India, the TIMES NOW channel spews venom against Pakistan on a regular basis and instead of initiating a healthy debate on issues affecting both countries, ritually engages in Pakistan-bashing completely undermining the *Aman ki Asha* (Hope for Peace) spirit invoked by the group.[13] This could be explained away as an effort to enhance the TRP ratings during the prime news-hour in the evenings through high pitched rhetoric against Pakistan every time there is an alleged violation of ceasefire by the Pakistani forces or infiltration taking place in Kashmir. Following the success of TIMES NOW, this strategy has also been adopted by many other news channels in their quest for larger viewership. On the Pakistan side also, there is no dearth of anchors and channels vilifying India in the wake of tensions between India and Pakistan. There is hardly any effort to bring down the temperature through reasoned analysis of the situation and appeal to the good sense of the people in both countries. The alternative route of seeking amity and reconciliation is hardly explored. For example, the issue of trade and commerce between India and Pakistan, which carries the potential to improve the state of bilateral relationship and create the environment for trust and dialogue, do not attract enough media attention. Interestingly, on both sides of the India-Pakistan divide, there are many academics, economists, businessmen and civil society activists who are busy churning out literature emphasising the need for India and Pakistan to bury their hatchet and come together to realise the potential of regional cooperation. However, such opinions, often based on sound research, fail to catch the headlines.

It is true that media reporting is not value neutral. Media houses have economic interests run as corporate concerns. Therefore, media is vulnerable to pressures from power sections in the government and feel obliged to pursue official line. It is equally true that there are corporate houses opposed to government policies who through their media outlets propagate a totally contrarian perspective on the way the government functions. The media, thus, becomes a powerful tool in the domestic political context by propagating a particular view point it considers profitable and serves its business interests.

Media and National Security

At another level, the national security interests of the state sometimes dominate the media's approach to issues concerning the foreign policy of a state. The security establishments in different countries are known to plant stories in the media depending on the outcome they expect in the foreign policy domain. In the case of Pakistan, the "collusion" of Pakistani military establishment and media is apparent. There was an instance where the reporters in Pakistan were even instructed to portray the Sharif-Modi meet in June 2014 and "give it a negative tint"[14] because the military leadership in Pakistan was apparently not happy with Nawaz Sharif's approach to India and his desire to be present in Delhi for Prime Minister Modi's swearing-in ceremony. In one of the articles written by an editor who previously worked in Pakistani media, another senior journalist was quoted as saying, that "Television anchors receive funds from the military establishment, if not the civilian Ministry of Information and Broadcasting. Today, all the Pakistani intelligence agencies and the military have media departments that ostensibly only disseminate background information and press briefings, but are actually guiding and managing discourses and the national narrative".[15] Indian media also tends to take an overtly nationalistic stance and promotes media jingoism in the context of India-Pakistan relations.[16]

There have been instances when India and Pakistan put several restrictions on accredited journalists to report from each other's countries even while two journalists are to be allowed as per international convention to be stationed in each other's country. There have been cases when journalists were expelled on the allegation that they were working as spies.[17] Most of the media houses are now recruiting journalists from the countries they want to track, and inserting regular guest columns from neighbouring countries to dodge the restrictions that could impair their ability to report on the developments in the neighbourhood.

Similarly, in Bangladesh, media owned by both right-wing and the left-wing political forces usually take a critical view of India though their views on domestic politics might be progressive at times. In the 1970s, as well as in the 1990s as discussed elsewhere, newspapers like *Holiday* and *Daily Inquilab* played a significant role in arousing anti-Indian sentiments and creating doubts in the minds of average Bangladeshis about the desirability of good relationship between India and Bangladesh and the signing of the 1972 Treaty of Peace and Friendship by Mujib government. Such instances persist over time.

The media's role in foreign policy is also evident in the Sri Lankan experience when the media was dealing with the alleged human rights violations during the last phase of the war. During the war, the Media Centre for National Security established by the government guided the discourse on war reporting and controlled the narrative pertaining to the war on LTTE and there were severe restrictions on media. Even after the war, the checks on media continued; there were concerted attacks on media personalities who were critical of the previous Rajapaksa regime. One also perceived media jingoism in Sri Lanka in 2014 when the UNHRC (United Nations Human Rights Council) voting took place over the issue of UN investigations into Sri Lankan government's role during the last phase of war. Most of the media reports and analytical pieces were seen to be portraying it as an assault on the sovereignty of Sri Lanka by the western countries. Interestingly, there was a marked sense of departure in media's outlook with the change of regime in January 2015. In spite of UNHRC publication of war crime report, the media reporting was balanced and nationalistic jingoism was conspicuously absent.

This suggests that while media shapes foreign policy and can be a potential binding force in South Asia, it is likely to be influenced by the nature of political leadership and toe the governmental line. Since business houses have their economic interest, confrontation with the political elite is generally avoided. Editors having independent views and not following the line of the owners are generally sacrificed at the political altar.

Impact of Visual Media

Visual media was popularised in the 1980s and only a very few people owned television sets in the initial decade. Moreover, the only sources of news in the visual media were the channels funded and controlled by the governments in different countries. India witnessed a boom in private media channels in the mid-1990s. Similarly, there was a surge of private media channels in most other countries including Bangladesh, Pakistan and Sri Lanka in the next decade. The visual media often shapes public opinion in a negative way which creates hurdles in inter-state relations. For example, the killing of 16 BSF soldiers in Boraibari in the India-Bangladesh border and later displaying one of the soldiers with his hands and legs tied and hanging from a bamboo pole, like an animal carcass, created an outrage in India in 2001.[18] Similarly, the visual of Felani—hanging from the barbed wire fence after being shot by the Indian Border Security Force for illegally crossing the border—created an outrage in both the countries in 2011. These visuals created an adverse impact on India-Bangladesh relations.

The beaming of the Kargil War to the drawing rooms of the people in 1999 was truly a media revolution that embittered India-Pakistan relations. Similarly, the live coverage of 26/11 Mumbai attack left indelible impact on the people in India who came face to face with the hatred emanating from a section of people within Pakistan against India and Indians. However, the media's portrayal of the tragedy generalised people's impression about all Pakistanis as India baiters. Bilateral relationship between the two countries has still not been able to get out of the shock administered by 26/11 in 2008. It is also true that the media focus on 26/11 caused a ripple throughout the world and created a negative image about Pakistan at the international level.

While social media and internet have erased barriers among people across international borders in terms of enhancing contacts at the individual level, the print and visual media have sometimes played the role of the spoiler. One often hears the Pakistanis complaining about the 'aggressive' visual media that can be described as the 'TIMES NOW' effect and similarly there are TV channels in Pakistan that engage in arousing public sentiment against India. The trend even becomes visible when the states engage themselves in speaking to each other through the media. The print media plays a relatively lesser role in fuelling jingoism since the advent of the visual media, which has taken the lead in delivering instant response to events with immediate impact on the government. Therefore, it is not surprising that many of the corporate-owned media houses not only dominate the English and regional language print media, but also own television channels.

Media and Corporate Interests

John Swinton, the former Chief of Staff at *The New York Times* once said while reacting to a guest who raised a toast to 'independent media' in the New York Press Club in 1953: "I am paid weekly for keeping my honest, opinion out of the paper I am connected with... The business of the journalists is to destroy the truth, to lie outright, to pervert, to vilify, to fawn at the feet of mammon, and to sell his country and his race for his daily bread. You know it and I know it, and what folly is this toasting (of) an independent press?"[19]

Increasingly, corporate houses have entered the domain of visual media and opened television channels in their bid to expand business and also further their economic interests. Ownership of media can be used as an effective bargain for political favours. It is likely that the corporate business houses having economic interests in terms of investment and capturing the market will utilise their channels to further their corporate interests. In any case, corporates economic interests sometimes dictate their political affiliation and the content of the news channel. According to a study of the media houses in Pakistan, some commentators have argued that "the corporate media sector would be the greatest beneficiary of communication regulation due to its political clout, lobbying expertise, and economic prowess".[20] Thus, regulatory bodies do not necessarily help the cause of independent media and provide a level playing field to various media houses.

There is a contrarian argument also that the government's influence is in clear discount as corporate greed has risen to an extent that government's inducements have stopped shaping media orientation. For example, in India, which could also be true of other South Asian countries, the phenomenon of media getting out of governmental control is summed up by Sanjaya Baru when he writes, "...given rising budgets of private media organisations, Government freebies and junkets have declining influence in shaping media thinking on major policy issues".[21] This could be true, however, despite its decreasing financial dependence on the government sponsorship, media is a willing partner in the official projects of nation building and championing particular world views.

At the same time, media maintains a close relationship with the government to get access to official information and sometimes to get goodies like a free trip with the official entourage and sometimes 'exclusive' leaks or 'exclusive interviews' that put them ahead of their peer news agencies. The government also uses media to gauge public opinion and, sometimes, select information is leaked to the media to send a message to the domestic constituency as well as to other countries. Therefore, media has its own interest and biases and with corporate overtaking of the media houses, the media-government collaboration is likely to continue. This led to the Minister of State for External Affairs, General V.K. Singh, to call the phenomena as "presstitute" creating uproar in the media. As a journalist writes: "The reality is that the media is not always above board when it comes to fair play. In many ways its biases are not only not apparent, but seldom disclosed".[22] There is also the 'bread and butter issue' for the journalists who also live in the modern consumerist world with their material aspiration.

Media and Nationalism

In South Asia, given the context of nation-state formation in the region, the media's perspective has an unmistakable nationalist overtone. Therefore, there is a tendency to project inter-state as well as intra-state conflicts in a particular manner to strengthen the dominant ideological orientation of the state. However, this is not to deny that the reporting is also coloured by the bias of the person covering the issue as well as the commercial and political interests of the respective media houses.

It is interesting to note that in the region, the vernacular media often tries to manufacture a nationalism that caters to the readers at the local level in rural areas whereas the English press is much more liberal and caters to the English speaking elite population in urban locales. Therefore, there is a clear constituency which each of the media caters to. In each country, one can identify media houses that take a particular foreign policy posture based on the kind of nationalism they seek to produce. For example: the *Telegraph Nepal* in its reporting takes a distinct anti-India stance while one does not see any such approach towards their reportage on China. In such cases, the ideological affiliation of the newspaper becomes quite visible. In Bangladesh, the left-oriented newspapers, for example, the *New Age* is extremely critical of India and the Awami League party and its foreign policy, while its coverage on China appears quite value neutral. Similarly, the centre right newspaper like the *Sangram* (Jamaat-e-Islami's mouth piece) and *Naya Diganta* have time and again questioned Indian investment and trade from a nationalist perspective. The reporting on border firing and fences are projected in a manner that it blames India without taking a critical look at the smuggling racket that flourishes in the border region and entices Bangladeshi citizens to act as carriers in the smuggling racket. Reports in these newspapers on border firings hardly mention certain common facts that such firings take places in the night and targets illegal activities that the people are engaged in. The foreign policy impact of these newspapers is negligible, however, they do create suspicion in the minds of the people about India. Similarly in Sri Lanka, the media houses like the *Daily News* did not hesitate to campaign against the UNHRC and unabashedly supported the Rajapaksa regime at the height of its power.[23] Any criticism of the war with the LTTE and arguments in favour of devolution was portrayed as anti-national by the media.

In some cases, some anchors in the visual media in the region in different countries try to peddle a particular nationalistic position, and in debates on foreign policy, they would exhort guests to take a 'for or against' position and try to paint the dissenting voice as anti-national.[24] Such type of television debates is more pervasive in India, Pakistan and Bangladesh. As a study on media's reporting in the India-Pakistan context pointed out: "For years now, the media of both nations (read India and Pakistan) have been fighting a proxy war that is blurring out factual and unbiased coverage of events in the subcontinent. Overly nationalistic posturing and jingoism lie at the heart of this".[25]

Such nationalism propagated by media whips up popular passions in favour of or against foreign policy choices of a government and constrains their ability to ameliorate interstate tension through proactive measures. Intense media scrutiny does not allow the governments to be innovative in their policies as their policies are often evaluated from the prism of a zero sum game in the media forcing them to advocate a conservative status-quoist line.

The display of nationalism is more perceptible among the journalists in India and Pakistan when they deal with issues pertaining to bilateral relations. Given the hostile relationship that has been in place for a long time, the reporters and commentators often feel it their duty to conform to the nationalist discourse churned by the establishment for fear of being branded as unpatriotic while dealing with these issues. If any journalist takes an independent view or criticises their respective government in a bilateral India-Pakistan problem, they can do it at their own peril of being labelled as 'agent' of the 'enemy'. The Urdu press of Pakistan is a victim of this mind-set and often raises the ante against India. It emphasises on the human rights violations in Kashmir, opposes the idea of trade and commerce with India, portrays India as an enemy which is not reconciled to the existence of Pakistan and accuses India of trying to desertify Pakistan by deliberately obstructing flow of water into Pakistan. As a Pakistani observer noted the context of media's role in India-Pakistan relations: "the Urdu press constitutes an important medium for Pakistani people to follow political developments. What is arguably more disturbing is that such reports are skewed and biased, quite often devoid of fact but dipped in myth."[26] In the English media, there is always a cautious approach while dealing with India-Pakistan problem which "generally avoids confrontation with official stand".[27]

Threats from Non-state Sources

Media in South Asia is threatened by militants and terrorists of all hues and reporters are often forced to be careful about serving news in deference to the diktats of such non-state actors. There are instances of fringe groups in India threatening journalists, the TTP (Tehrik-i-Taliban Pakistan) threat in Pakistan, recent threats to the Bangladeshi journalists not to publish anything against the killing of 'atheist' bloggers and warned women journalists to stay at home.[28] In the past, the LTTE also had embedded journalists to report their side of the story to the world.[29]

Media and Regional Cooperation

Regional cooperation gets least priority both in the print and visual media. Findings from the 'content analysis' of 15 newspapers from the neighbourhood over the last three months revealed that there was very limited report on South Asia, whereas other parts of the world received more attention and space; there was no effort to enhance knowledge about developments in the neighbouring countries; India received maximum attention in the media in the neighbourhood compared to any other country; and there is a disproportionate focus on India's security and foreign policies as opposed to its society and culture even if Bollywood was covered well in the neighbourhood.

Apart from the usual reports on the region when the South Asian Association for Regional Cooperation (SAARC) summits take place, there is little focus on the state of regional politics in the media. The visual media takes a lead to showcase cultural exchanges among states in the region even though it is more pronounced in case of the media of India and Pakistan. For example, the private media channels like *Zee Zindagi* that shows Pakistan television drama in India has become quite popular and provides a glimpse into the life of a particular class of people in Pakistan. Similarly, Indian channels like Star and Zee television networks are popular in Pakistan. Indian television channels are in fact popular in many other neighbouring countries and have a significant viewership in the region. Some of these popular soap operas are even dubbed into Sinhala language and watched in Sri Lanka. The Bengali channels are popular in both India and Bangladesh. However, these channels are not in the business of inducing intercultural learning or propagating regional cooperation. While the primary motive is making profit out of advertisement through increased viewership, the channels may be sometimes attaining such objectives by default than design.

However, the media can certainly play a positive role in promoting regional cooperation. Those controlling media need to take into account their influence and function in a responsible manner. In recent years, one has seen how even social media was used to launch hate and fear campaigns. For example, morphed pictures that were circulated in the aftermath of the tribal-Muslim conflict in Assam in May 2012, generated violent protests by Muslims in Mumbai. It was later found that photos of people killed in Assam flood were circulated to show as Muslims killed in Assam. Similarly, a morphed picture led to violence against Buddhists in Ramu in Bangladesh. While social media has played a great role in bringing people together through the cyberspace by deconstructing the narratives built by the states, it also has the potential to generate violence and misunderstanding. As one of the internet media outlets argued in an editorial, referring to Pakistani newspapers reportage on India: "the media has rarely faulted, let alone questioned the government and the military with regards to ties with Delhi....The propaganda is often focused on a select few issues, which are repeatedly stated in various forms and to different degrees of severity".[30]

It is assuring to note that many media groups have joined hands to promote peace and greater understanding in the region which can create conducive atmosphere for regional cooperation. For example, as has been cited earlier, the cooperation between Jang and Times group to launch *Aman ki Asha* was quite a success in promoting people-to-people contact between India and Pakistan. The South Asian Free Media Association (SAFMA) is also contributing to exchange of media personnel within the region and exchange of views among the members of the media community in the region. Despite the fact that various laws passed by the countries of the region are aimed at muzzling the press, the media is largely doing fine in terms of expanding its reach and enhancing its use-value and influence in most of the countries in the region.

Media's capacity to promote a soft and inclusive culture of trust and tolerance and be an agent of change in the region is greatly underestimated and often left untapped. Given the favourable mind-set displayed by the politicians in the region today, media can be a real agent of change and herald a new beginning in regional cooperation. Rather than playing overt or covert nationalist games that perpetuate interstate tension and spoils interstate relations, the media can highlight events that depict the unmistakable change taking place at the people-to-people level in favour of greater interaction and cooperation; it can provide forum for constructive engagement by bringing in stories that are much humane as is reflected in the website of *Aman ki Asha*. In spite of the corporate's political agenda, media can play a role in bridging the gap in the perceptions of the people about one another.

Conclusion

There may not be something called "value-neutral journalism" as journalists are products of the socio-cultural environment in which they are raised. It would be important, however, for the media to verify and interrogate its functioning and play its role as a change agent and catalyse the process of interstate cooperation. In the 24x7 news format, where each of the media house is in competition with the other for larger public attention there is a temptation to indulge in sensationalisation of information. However, through coordination and networking with regional media houses and imaginative coverage of the neighbourhood, the media can change the discourse on regional cooperation and integration and create an atmosphere of mutual trust and understanding among states who distrust each other and regard each other as enemies. By shaping public opinion favourably, media can moderate the views of fringe constituencies in most of the countries who develop a vested interest in perpetuating the atmosphere of hatred and fear.

Media is considered the fourth pillar in a democracy. A vigilant media is intrinsic to democratic governance. Given the increasing salience of neighbourhood in the domestic discourses in every country in the region, media can play the role of a moderator in the foreign policy domain. While the media needs to portray the situation as it is, it needs to downplay jingoism and should not appear to take sides or give space to alarmist views. Rather than highlighting conflicts, the media can bring in humane stories where citizens have stood for each other regardless of the governmental narratives that propagate distrust. Apart from this, emphasis on common cultural linkages in the weekly magazines or doing such a story in the visual media once a month will certainly go a long way in instilling a sense of regional consciousness that will transcend narrowly constructed nationalist discourses in individual countries. The media has the potential to promote regional cooperation and it must realise it.

Data on Media in South Asia[31]

Country	*Print Media Newspapers/magazines (Eng.+Vernacular)*	*Radio Stations*	*TVChannels*	*Internet users/ Population*
Afghanistan	7 daily + 100s of publications	175 FM stations	75	1 mn/31.8 mn
Bangladesh	40+ Bangla, 10+ Eng	15AM and 13FM radio stations	100+	617,300/166 mn
Bhutan	11 (7 in English and 4 in Dzongkha)	5 radio stations (including BBS Radio since 1973)	BBS TV (introduced in 1999 but picked up in 2006)	133,289 / 742,737
India	82,237 newspapers[32]	AIR + 245 pvt FM	30 state owned + 798 (397 news + 401 entt)	61.3 mn /1238 mn
Maldives	12 (print and online)	12	3	3296/393,595
Myanmar	3 daily (state owned, free of charge) + 4 dailies (Pvt), + 12 licenses issued + 187 weekly (Pvt.)	6 (1 AM + 2 FM + 3 SW)	7 (state owned) + 1 pvt	110,000/55.7 mn
Nepal	3,741 (251 daily, 1304 weekly, 1122 monthly)	57 (6 AM + 50 FM + 1 SW)	22 (2 state owned + 20 pvt)	577,800/30.9 mn
Pakistan	~945 (from about 4000 in 1997, 424 members of APNS)	200 radio stations	8 state owned+ 91 PVT	20.4 mn/196 mn
Sri Lanka	41 *(21 Sinhala+ 12 English + 8 Tamil)* 25 daily + 6 monthly and 10 weekly	67 stations (34 Sinhala + 14 Eng + 11 Tamil + others) 3 S-E-T)	46 (9 state owned) 26 Sinhala + 7 Eng + 5 Tamil + 5 S-E +	1.8 mn/21.8 mn (2009)

NOTES

1. For details see the Table at the end of the chapter.
2. Piers Robinson, "Media as a Driving Force in International Politics: The CNN Effect and Related Debates", October 8, 2013, at http://www.globalpolicyjournal.com/blog/08/10/2013/media-driving-force-international-politics-cnn-effect-and-related-debates (accessed October 10, 2015).
3. Ibid.
4. Matthew A. Baum and Philip B.K. Potter, "The Relationships Between Mass Media, Public Opinion, and Foreign Policy: Toward a Theoretical Synthesis", at http://www.hks.harvard.edu/fs/mbaum/documents/BaumPotter_AnnualReview2008.pdf, p.57 (accessed October 2, 2015).
5. See the Government of Bangladesh "National Broadcasting Policy 2014". Gist of the policy is available, at http://www.mediabangladesh.net/national-broadcasting-policy-2014-bangladesh/(accessed October 10, 2015).
6. S M Shameem Reza, "Media Governance in Bangladesh: Rhetoric and Reality of Broadcasting Policy", *Forum*, May 5, 2012, at http://archive.thedailystar.net/forum/2012/May/media.htm(accessed October 14, 2015).
7. AFP, "Sri Lanka shuts down war-time propaganda centre", *Business Standard*, December 3, 2013, at http://www.business-standard.com/article/pti-stories/sri-lanka-shuts-down-war-time-propaganda-centre-113120300003_1.html(accessed October 14, 2015).
8. The chapter is restricted to the analyses of print and visual media only. Social media falls into a different genre as far as presentation of news and views are concerned. The chapter will focus on foreign policy reporting and its impact on inter-state relations.
9. Atul Aneja, "Where big can be bothersome", *The Hindu*, January 7, 2000, at http://www.thehindu.com/2001/01/07/stories/05071343.htm(accessed September 1, 2015).
10. Pratyoush Onta, "The Paradox of the Nepali Mindset: Hate India, Love India", *Himal Southasian*, February 2001, at http://old.himalmag.com/component/content/article/1943-The-Paradox-of-the-Nepali-Mindset-Hate-India,-Love-India.html (accessed September 1, 2015).
11. In spite of India providing largest aid the *Kantipur* chose to title its news story as: "China, Japan announce major support to Nepal", June 25, 2015, at http://www.ekantipur.com/2015/06/25/top-story/china-japan-announce-major-support-to-nepal/407024.html; In the context of Kailali killing, there was also motivated reporting, Bhrikuti Rai, "Beware of fake News", *Nepal Times*, September 4-10, 2015, at http://nepalitimes.com/article/nation/in-nepal-beware-of-fake-news,2556; Rohit Karki, "Aid and Interests", *The Kathmandu Post*, August 5, 2008, at http://kathmandupost.ekantipur.com/printedition/news/2015-05-07/aid-and-interests.html (accessed September 5, 2015).
12. For details see: *Aman ki Asha*, at http://amankiasha.com/ (accessed October 17, 2015).
13. See Shamsad Ahmed, "Media's Constructivism and the India-Pakistan Peace Process", *IDSA Strategic Comments*, February 2, 2010, at http://www.idsa.in/idsacomments/MediasConstructivismandtheIndia-PakistanPeaceProcess_skhan_020210(accessed October 19, 2015).
14. Neha Ansari, "Not Fit to Print: An Insider Account of Pakistani Censorship", The South Asia Channel, *Foreign Policy*, November 20, 2014, at http://foreignpolicy.com/2014/11/20/not-fit-to-print-an-insider-account-of-pakistani-censorship/ (accessed September 7, 2015).
15. Ibid.
16. Smruti S.Pattanaik, *Elite Perceptions in Foreign Policy: Role of Print Media in Influencing India-Pakistan Relations, 1989-1999*, Manohar Publishers, New Delhi-RCSS, 2004.
17. For example, Nirupama Subramanian of the Hindu group reporting from Islamabad was

asked to leave and her visa was not renewed. See Nirupama Subramanian, "A Foreign Correspondent From India as Suspect in Pakistan", at http://niemanreports.org/articles/a-foreign-correspondent-from-india-as-suspect-in-pakistan/(accessed October 5, 2015).

18. Harinder Baweja, Shisir Gupta and Wasbir Hussain, "Bordering truth", *India Today*, May 7, 2001, at http://indiatoday.intoday.in/story/barbaric-killing-of-bsf-jawans-puts-india-bangladesh-relations-under-severe-strain/1/233646.html(accessed September 5, 2015).
19. John Swinton on the independence of the press, at http://www.constitution.org/pub/swinton_press.htm(accessed September 10, 2015).
20. Azmal Rasul and Stephen D McDowell, "Consolidation in the Name of Regulation: The Pakistan Electronic Media Regulatory Authority (PEMRA) and the Concentration of Media Ownership in Pakistan", *Global Media Journal*, Vol. 12(20), Spring 2012, at http://www.globalmediajournal.com/open-access/consolidation-in-the-name-of-regulation-the-pakistan-electronic-media-regulatory-authority-pemra-and-the-concentration-of-media-ownership-in-pakistan.pdf, p.4 (accessed September 17, 2015).
21. Sanjaya Baru, The Influence of Business and Media on Indian Foreign Policy, *India Review*, Vol.8(3), 2009,p.279.
22. R. Jagannathan, "VK Singh and the P-word: Media Should learn to Take it on the Chin", *First Post*, April 10, 2015, at http://www.firstpost.com/india/vk-singh-and-the-p-word-media-should-learn-to-take-it-on-the-chin-2190245.html (accessed September 17, 2015).
23. "Expose: Media Heads To Bow; Rajapaksa Gives 547 Journos Interest Free Car Loans", *Colombo Telegraph*, January 20, 2014, at https://www.colombotelegraph.com/index.php/expose-media-heads-to-bow-rajapaksa-gives-547-journos-interest-free-car-loans/; "A Sri Lankan Journalist Eagerly Toes the Line", *The New York Times*, October 18, 2013, at http://www.nytimes.com/2013/10/19/world/asia/a-sri-lankan-journalist-eagerly-toes-the-line.html?_r=0 (accessed September 15, 2015).
24. Sanjaya Baru, no. 21.
25. Dwaipayan Bose, *Journalism Caught in Narrow Nationalism: The India-Pakistan Media War*, Reuters Institute for the Study of Journalism, Oxford University, Hillary and Trinity Terms, 2011, p.5.
26. Editorial, "How free is Pakistan media?", *Strategic Insight*, Policy Research Group, March 17, 2010, at http://policyresearchgroup.com/regional_weekly/hot_topics/638.html (accessed September 15, 2015).
27. Smruti S.Pattanaik, *Elite Perceptions in Foreign Policy: Role of Print Media in Influencing India-Pakistan Relations, 1989-1999*, p.178.
28. IHS Jane's *Country Risk Daily Report*, "Threat against Bangladeshi journalists increases risk of targeted crude attacks against individuals", at http://www.janes.com/article/55419/threat-against-bangladeshi-journalists-increases-risk-of-targeted-crude-attacks-against-individuals (accessed October 20, 2015).
29. Between 2007 and 2009 the Sri Lankan government was critical of the journalists who did not side with the government narrative of the war. The Ministry of Defence in its website criticizing the journalists wrote: "Those who commit such treachery should identify themselves with the LTTE [Liberation Tigers of Tamil Eelam]rather than showing themselves as crusaders of media freedom". See, "EXCERPT: Journalism on the front line", *Dawn*, May 11, 2015, at http://www.dawn.com/news/1181155 (accessed October 20, 2015).
30. No. 26 (accessed October 20, 2015).
31. Compiled from government as well as private sources in each of the countries covered here.
32. Hindi (7910), followed by English (1406), Urdu (938), Gujarati (761), Telugu (603), Marathi (521), Bengali (472), Tamil (272), Oriya (245), Kannada (200) and Malayalam (192).

2

The Media and Foreign Policy Discourses in Pakistan

Rasul Bakhsh Rais

Introduction

Freedom of expression is one of the most refreshing and robust aspects of Pakistani society; it stands out spectacularly in the otherwise depressing elitist politics and dominance of dynastic political families.[1] No fair person can remain unimpressed by the degree of self-critique, sometimes bordering on cynicism, which the Pakistani media demonstrates. The commentators in the press and participants in political talk-shows express their views in an unprecedentedly frank and open manner. This is a great progress and one of the hard-earned rights, resting on the sacrifices of journalists who suffered humiliation, prisons, tortures and even murders, the public intellectuals and the civil society of Pakistan.

The development and growth of media in Pakistan has a long history, traditions and institutions, that go back to the colonial times. This is a history of struggle between freedom of expression and tendency on part of the autocratic leaders to suppress dissent.[2] The media in Pakistan has risen with the growth of democracy, like in other societies. The two grow together and reinforce each other. It is, therefore, no coincidence that some major developments in the print media of Pakistan occurred with democratic openings. The media found a bigger space for the first time when the late Prime Minister, Mohammad Khan Junejo, asserted his autonomy against General Zia-ul-Haq. Junejo encouraged debates and controversies in the press that quite often reflected on the role of the military in politics and society. Women speaking on gender issues and fledging civil society organizations added a great deal to the tradition of dissent during his brief tenure in office.

After decades of stagnation, the entry of two new newspapers, *The Muslim* and *The Nation*, in early 1980s, broke the monopoly of the *Pakistan Times* and *Dawn*. Younger men and women, representing a new generation pursued journalism as a career and new writers began to contribute columns to the editorial pages. *The News*, *Frontier Post* and *Daily Times*, later in the decades, further added to the diversity and space for comment in the print media.

With these publications and many more in the vernacular languages, Pakistani media entered a new phase. The development of the print media had its own momentum that could not be controlled or restrained by traditional methods of intimidation, threats or denial of printing paper and withholding of advertisement. These methods were tried but began to lose the impact they once had on publishers and editors.

Globalization of information and ability of foreign media to reach homes and work places in Pakistan set the stage for media revolution in the country. With the foreign media leapfrogging the territoriality and sovereignty of all states, governments began to lose control of what citizens could hear, read and watch. Today, virtually thousands of newspapers in hundreds of different languages around the world are just a few clicks away everywhere in the world, more so, in South Asian countries that have some of the well-established traditions of free press.

Our governments and others have had to adjust to this global change that the technology of communication has brought about. Rulers who have tried to control the global flow of information have ended up looking pretty silly, with very little success in denying access.

Pakistan can rightly claim merit in recognizing the limits of state and sovereignty in exercising raw power over the print and electronic media. The media outlets here are now too many, have greater resources and can reach wider audiences than they could do ten years ago. All private networks have flourished and achieved remarkable sophistication and incredible capacity in acting as a popular forum of debate on current national and international issues. One is amazed by the stridency of the questions of the anchor-persons and the frankness of the participants' views and comments in various programmes on television channels and in opinion page articles.

The media in the process of maturing has accommodated all kinds of views, taking a pluralistic character. It is no longer confined, as it was in the past, to tirades and one-sided information provided by government spokespersons. Viewers now have the opportunity to watch and listen to the other side of the story and read all types of views on the editorial pages and make up their own minds. This is precisely the role that progressive and independent media can and should play in a society like Pakistan, which is undergoing many changes and transformations, visible and not so visible.

Today in Pakistan, the media is an extremely powerful tool and a major resource for influencing public opinion. It has built up a capacity to generate narratives and engage in public discourses on national and international issues. The central argument of this paper is that Pakistani media has developed into an autonomous, robust and effective institution representing diverse and even conflicting social, economic and political interests of the society. Embedded in this view, the paper will focus on dominant public discourses in Pakistani media on three sets of foreign policy issues—relations with India, the United States and the Muslim countries.

Methodology

The major challenge one faces while looking at the media in Pakistan is that it has several categories or media types, outlets and too many channels through which it expresses itself. There is electronic media, and within electronic media there is at least one channel in English language, Urdu channels, Sindhi channels, Baluchi channels, Pashto channels, Punjabi channels, etc. Among all of them, the Urdu channels dominate the electronic media scene. It can only be part of a much larger study to monitor all brands of media and compare them for what they focus on and what orientations they have. Rather, this study is based on a small sample and focuses only on the print media, which has historical roots and is well-established. Print media in Pakistan is a much matured medium of communication and has stable, nationwide readership.

There are hundreds of Urdu newspapers and at least eight major English newspapers in Pakistan currently in circulation. The scope of this article is limited and reflects mainly representative sampling of writings on foreign policy issues from four newspapers, two Urdu and two English. Among the English papers, *The News* and *Dawn* have been selected. *Dawn* has been in publication since early 1940s, it was founded by Mohammad Ali Jinnah, the founder of the country. The paper has the largest circulation in the English language. The Jang group of newspapers added to its publications an English daily *The News* in 1980, challenging the dominance of *Dawn*. Over the past two decades, *The News* has established itself as one of the major English dailies. Among the Urdu newspapers, *Jang*, that started in early 1940s, before the creation of Pakistan and *Nawaiwaqt*, also one of the major newspapers which exercises great deal of influence with a nationalist, conservative orientation. It is hard to define *Jang* as it has no ideological line and runs mainly as a commercial venture. *Nawaiwaqt*, on the other hand, has remained a campaigner for Pakistan's ideology and the Kashmir issue.

Media in every country focuses on current issues, generally the politics in broader terms and every day happenings of public interest and national importance. In this sense, Pakistani media casts a wide net with daily focus on quality of democracy, incidence of terrorism, Islamic radicalism and militancy, and of course, relations with major countries and proximate regions. Since the foreign relations of Pakistan extend over all continents, the coverage of foreign policy issues in this paper is limited to three countries—Afghanistan, India and the West/the United States—in order to make it more focussed and practicable.

Another challenge is with regard to a suitable time frame—as to how many years one has to cover in order to get a fair idea about the issues, debates and controversies. Hence, the timeframe has been narrowed to two months—August and September, 2014. The choice of the months was random, assuming that a set of another two months may not make a difference. In future, comparative study of different set of months for different years can be made that will confirm or challenge the findings. The views and conclusions are based on the survey of articles in the newspapers concerned. The content, therein, has been closely read before analysing or commenting upon it.

Some Tentative Findings

In two months, the four papers published 2,318 editorials and the opinion page articles on a wide range of issues, as all newspapers do. Surprisingly, out of 2,318 articles only 90 articles cumulatively dealt with foreign policy related issues. Rest of the opinion page articles and the editorials were about Pakistan's domestic politics and other internal issues.

Why do foreign policy issues figure so low in the debate and discussion in the print media? There are two possible reasons to explain the peripheral interest. In the month of August-September 2014, the newspapers in Pakistan carried extensive coverage about the *dharna*, the sit-in and the long march led by the Pakistan Tehreek-e-Insaf (PTI) of Imran Khan. The print media as well as electronic media excessively devoted time to cover developments in Islamabad including the evening speeches made by the leaders of the PTI every day and also the issues that were highlighted. Secondly, it is felt that even without a focus on an ongoing political crisis of immense national interest such as the PTI protest, the foreign policy issues still have remained less attractive. The reason is that foreign policy discourses require serious thought, expert opinion and sharper focus than the gossip, the juicy controversies and 'breaking news' coverage of political events. Never have foreign policy issues been popular either with the electronic or print media, except in the case of Afghanistan, India and the United States—the three countries selected for sampling in this paper. Also, the comments and editorials published in both types of media are incident or event-driven. Foreign policy issues, mainly security, defence and strategic problems relating to these countries are extensively debated, and even consistently, but much of the debate or controversy is triggered by events.

Comparing the English and Urdu newspapers, one gets a very contrasting picture. For instance, one of the most influential Urdu newspaper, *Nawaiwaqt* published only ten articles on foreign policy issues in two months, while the *Jang*, its traditional rival, carried 14 articles. Compared to this very small number, the *Dawn* published about 28 articles and *The News* carried 34 pieces, the largest number of articles among all the newspapers. In percentage terms, it comes roughly between 7 and 8 per cent for English newspaper articles. For Urdu newspapers, it is much lower at about 1.7 per cent in case of *Nawaiwaqt* and 1.6 per cent in the case of *Jang*. This is all what was devoted to foreign policy and national security discourses in the widely read, and most popular Urdu language newspaper in Pakistan.

India

During the brief period this paper covers, it was found that wide range of issues relating to India have been the subject of debate and discussion in the four newspapers. These are as follows: Kashmir dispute, democracy in India, electoral process and the outcome of the 2014 general elections, the rise of the Bharatiya Janata Party (BJP), India's regional ambitions and search for dominance.

On floods, there was interesting debate whether it is a natural disaster or a man-made disaster? When it comes to a man-made disaster, due to the nature of politics in Pakistan, the governments in power have done little in terms of precautionary measures needed to avert seasonal floods or meet adverse consequences of floods upon different sections of population. There was a debate in Pakistan whether India was behind the floods and that it had done so by releasing water where it was not supposed to, particularly the Chenab, causing huge floods and devastation.

Interestingly, while writing on the 2014 monsoon floods in Pakistan, a good number of commentators pointed finger towards India for releasing waters so as to harm Pakistan. The Islamist parties and groups, in particular, blamed India for the floods as its strategy to destabilise the Pakistan economy and society.[3] In Pakistan, there is intellectual pluralism—neither the commentators write with one voice, nor do the political leaders make similar statements. On the flood controversy, Ayaz Amir, one of the strident liberal voices in the media wrote: "India is not trying to destroy us, or wreck our agriculture, through manipulating the Jhelum and the Chenab. It is only managing its share of the waters far better than us".[4]

What is noticeable is much praise for the Indian society on the issue of democratic development. There appears to be a unanimous view in Urdu and English press that India is democratising better and Pakistan must learn from the Indian experience.[5] The thinking is that if India can be a successful democracy with so much diversity and with so many problems, so can Pakistan be a democracy, and must be with all the problems that it is facing today. Overall, there is a great deal of admiration for Indian democracy in Pakistani press.

The second trend, which is very important, is that India is an emerging regional as well as global power. India has ambitions and one gets two views on Indian ambitions as rising power: pessimistic and optimistic. The same could be the view in India or elsewhere. The optimistic view is that India has made it and will continue to be through it. India is growing economically and is much more coherent than it used to be and Indian ambitions are perhaps realisable. The other pessimistic view is that India's problems are such that, perhaps, there is a mismatch between capacities and resources of India and the dreams or the aspirations that it has set for itself.[6]

On the issue of the rise of the BJP again, we get a plurality of views in Pakistani media. One view holds that a hidden part of India is conservative, Hindu-orientated, anti-minority, etc. This side has become much more salient and dominant. It appears to be in sync with the conventional view in Pakistan about India being a Hindu nation, not a secular one. A secular India has always been a farce and that is what has materialised with the rise of the BJP. But with regard to English newspapers' articles, there is a nuanced view on the emergence of the BJP as a dominant political force. As there is a debate within India, whether it is the rise of the BJP and the *Hindutva* crowd with only 33-34 per cent of the popular vote, or is it a referendum against the performance of the Congress Party's 10 year rule in the country. So, the opinion in this case also seems to be divided in Pakistan.[7]

On the Kashmir dispute, however, there seems to be unanimity of views in Pakistan—that this is an issue which needs to be settled. But again, the variation in views persists for the ways to settle the Kashmir issue in Pakistan as well. There might be a similar situation in India. However, as far as the dispute and the problems in India-Pakistan relations are concerned, and the need for its resolution, there seems to be a general agreement that India and Pakistan need to take up resolution of the Kashmir issue seriously. In Pakistan, the opinion is rather much divided on the Kashmir issue—as to whether to put Kashmir on the back burner, to freeze it or develop close relations with India.[8] Urdu newspapers, and among them, particularly *Nawaiwaqt* that is considered very influential, is consistent in arguing that without self-determination by the people of Kashmir, close relations with India will never be allowed to develop. It continues to assert that no progress in India-Pakistan relations is possible, or should be even considered as desirable, if the Kashmir issue remains unresolved. This argument is in convergence with the dominant view in Pakistani society as well.

Afghanistan

Afghanistan has been a dominant foreign as well as a national issue in Pakistani discourses since the communist takeover of the country in April 1978. This country's unending war for the last 37 years has greatly impacted Pakistan's internal security, demography with the influx of mainly Pashtun refugees in

Baluchistan, terrorism and militancy. From the Soviet intervention in 1980 to the US war on Afghanistan in 2002, Pakistan has remained directly or indirectly involved in the Afghan conflicts with many terrible blowback effects. A close reading of the articles on Afghanistan for the months of August-September 2014 gives us an idea about certain key issues that dominate the thinking in Pakistan.

First, the Afghan leaders have not taken the responsibility of their own country. Never have they arisen to the occasion and pulled the country out of wars, which were essentially their own power struggles. They encouraged foreign powers to help them attain power, protect them or dislodge a sitting government. The divisions among the Afghans have invited foreign troubles, foreign interventions: regional and international. One part of Afghanistan has been on the side of the invaders, the Soviets and the Americans, and the other side has always resisted these invaders. A part of Afghanistan thought that Soviet intervention was for their good while another section believed that it was the loss of nation, country, state and sovereignty. Similarly, the American led intervention in Afghanistan is seen in the same fashion in Pakistani media—both electronic as well as the print media. Picking evidence from the print media, one understands that the Northern Front of Afghanistan, comprising many groups and several militia leaders, found the American intervention as a way leading them to success and power. To end the Taliban rule, the American forces forged an alliance with the leaders of the Northern Front. The Taliban—their common enemy and the other part of Afghanistan, has been resisting and reorganising itself, which poses a grave threat to the stability, order and security of Afghanistan.

Secondly, what will happen in Afghanistan post-2014 has been the subject of lot of writings in Pakistan. American decision to end fighting and withdraw from Afghanistan by the end of 2014 generated a lot of debate and questions in Pakistani media. The most important of all was—will Afghanistan be able to stand on its feet and become politically self-reliant? In response to this question, a pessimistic view about Afghanistan, which is very dominant in Pakistani media, prevails. Pakistani commentators do not share an optimistic view that Afghanistan will be able to defend itself against the rise of the Taliban. The pessimistic view is that with the withdrawal of foreign forces, Afghanistan may plunge into yet another civil war and Pakistan should be prepared to face the consequences.[9] At the same time, Pakistan needs to make sure that Afghanistan does not fall apart again, because failures of Afghanistan have always produced tremendous negative consequences for Pakistani security, stability, social order, demographic balance, particularly in Baluchistan. Therefore, Pakistan has a vested interest in the stability and security of Afghanistan. Ultimately, however, Afghanistan's leaders have to take up responsibility for themselves.

Thirdly, an important debate on Afghanistan is regarding the weakness of the state and its effects on Pakistan. It is believed that weakness of the Afghan state—its foreign dependence and, hence, vulnerability—has provided space to the forces adversarial to the interests of Pakistan. Therefore, Afghanistan's vulnerabilities impose on Pakistan an abiding policy to secure its legitimate security interests in Afghanistan. What is that legitimate security interest? It is what is generally referred to as "strategic depth" which is defined in different ways in Pakistan. The concept of "strategic depth" is essentially a defensive doctrine, meaning that no other country should use Afghan territory against Pakistan's national security interests. The moot point about Afghanistan is that peace and harmony between Afghanistan and Pakistan is in the interest of both the countries. Pakistan is culturally, ethnically, and historically integrated with Afghanistan. What explains this complex relationship is the glaring fact that approximately 50,000 to 60,000 people cross the border between the two countries without any visa. There are no two other countries in the world, perhaps with the exception of Canada and the United States, where such cross over movement of populations takes place on a daily basis. This kind of movement has been going on for centuries, only numbers would vary in different periods. This explains well about the borders, geography, ethnicities and intertwined fates of the two countries. It is only recently, with inter-crossing of terrorists and militant groups that Pakistan has begun to consider it a problem and has been thinking on how to control the borders. What has been an accepted norm of licencing the tribes on both sides to travel without documents is likely to get changed. The complexity of borders, movement of militants, and intervention in support of insurgencies explains Pakistan's legitimate interest in stabilising Afghanistan.

Islam and the West

The third consistent theme or discourse in Pakistani media which is equally important and needs to be highlighted is Islam and the West debate. What is that debate? What comes out very clearly in the discourse is that there is a sort of 'clash of civilizations', cultures or identities. There is a historical, political and cultural notion of the West which is essentially embedded in the memories of colonialism and American hegemony. The Indian Muslims and now Pakistan have historically been Pan-Islamists more than the Muslims in any other part of the world. However, their traditional zeal for Islamic solidarity has been taken over by Arab radicalism, religious extremism and militancy.

The events in the Middle East, Afghanistan and in other parts of the Muslim world and the affairs of the Muslim minorities get lot of media and political attention in Pakistan. And there is an Islamic world with all the diversity that we have. The American-led interventions in Iraq—now being debated in the US as a policy blunder—conflict in Syria and American strategy in general in the proximate regions have always remained a subject of great intellectual and policy interest in Pakistan. We find two contrasting views—the one found in the writing and reports of the western think tanks and the other in the Pakistan media. One cannot escape noticing the perception in Pakistan that either the Muslim societies, including Pakistan are misunderstood or deliberately misrepresented. One finds 'orientalist' analysis as a dominant mode of thinking in every layer of Pakistani society—from laymen to the high dominant class elites.

The American articulation of its strategy aiming to stabilise the turbulent Muslim regions is seen with great suspicion. The mainstream Pakistani intellectual, mostly writing for the vernacular media, believe that the motive of the US and its allies is to spread 'disorder'. Even if it is not a hidden objective, its security policies, interventions and selection of local allies has produced counter-effects of instability and disorder in many parts of the Muslim world. The interactions between the Muslim world and the West continue to be explained essentially through the lenses of conspiracy theories. A general belief is that the US wants to perpetuate its hegemonic order in the Middle East and beyond.

American strategy of changing regimes has, in fact, been very destabilising. The interventions in Iraq, Syria and Libya have not produced the desired and promised stability, order, democracy and peace. Rather, the entire fabric of the societies with the old order have vanished, giving rise to civil wars. These might be the unintended consequences, but their interpretation in the Islamist constituencies and the conservative sections of Pakistani society is through the framework of either 'orientalism' or conspiracy theories. This very much echoes with the thoughts and ideas emanating from Iran about the western world.

A very important point in the debate is that the United States is declining and China, a very close strategic partner of Pakistan, will counter the US hegemonic order. Wishful, as it might be, it does explain a culture of distrust of the West and an aspiration of countering the western domination and influence. The other point is about the West itself. We understand the West in a particular way—industrial democracies and social transformations with rooting of liberal ideas stemming from enlightenment traditions. In the idiom of Pakistani journalistic writings and newspaper articles, the West and the US are clubbed together or used interchangeably. They do not see the distinction between the European Union and the United States. The United States is the West, and the West is the United States.

Lastly, the understanding of American policy on developing democracy and protecting human rights is equally interesting. The prominent view is that the United States and its European allies advocate democracy where their geopolitical interests are compatible with democratic change in that particular country. If their strategic interests are conflictive with the democratic change in that country, they prefer dictatorship, or monarchy, or *Sheikhdoms*. Pakistani media rejects the view that the US pursues democracy as a global ideal. Rather, its interests in democracy, dictatorship or monarchy are driven by the real political interests.

Conclusion

In the coming years, the Pakistani media, both print as well as electronic, is likely to grow more in numbers, influence and power, and contribute greatly to the quality of dialogue and debate on issues that confront Pakistani state and society. The governments that have controlled information and debate in the past may not be able to do so in future. On the contrary, today, it is difficult for the government to think of suppressing the media successfully by applying rough and tough methods.

The desire to influence public opinion on any issue of political concern is a legitimate effort on the part of the government. It can do so either in acceptable or objectionable ways. One of the most acceptable ways is that the government may employ spokesperson who can better fashion an argument with communication skills so as to present the official view point logically and convincingly. How one conveys things on the modern media platform is as important as what is being said or who is communicating it. So far, most of them who represent the government side, sadly lack these qualities. They seem to be lacking credibility when they try to spin facts and twist an argument before an increasingly aware audience. Such spokespersons are probably not trained in media management; certain circumstances and their being available catapults them to those positions. They do not seem to understand that acknowledging failures and errors, quite often, reduces adverse political consequences of a government's actions, both on domestic as well as foreign policy issues. A strategy of denial in the face of glaring facts has often damaged the position of government on many national and foreign policy related issues.

One of the objectionable means has been the use of power and patronage that the successive Pakistani governments, both civilian and military, have extended to the media persons affiliated with press clubs and unions. The governments have very generously doled out public resources in their effort to buy off the loyalties of media persons. Disregarding the fact whether they are accomplished or not, the practice of allotting plots in expensive urban areas, developing residential colonies for the journalists and offering invisible benefits to opportunistic media persons is a common practice in Pakistan. Such issues of impropriety definitely reduce the autonomy and freedom of the media.

Media in our times is an extremely powerful tool and this resource belongs to the society and its interests. But there are multiple forces within the society—economic interests, political parties, groups, social movements and, of course, the government—that influence media by several means. In this regard, Pakistani media while developing and proliferating, is and will be a contested institution.

Even in the face of challenges, Pakistan has been able to protect cultural, ideological and political pluralism that is deeply embedded in traditional social structures of the country. For this reason, we see debates, discourses and competing narratives on national as well as international issues.

On India-Pakistan issues or Islam and the West interactions, the Pakistani media does not seem to be very objective or neutral. It is perhaps in the character of the developing media around the world that they must go with the dominant views of the society. By doing this, the media plays an agenda-setting role—not for change but for affirming the traditional view of things. On these two foreign policy themes, the media, in my view, has been provoking public emotions and has continuously fed itself on these emotions. The end result is a pervasive conspiratorial mind-set, emotionalism and negativity.

NOTES

1. "Herald Exclusive: Political Dynasties in Pakistan", *Herald* (Karachi), May 9, 2013; Zahid Hussain, "Dynastic Politics", *Dawn*, July 24, 2012.
2. Zamir Niazi, *Press in Chains*, Oxford University Press, Karachi, 2010.
3. Mehreen Zahra-Malik and Asim Tanveer, "Pakistani Islamists use floods to turn opinion against India", *Reuters*, September 17, 2014, at http://in.reuters.com/article/2014/09/16/southasia-flood-militants-idINKBN0HB2IR20140916 (Accessed on November 1, 2015).
4. Ayaz Amir, "The Timeless Fatalism of the Subcontinent", *The News*, September 12, 2014.
5. "Left behind as India forges ahead", (editorial), *Dawn*, September 16, 2014.
6. Munir Akram, "India's Great Power Game", *Dawn*, September 28, 2014.
7. Aijaz Zak Syed, "Modi's moment and the coming crisis", *The News*, August 22, 2014.
8. See for instance, Asif Ezdi, "Geopolitical realities", *The News*, September 15, 2014; Sherry Rehman, "India's Greta Garbo moment", *The News*, August 24, 2014; Maleeha Lodhi, "A no-talks strategy going nowhere", *The News*, August 25, 2014.
9. Maleeha Lodhi, "Price of discord and delay", *The News*, August 5, 2014; Rahimullah Yusufzai, "The never-ending election", *The News*, September 14, 2014.

3

Impact of Media Ownership on Reporting: When Journalism is Prey to Predatory Instincts

Syed Badrul Ahsan

Imagine the following circumstances in journalism, in the context of Bangladesh:

One

Two siblings operate one of the leading daily newspapers in Bangladesh. They are, respectively, executive director one and executive director two of the media house they have inherited from their deceased father. One of the siblings is a diehard opponent of the military regime which has its grip on the country. The other one is part of the regime, as a minister serving cheerfully under a general whose political legitimacy is open to question.

And that is not all. Late in the night, one of the siblings, unable to agree with the tone and content of one of the two editorials scheduled to be published in the following day's issue of the newspaper, kills the editorial. Through sheer coincidence, the other sibling does not agree with the second editorial and spikes it. In the middle of the night, with all the editorial writers having gone home, the responsibility falls on the sports editor, working as he does till late, to fashion a new editorial that is not quite an editorial. Somehow the newspaper is saved from embarrassing itself, only just.

Such incidents have happened in Bangladesh's newspaper industry, with bad consequences. The newspaper we speak of gradually lost ground to other and newer newspapers, predictably.

Two

Take another instance of the many maladies newspapers in Bangladesh continue to suffer from. The management of a newspaper, an English language one, for years has failed to pay regular monthly salaries to its working journalists and other staff. Months go by before the owners decide that at least some segment of the salaries, now in arrears, needs to be cleared. And, presto, salaries for two months out of the five that have gone by are paid, before the process of non-payment begins all over again.

Such a condition goes on for years, with results that are devastating for the newspaper. Where it began its journey in the early 1990s with a circulation that worried its rivals in the market, it now finds itself in steep decline, with a good number of its journalists moving off, at regular intervals, to other newspapers. The newspaper in question goes for a relaunch. The move does little to change its fortune. Its management is unable to bring about the change it wishes to, for reasons that are obvious. The decline continues.

Three

Take a third instance of how media house owners sometimes maim the very newspapers through which they mean to consolidate their presence in Bangladesh's market economy. A leading industrial group decides, in the infinity of its wisdom, to come forth with an English language newspaper. Its offer of stupendously high salaries draws leading journalists from other newspapers to its fold. Everything seems to be in place, until weeks before the launch of the newspaper, the owners decide to give marching orders to some of the senior journalists it had earlier brought on board. The editor is not informed of the action. Unable to assert his authority on the issue of hiring and removing journalists, he resigns.

The owners then go on a search for a new editor. And they find one in a non-journalist, an academic who has been part of the Department of History at the country's leading public university. Months into his job, the academic-cum-editor loses the support of the owners, who ask him to resign. He does so. And so do others, who too have been asked to put in their resignations. Those who stay on, but only just, discover to their mortification that the high salaries they had been promised when they were recruited at the newspaper have been reduced by half, no explanations offered. Predictably, the newspaper suffers. The promise with which it began has worn off. It has turned into sheets of paper that do not reflect anything of the media. Its owners have left it grievously maimed. It remains stillborn.

Four

The management of a leading newspaper in the country suddenly light upon the brilliant idea that those on its staff, journalists as well as non-journalists, who have reached the age of sixty years will automatically retire from service. It will be up to the management to offer or refrain from offering fresh contracts to those on the way to retirement, but the message is clear: the newspaper now has a policy resembling that of a government bureaucracy.

Experienced hands are handed retirement letters. The more fortunate ones among them are offered contracts for a year, six months or a period of time decided by the management, among which group is the editor of the newspaper. In most bizarre fashion, the editor, despite being in his mid-sixties, will not retire, will indeed stay on. The contradiction, or call it hypocrisy, is not lost on anyone.

Politics and the Past

If that is an image of how the media, especially newspapers, operate in Bangladesh at present, there is, too, the past that cannot be papered over. A good deal of the legacy or mind-set behind the workings of the media in the country has to do with the various shades of politics that in the past conditioned attitudes in the media industry. Let us start from the beginning.

One

Between 1958 and 1969, the media were fundamentally compelled to be subservient to the wishes of the military regime of Field Marshal Mohammad Ayub Khan. For more than a decade, the press worked in regimentation. Newspapers espousing the popular cause—and here the Bengali *Daily Ittefaq* takes centre stage—were banned and their editors carted off to prison.

The legacy of media activities in Bangladesh and in pre-1971 Pakistan has never been a healthy one. During the course of Bangladesh's War of Liberation in 1971, total censorship of the press was imposed, with the result that people in West Pakistan had precious little idea of the repression the Pakistan army was carrying out in East Pakistan. Newspapers in both East and West Pakistan carried, on a daily basis, reports of 'normalcy' in Dhaka and elsewhere. The realities, of course, were something else.

Two

In independent Bangladesh, the earliest assault on the freedom of the media came in early 1975 when the government of the day pushed through the Fourth Amendment to the constitution, a move that replaced multi-party democracy in the country with single-party politics. In line with such action, the government decreed, in June 1975, a ban on all newspapers save four—two in Bengali and two in English.

Three

In the period of Bangladesh's first military ruler, General Ziaur Rahman, the ban on the media was lifted. But that again was cold comfort, given that newspapers were not permitted to express their opinions in the kind of freedom necessary for the media. In the Zia period, a stretch of five years in which an airbrushing of the nation's history turned into a routine, newspapers found themselves unable to mention certain historical truths on significant national occasions as Independence Day and Victory Day. The Pakistan occupation army was blandly referred to as a mere occupation army. No mention was made of Sheikh Mujibur Rahman and his close associates who waged the guerrilla war against Pakistan.

Four

In the era of Bangladesh's second military ruler, General Hussein Muhammad Ershad, there was no overt mention of news censorship being in place. But a more shrewd mechanism came to be applied to the workings of the media. Often, only moments before newspaper pages were to go to press, the military authorities would despatch what they euphemistically called 'advice', but which was in truth a clear instruction to the media not to publish particular news items. Not one newspaper dared to disregard the 'advice', for reasons not hard to fathom.

Five

During the second term of the Bangladesh Nationalist Party (BNP) in office under Prime Minister Khaleda Zia, censorship as one generally understands the term was non-existent. That did not, however, prevent some of her close advisors from filing cases against editors of certain newspapers on the ground that the latter had damaged their reputation through publication of 'malicious' and 'false' news. The editors were, thus, kept busy approaching the higher judiciary for bail. In the end, though, the howls of these politicians amounted to little.

During the period of government by the Awami League between 1996 and 2001, a ruling party lawmaker achieved notoriety when he had his goons severely beat up a reporter whose singular fault was that he had been reporting on the questionable activities of the honourable Member of Parliament.

Six

And over the past few years, a fairly big number of outspoken journalists in the south-west of the country have been murdered by extreme left-wing elements. The wheels of justice have moved in tardy fashion, with the families of the dead newsmen slowly losing faith in the ability of the government to bring the assassins of the journalists to justice.

In more recent times, the move by the government to regulate journalism through measures adopted by parliament has drawn flak across the spectrum. The government, of course, calls it a measure aimed at encouraging quality and objective journalism. One must wait to see how things pan out.

Politically Partisan Journalism

At this point of time, a reality we cannot ignore about Bangladesh is the deeply divisive nature of society along disturbingly clear political lines. You could argue that political tribalism, today, underscores the pursuit of life in the country, to a point where such professional bodies as lawyers' associations, teachers' associations and doctors' organisations have all divided themselves right down the middle to align themselves with one or the other of the two major political parties in the country.

The malady has naturally affected the journalists' community, which has for the past couple of decades or more operated along clearly defined partisan lines. The consequences have, predictably, been grave in that political considerations have often come into the presentation of news and editorial comments and have, more often than not, been reflective of the positions adopted by the two major parties on important national issues.

Today, in Bangladesh, we have journalists' unions, notably the Dhaka Union of Journalists (DUJ) and the Bangladesh Federal Union of Journalists (BFUJ) factionalised into two clear camps, owing fealty to one or the other of the leading political organisations in the country. The casualty, again, has been journalism—in content presentation and in objectivity. All too often, the subjective has gained the upper hand.

Journalistic Prejudices

There are, again, all those typical maladies, associated with any profession we come across in the world, of journalism in Bangladesh. Obviously, they do impact our work and, sometimes, even lead to situations where calling of the profession appears to be getting into a quagmire.

Imagine the following:

The owners of a leading newspaper have never permitted anything remotely critical of capitalism or the US policy around the world to be published in their media outlet. Their bias against socialism or left-wing politics has, thus, opened some gaping holes in the way their newspaper, despite the presence of experienced journalists on the team, has looked at the world.

Imagine a little more:

A non-journalist catapulted to the position of editor of a newspaper sees nothing wrong in launching vicious personal attacks on individuals, among whom are respected journalists working for other newspapers. Additionally, he advocates, through his write-ups, his unambiguous support for such extremist and medieval elements as the *Hefazat-e-Islam*, an organisation engaged in whipping up fear and terror against a legally established government around the issue of religious fanaticism.

Imagine, again, the following:

In the period of Bangladesh's last caretaker government between early 2007 and early 2009, the editor of a popular newspaper advocates a purge in national politics. He did so in a front page commentary by pointing to the need for the two leading political personalities of the country to retire as a first step toward political reform in the country. It is the so-called, rather discredited Minus Two formula he speaks of—and swiftly comes criticism across the board.

Imagine, additionally, this situation:

The editor of a reputed newspaper is unwilling to entertain or publish any write-ups from individuals who tend to disagree with certain points of view put across by the country's Nobel Laureate. The attitude runs counter to the professed policy of the newspaper, namely, acting as a platform for liberal thoughts and open public debate on issues. The editor's personal equation with the Nobel Laureate is unabashedly given out as the policy of the newspaper.

These are realities that have happened and may happen again. If one considers these and all other factors as part of a pattern, it becomes easier to comprehend the circumstances which define the manner in which contemporary media works in Bangladesh.

Media as People's Voice

All said and done, the media maintains a vital and energising presence in Bangladesh. In a political situation, where parliament has remained largely dysfunctional over the last many years (thanks to the refusal by the opposition of the day to be part of the legislative process of debate and deliberations in the House) it has, in effect, become the responsibility of the media to bring into the public domain issues of significant national concern. This is the job which both the print and electronic media have been doing more or less to public satisfaction. With close to thirty private television channels operating in the country, it is now possible for intellectuals of various shades of opinion—journalists, academics, politicians and others—to engage in lively debate on the issues. Indeed, it is often difficult for viewers to choose a television channel they would like to tune in to at prime time, for the simple reason that a goodly number of channels may be airing similar programmes at the same time.

If television is today a twenty-four-hour undertaking, it is for newspapers to struggle to keep up with them as much as they can. Almost every newspaper (and as many as 70 daily newspapers, 9 of them in the English language, happen to flood the news arena at present) has developed its online version where the number of hits from readers remains testimony to the keen interest they take in national as well as global events.

The newspapers, in their print form, have gone for more public-interest news together with regular analyses and commentaries on the defining issues of the times. That has been a most encouraging development in Bangladesh's journalism. Add to that the trend which has recently developed in newspaper organisations toward arranging round table discussions on issues pertaining to the public interest.

What has been less than encouraging is the inability of a number of media organisations to sustain themselves resource-wise in the way they would like to. It remains a truth in Bangladesh that journalists keep switching jobs and move from one media organisation to another for a particularly glaring reason—need for respectable, regular salaries and other benefits that media people around the world are generally offered.

This paper provides only a glimpse into the exciting and, at times, frustrating world of Bangladesh's journalism. Obviously, there are other realities that need to be factored into this discussion, the objective being an exploration of a new ground the media in a geographically circumscribed country of a hundred and sixty million people may be able to break and cover in the times ahead.

4

Media in Post 9/11 Afghanistan

Amrullah Saleh

The surge of social media in Afghanistan has been the major and swift movement in the region. In this regard, while South Asia and Central Asia started from a solid base, Afghanistan, as such, had to start from almost zero. Afghanistan has been deprived of a vibrant and neutral media and communication channels for long. During the Soviet intervention in Afghanistan, the state-run media was tilted heavily in favour of the erstwhile Soviet Union and, thereby, glorified their intervention in the country. However, media based in Pakistan and West came down heavily on the Soviet intervention in Afghanistan. They were sharply critical of the external intrusion in Afghanistan and the then regime there. In the 1990s, Afghans would largely listen to western or regional outlets for news, information and entertainment. Prominent and common channels were the British Broadcasting Corporation (BBC), Voice of America (VOA), Deutsche Welle (DW), Radio France, Radio Mashhad and Radio Liberty broadcasting in local Afghan languages.

Until the collapse of the Taliban, there were only two television stations in the entire country. The national television station of the country was shut by the Taliban in September 1996 as they besieged the capital, Kabul. The other remained operating with limited reach in the north-eastern corner of the country. It mainly used to broadcast the messages of the anti-Taliban Islamic State of Afghanistan. Again, at the dawn of the 21st century,

Afghanistan's only state television channel was shut down by the Taliban and the state radio was turned into a war mongering clerical outlet which mainly spread hate propaganda. The only other television and radio station with limited reach was situated in Badakhshan province and run by the anti-Taliban Islamic State of Afghanistan.

What Happened Post 9/11?

In October 2001, prior to the collapse of the Taliban regime, a number of nameless satellite-based radio channels were created which began broadcasting non-stop music and the US (United States) government war announcements round the clock. These were part of the CIA (Central Intelligence Agency) and Pentagon's psychological warfare programs.

FM (Frequency Modulation) in Afghanistan is a post 9/11 phenomenon and turned to be a wonder when Afghans, craving for news and entertainment got these news feeds for the first time in their lives on portable radios tuned to FM stations. Crank radios were dropped in rural areas of the country to allow Afghans to listen to the FM channel that were created for the purpose of delivering the international coalition's messages. Through the radio, Afghans all over the country were encouraged to rise against the Taliban, providing information against Al-Qaeda and by doing so contribute towards a better future for Afghanistan. The distribution of radios and the operation of channels was an effective way of getting pre-emptive messages out in the population.

With the formation of the Interim Government in 2002, more options were presented to ordinary Afghans. In the year 2003, a series of new FM channels were established at national and provincial level with funding from USAID (United States Agency for International Development) and EU (European Union).

Subsequently, in 2004, private television channels started operation. Access to the internet became easier and cheaper, a trend that continues till date. For Afghans, the idea of private media has had been a dream which seemed impossible to fulfil at one point. The media has always been associated with power. It has always been a tool at the hands of powerful, not a power by itself. Because of western intervention in the country, the Afghans were acquainted with free media (after 9/11) which was earlier an alien concept. Today, Afghanistan has one of the most vibrant media in the region vis-a-vis its size and population. Currently, Afghanistan has nearly 1800 hours of radio broadcast and about 1300-1500 hours of television broadcast per day. Afghanistan has one or two state-run television channels. The remaining dozens are private, either subsidised by foreign donors or running on revenues accrued from commercials. Hundreds of FM channels are mushrooming around the country focussing mainly on provincial issues, sub-national issues and several other significant matters. But then again, this exposure has had its limitations too. While the Constitution of Afghanistan guarantees the freedom of expression within the limits of Islam, the article where this particular clause is stipulated is very vague and leaves room for a lot of interpretation or misinterpretation. This particular article in Afghanistan's constitution has been misused by powerful people to hurt journalists and create obstacles in their endeavours. Such abuse has forced several journalists to opt for self-exile fearing retribution.

The role of media in post-Taliban Afghanistan has been a vital voice in creating public awareness. This is in contrast to past when media was merely an outlet to spread propaganda of a particular faction, the ruling party or the State. Post 9/11, media has become a tool for accountability whereas in the past it was always used for justifying wrong, yearning for power, unlawful domination, etc. Today, media is also becoming a platform for the rise of new leaders in the country whereas in past established leaders would exploit media to suppress others. Repressive regimes in Afghanistan never allowed new leaders to flourish. Afghanistan has been witnessing the evolution of an effective and strong media and, thus, considered a predominant factor towards strengthening national unity and the sense of *pan-Afghanism*. Media has effectively spread a strong belief across Afghanistan regarding the significance of a strong state. It is promoting the sense of statehood amongst Afghans. In fact, the private media is staunchly promoting the legitimacy of the state structure in the country.

Media in Afghanistan also has certain shortcomings. It has been accused of creating frictions in the Afghan society. The other adverse impact of expansion of media in Afghanistan is that it continues to politicise the Afghan society. Private funding also buys political influence through the media without much awareness in the public domain regarding the sources of income.

Broadly, media had an enormous impact on lives of people within Afghanistan. Free media has been instrumental in helping Afghans gain access to essential fundamental rights and freedoms. Today in Afghanistan, the free media plays multiple functions in society:

1) As a voice for justice: Almost on a daily basis, there are cases where one can see people raise their voice through the media on being denied justice from the government, from powerful sections of the society, brokers or other traditional institutions. Once the media stimulates such issues, the government institutions act swiftly on certain cases. They have no option but to attend to people's grievances. Issues such as violence against women, corruption, embezzlement, fraud, murder, abusive government authorities do find regular coverage in the Afghan media, encouraging the wider population to view media outlets as a source of support for the victims and for the oppressed sections of society.

2) As a tool of influence: The free media in Afghanistan has created a strong sense of connectivity among the various parts of the country. Dozens of new figures have emerged in the national scene with the help of the media, directly appealing to various constituencies and audiences in the country. The existence of free media in Afghanistan, no doubt, has strengthened the sense of nationhood. However, in the meantime, it has also encouraged assertion of communal, provincial and ethnic identity. With the media providing wide scale exposure, it is natural that it has been used both positively and negatively by those seeking influence amongst people.

The negative did not and does not, however, offset the positive. While on the one hand, the media gave rise to groups seeking self-interest, it also provides an effective platform for a number of parliamentarians and provincial council member to propagate programs for their respective constituencies, garner support and get elected in due course.

3) As a medium for promoting activism, raising awareness and propelling action: At times of calamity and or any other hardship, people share their sense of grief and sympathy via media and mobilise support for their cause. For instance, recently in 2014, land erosion and avalanche buried an entire village in the north eastern province of Badakhshan. Aid poured in from all corners of the country after images of the disaster were broadcasted/shared through the social media. A strong sense of national solidarity, that too of this scale, had little precedence in Afghan history and the credit for arousing an overwhelming national response to a disaster goes directly to social media.

It is sometimes alleged whether the media in Afghanistan is involved in glorifying acts of violence committed, by reporting them regularly on a daily basis. However, one has to see that in a war-ridden country like Afghanistan, that witness innumerable incidents of violence, murders and killings every now and then, the media is reflecting the reality. Therefore, it is not entirely correct to accuse the media of capitalising on the lives lost and bloodshed of common Afghans.

4) As a tool for strategic change: The media has been instrumental in raising the level of awareness on Afghanistan's role and influence in the broader region—the potential of the country, its weaknesses, foreign policy, past mistakes and options for a better future. Such themes are continuously explored through series of talk shows, editorials, social media discussions, documentaries and commentaries. The quality of the discourse and the debate has significantly improved in this regard. With more and more Afghans having access to quality higher education inside and outside the country, they are turning to social media outlets to share their favourite subjects/topics, freely express their opinions—criticise or approve government policies and societal behaviours. Freedom of expression has, undoubtedly, resulted in a strategic change in the behaviour of Afghanistan as a country and also as a state.

For instance, exposure of information through the media and discussions on why and how Pakistan supports the Taliban and spurs instability in Afghanistan has given rise to a pan-Afghan sentiment against Pakistan. Whereas in past this particular issue might have been a local problem or a subject of discussion, it has now evolved into a pan-Afghan factor of unity in recent years. The mushrooming media outlets enabled Afghans to express themselves and share their findings, frustrations and experiences with the Taliban and Pakistan's unrelenting support for the extremists groups.

The free media has similarly enabled Afghans to get more information on how Afghans are treated in Iran, a country hosting millions of Afghan refugees. In past, the Afghans would hardly know what happened to their dear and loved ones working on Iranian construction sites, farms or as illegal workers in their municipalities. However, with the help of the media, Afghan people could now hear/read about the oppression, injustice and inhumane treatment of refugees and labour migrants in Iran. Consequently, they were able to put pressure on their government to take adequate measures such as ensuring better counsellor service for Afghans in Iran and adopting a tougher stance while talking to the host Iranian authorities about the situation of the Afghan refugees.

Foreign policy is a strategic area that is largely shaped by public opinion inside Afghanistan. Public opinion on the other hand is shaped by what appears in/via the media. The other strategic area is the annual allocation of resources for various regions inside the country. Media exposure and pressure has decreased the amount of favouritism and nepotism in distribution of resources to various provinces in Afghanistan. When injustice is felt in the distribution of resources, social groups rise up and raise their voices demanding justice and equal access to the country's resources.

5) As a body for monitoring human rights: Media in Afghanistan has been extremely helpful and effective in bringing to light certain horrific cases of human rights violations. However, much more needs to be done to expand the coverage of such exposures from all nooks and corners of the country. In many ways, women in Afghanistan, are safer than what they were years ago. Due to media intervention, violence against women has also become some kind of a social stigma, at least in large cities. Cases of shameful rape, acid throwing on the face of young women students, violation of inheritance rights and many more such instances have found wide dissemination in the Afghan society with the help of a free media. This has not been enough though.

The Afghan media, with the help of human rights groups, has been able to create awareness about gross human rights violation during the years of war, but it has not been able to put enough pressure on the government to enforce the implementation of the transitional justice, a process which at least forces the culprits to acknowledge their crimes, if not stand for the trial. In a divided society like Afghanistan, transitional justice along the ethnic, political and sub-national lines is not an easy task or process which probably may never be implemented. Feelings about criminals and heroes are mixed. Nonetheless, the achievement of media in this area has been significant. At least a wider section of Afghan population now knows that it is no longer possible or as easy to conceal crimes or cover up evidence, realising that it could come out some day. In 2013, the names of nearly 5,000 prisoners executed by the leftist regime in the 1980s finally came out as the list was published in mainstream newspapers in Afghanistan. Almost three decades after the crime, the nation stood united in condemning it and remembering the victims by congregating in mosques and suspected sites of massacre.

6) As a medium for division within society: It is necessary to highlight that the media, by default, has been used as a medium for further entrenchment of divisions within Afghan society as well. It is no secret that Afghanistan suffers from deep divisions within as a result of how the state has evolved in the distant and recent history, how ethnic and sub-national groups have risen to defend themselves or grab power, how certain sections of the society have stood aside with various invaders against their own people. These are all fresh memories. A lot has been forgiven but nothing really forgotten. Politicians and political groups entrench their interest by exploiting these default differences in the society and keep them alive by adding fuel to them. The recent history of Afghanistan has witnessed bloody conflict between leftist and rightist extremist groups. Today, however, the Afghan society is devoid of that nature of hatred. Presently, the most dominant political theme in the country is ethnicity and sub-nationalism. All ethnic groups have media outlets of their own.

7) A tool at the hands of the enemy: Access to social media is also an effective tool at the hands of enemies of Afghanistan. They are those who misuse it to spread their divisive narrative, exploit ethnic and communal differences, spread their ideas and enhance their recruitment strategy. Legitimate television and radio channels have to broadcast what the terrorists, radicals and hate mongers do. While on one hand it helps to unite people against those forces, on the other, it applauds the achievement of the terror groups as well. The Taliban and other smaller terror groups run their own weblogs, websites and fake Facebook accounts. They put footages of attacks and share their negative propaganda.

8) Print media: The youth make the bulk of clients for news, information and entertainment. Such information is catered to youth via social media, television and radio. Although dozens of newspapers are printed in Kabul and other big cities of the country, they are all subsidised. The subsidies for these newspapers come from EU and USAID and several other unknown sources. The distribution of the newspapers in most cases is free as the purpose is to get a particular message out. The prevailing situation may change, but as it stands now, the print media is not something viable.

Afghan Media's Focus on Pakistan

Pakistan is foremost important factor and is extensively covered by the media in Afghanistan. Questions such as why Pakistan supports the Taliban, sponsors killings in Afghanistan, why they do not cooperate enough with legitimately elected Afghan government or why Pakistan consistently sponsors proxies or terror in the country dominate the media discourses in Afghanistan. Those are some of the key issues highlighted in Afghan media, both visual and print media and radio stations. Majority of Afghan talk shows and roundtable discussions are based on terrorism, Pakistan and the reason why Pakistan relentlessly supports Taliban?

Conclusion

In conclusion, Afghans see media in their country not only as the major achievement of the post 9/11 quasi democracy but also as the fourth pillar of the state. Many give the credit for the same to former President Hamid Karzai. Could he opt not to do so? The answer is no. The NATO/ISAF (North Atlantic Treaty Organisation/International Security Assistance Force) intervention was to help Afghans have a better life-democratically liberal than before. No doubt, Hamid Karzai in his heart was for the freedom of press, but he hardly had the option of not allowing the same. The media has enhanced Afghan peoples' awareness about their country, the region, and made them alert to issues of human rights, gender, and justice and government policies. It has also helped them regain confidence in themselves and dare to stand against injustice at different levels in the state and society. For instance, the role of Afghan media in creating unity at times of calamity, distress and natural disaster. There was land erosion in Badakhshan province in the north east. The first community which delivered aid and relief to Badakhshan were people of Kandahar. People there felt similar pain and rushed to help those affected in Badakhshan. In this incident, the role of media was instrumental in connecting people from two provinces by disseminating timely information and updates.

The media has also been a big factor in the political defeat of the Taliban. Each massacre and attack against civilians gets magnified at the national level, generating more hatred and more resistance against terror and extremism. It has helped Afghans become more united at macro level while retaining disunity at the micro level.

The media in Afghanistan is unfortunately dependent on covert funding from outside sources and that remains a source of concern for all Afghans. Hopefully, with a better economy, the Afghan media will become independent and free, both in its conduct and regarding sources of income. In the meantime, media is a national treasure and something that Afghans would not be able to live without.

To conclude, while media can be a source for massive understanding, it can also be a source for massive misunderstanding. The perpetuators of either understanding or misunderstanding is not media itself. It is rather the thinking of the establishment in the countries that one represents.

5

Media in the Age of Intolerance and Terrorism

Kunda Dixit

A survey was conducted in the United States a few years ago to figure out which profession was the most unpopular. Guess who was voted the most disliked: lawyers. The second most unpopular were journalists. It seems only lawyers are more disliked than journalists. Fortunately, no one has yet done a similar survey in South Asia. Perhaps, journalists in South Asia have a slightly better reputation, but are still seen as a bunch of cynical, arrogant, insensitive and inquisitive hacks. For instance, think of the way journalists are portrayed in Bollywood movies. Journalists are stereotyped as know-it-alls who poke their noses into other people's business and do not let those being interviewed get in a word edgewise. It is not difficult to explain why this is so. Switch on any of the 400 plus television channels on cable, and it is getting increasingly difficult to tell the difference between a news bulletin and a sports or entertainment channel. It is quite possible now a days that there are 12 talking heads being interviewed simultaneously by a television anchor, and all 12 heads are shouting at the same time.

In addition, the space for news items and current affairs is clearly getting contracted. Journalism is now only a tiny segment of what we call mass media. Even among the few news programs on those 400 channels, it is difficult to find one that tells us clearly and simply what is actually happening in India or the region. What makes it worse, of course, is not just the argumentative, multiple talking head format but the news line-up. It was bad enough with the cricket, now we are forced to watch football as well—not on a sports channel but in a prime time news bulletin. All Indian news channels replay the coverage of cricket that had previously been broadcast live all day. The anchor then comes on and, without a shred of irony, says "now for the rest of the news" then going on to devote the last ten minutes of half-hour bulletin to major events in the country and around the world.

And even when the news and current affairs are about politics, they are superficial and sensational caricatures of reality. Which is why when foreign policy and security issues are covered, we get an outpouring of jingoism. There are some anchors who sound like they are actually in the payroll of the security forces or the Ministry of Foreign Affairs. And when there is a terrorist attack or a minor skirmish at the border, it is an excuse to unleash patriotic fervour that makes it sound like war has broken out. What is worrying is that one day this sort of irresponsible and incendiary coverage will actually be a self-fulfilling prophecy.

Constraints on Media

There are two extremes of journalism that make it difficult to steer a moderate foreign policy: too little control and too much. In dictatorships or controlled democracies, the impact results from the lack of information, disinformation and censorship. In free market economies with western notions of free press like in India or Nepal, we see a worrying trend of an ultra-commercialised media dumbing down content to such an extent that it either sounds like provocative propaganda or populist trash.

Let us not forget that it is also happening on the other side. News coverage in Pakistan TV is only slightly better and we do not even discuss Mandarin CCTV (China Central Television). In an age of political extremism, the moderate middle ground is squeezed by intolerant and bigoted loud mouths who are given air time because they are shriller. The first casualty is the truth, and as we all know, a lie repeated often enough can become the truth in the hyper-reality world of the manufactured consent of modern mass media.

A large part of the problem with the mainstream television and print media is the practice of beat journalism. Reporters assigned to the Ministry of Foreign Affairs or the security forces develop close contacts with their spokespersons, and are suspicious of displeasing them because it may cut their access to interviews, field trips or junkets. Which is why coverage of foreign policy, nuclear or security issues are identical right across the news media on any given day. Very few journalists and commentators will stray from the party line for fear of inadvertently telling the truth. Such self-censorship would be perfectly normal in closed societies, of course, but in democracies it is insidious. The result is that coverage is rarely honest—we are fed slogans and half-truths by embedded journalists who are stenographers. A half-truth is actually a lie.

Such camaraderie or nexus between officials and journalists is unhealthy for truth-telling, for democracy and for long-term peace-building. It will lead to officialdom, government agencies and the media itself to start believing its own lies. When the truth finally needs to be told, no one will believe it. And such chest-thumping coverage will, of course, widen the gap with neighbouring countries and polarise opinion even more.

Media and Social Responsibilities

Some of the more populous countries in South Asia have some of the worst social indicators in the world. Certain regions within them are worse off than sub-Saharan Africa. Infant and maternal mortality rates, stunting in children due to under nourishment, open defecation—take any parameter of development and the Indo-Gangetic plains have been consistently lagging behind. Some progress has been made in national average, notably in Bangladesh and Nepal—but there are still parts of our countries where more than half of the children go to bed hungry every night, and where teenage mothers die at child birth. The social indicators are bad enough, while the income gap between rich and poor, caste-based discrimination, exclusion and marginalisation of tribal communities have made our societies one of the most unequal in the world. Delivery of services, especially in underserved parts of our countries, is still poor. Public utilities and infrastructure have not kept pace with demand.

What has all this got to do with foreign policy and security, one may ask? The time has come to redefine the term 'security'—it now has to go beyond the military to include 'human security'. The level of human development of our societies, our economic status, and the well-being of our citizens has a direct impact on how seriously we are taken by the international community.

A country may have the second-largest standing army in the world, it may be the world's biggest importer of conventional arms, it may have the capability of making nuclear weapons and missiles to deliver them, but if more than half of its population defecates in the open and most of its children are underdeveloped, it will not be respected.

Inequality, deprivation and exclusion also have a direct bearing on internal security. Popular insurrections, communal riots, insurgencies are fuelled by disenchantment and disillusionment of the youth. Underdevelopment, therefore, is a national security issue. This, in turn, has implications for stability, external security and foreign policy options for a country.

In this regard, the mass media is a powerful force in setting the national agenda and priorities. But when it ignores a country's underdevelopment, poor social indicators and service delivery, the issues fail to get traction in national debates. When a new prime minister tries to focus national attention on cleanliness, he is ridiculed by media—opinion-setters because they have been drilled to do so. As a result, the policy-makers are under little pressure to address them. Indirectly, therefore, the media has a role in making human security a matter of policy priority since it has an important bearing on the traditional way we look at 'national security'.

The prevalent news formula is inadequate to address the challenges of equity, social justice, and conflict. The planet is in crisis partly because the poor and the voiceless have never mattered. They have not been counted because the media on most occasions ignores them. But what happens to the meek and weak need not be "soft" journalism or being always pushed to the inside pages or the features section. Even as the world becomes more and more interdependent, most mass media still reduce racism, migration, terrorism, or recession to discrete isolated factoids and fail to link them to the complex global conditions that cause them. Journalists are also required to show prodigious aloofness and not be moved by injustice and greed. If, by some misfortune, they get caught up in the events around them, they are not supposed to express their feelings.

We know that status-quo journalism is biased because it cannot take sides against wrongs. However, by denying this bias, the mainstream media actually shows partiality. Observers change reality by the very act of observing, and whether one likes it or not, reporters become a part of the story they go out to report. And yet, supposedly "objective" stories appear every day in the papers and on television: reporting that is scrupulously accurate on facts but miss the nuances of the larger truths because they do not analyse events and offer a way out. When the financial press unquestioningly takes it as a given that economic growth is good for the quality of life in a country, it exhibits a partisanship for orthodox economics.

One of the underlying causes of internal and external insecurity in South Asian countries is the failure of governance that has perpetuated the cycle of poverty, social injustice and inequality. These are serious challenges to the future of a stable South Asia. Therefore, reporting developments in the South Asian context calls for a new breed of journalists: ones without mental borders who have the energy and understanding to move beyond the traditional classroom concepts of reporting and writing, reporters who do not just report but look behind the headlines to examine cause and effect, and constantly explore regional or international linkages to national problems. They need to be multi-disciplinary and be able to investigate how development is linked to politics, the economy and national priorities.

Traditional media schools across South Asia teach aspiring journalists to look for the counter-point to make stories interesting. It is noted that it is the controversy, the disagreement, which gives the story a dramatic tension. Most coverage, therefore, sounds like a quarrel, opposites pitted against each other, even when the point of argument may be minor and the two sides are in overall agreement. Editors and publishers argue that they need to dramatize the story otherwise "no one will watch". This presumption that the news content reflects what the public wants has never been tested. It is an assumption, an excuse for lazy and cheap 'talking head' format of journalism. What it ends up doing is fuelling and perpetuating conflict and confrontation in the region and beyond.

Conflict is the adrenaline of a chauvinist media, and this kind of "on the one hand this, on the other hand that" reporting can be an obstacle in spreading clarity about national and regional problems. Readers and audiences worldwide are fed a diet of formula news that are superficial mainstream viewpoint on domestic politics and stereotyped cross-border coverage. Such coverage only reconfirms pre-held pigeon holes and existing national stereotypes.

Deborah Tannen, Professor of Linguistics at Georgetown University, asks: "Why do journalists need to make others wrong for them to be right?"[1] It is presumed that readers and audiences enjoy watching a fight, so the most extreme views are presented even though the journalist knows that "the other side" is telling a lie.[2] Tannen observes great danger in modelling intellectual inter-change as a fight: it contributes to an atmosphere of animosity that spreads like a fever.[3] This makes journalists responsible only for the method, not the content. It exposes them to manipulation by the powerful, who will make sure that the disclosures made by them deliberately get into the front page of the next day's papers. The role of the media should not be a public address system for the already influential rather it should place responsibility for the failures of our society on the people and institutions that control the society.

The biggest problem with the doctrine of narrative neutrality that we teach in media schools and is practiced in newsrooms across the region is that it is conservative and inevitably favours the institutions that control society. The media in South Asia, especially on television, therefore swings between neutralised and non-committal factoids, and needlessly confrontational cockfights. By being scrupulously "balanced", traditional reporting, thus, gives those who have power and wealth an unfair advantage—and perpetuates the imbalance in news coverage. It is biased against change and ignores the fact that impartiality can also mean taking sides. In short, objectivity is highly subjective.

Media and Democracy

Democracy as such, too, has its shortfall. Sometimes, it is considered messy-elected politicians, sometimes, tend to be crooks. However, it is still the best among the bad political models we have. At least in a democracy, there are mechanisms in place to set things right, and the rules of the game do not allow violence to be used as a political tool. For this, it needs to be ensured that democracy is enhanced to a better level—democratic institutions should be protected and strengthened so that it helps deliver development. The misdeeds of some politicians should not tarnish the system. Democracy is not desirable just for the sake of democracy—it is the competition of political ideas and the leadership skills of candidates that must lead to improvement in people's lives. An essential part of this mechanism is journalism. Independent media and free politics go hand in hand. Press freedom and democracy are two sides of the same coin. Curtailing press freedom harms democracy and vice-versa. However, there are enormous challenges for the media to fulfil this role. Some are old while others are new. In some countries of South Asia, even democratic ones, professional hazards for journalists have become so serious that reporters risk their lives every day to investigate stories.

The lesson is that press freedom does not come with any warranty. The freedom it has needs to be defended by its maximum application. The threats to media freedom do not just come from tyrants and dictators, they come from owners who see it as just another business, from under-motivated journalists, from publishers who turn their products into trivial tabloids because that is where the money is. Dumbing down content destabilises democracy. This is why we need to unleash the full power of investigative journalism to go in-depth and behind the scenes so that it could in the process effectively strengthen democracy and defend the free press.

On the other side, many journalists in the main-stream media are brought up to be fearless. They inherit either aggressiveness and cynicism or unquestioning conformity from their journalism *gurus* and peers. Often, these traits mask simple laziness. The media is obsessed with hard core politics, conflict, and confrontation for the simple reason that it does not need much effort and costs less than incisive, investigative reporting. It is relaxing to be on a freebie than to spend time with local authorities to interview local people. It is easier to find government officials and experts to talk about big plans for new superhighways and flyovers than to interview proponents of electric public transport. Agriculture, land reform or the environment get scant coverage because they do not tend to be relevant to city-dwellers. It is not surprising, therefore, that stories about the new economic paradigms that offer simpler, cheaper, and more relevant alternatives for a majority of population, are either ignored or covered scantily by the mainstream press.

This is why across India, Pakistan, Bangladesh and Nepal, hundreds of millions of people have no access to sanitation but still there is not much mention of this in media coverage. In these four South Asian countries, a total of some 300 million, most of them women, cannot read or write, 300 million people drink water from contaminated ponds and streams. India and Pakistan have six times more soldiers than doctors. Pakistan is spending twice as much for its military than what it spends on health and education combined. With the money, the Indian Air Force paid to upgrade its air force, the country would have been able to educate all of its 15 million girls who are out of school. India and Pakistan have only recently begun to realise that their domestic poverty is more destabilising than each other's arsenals. A nation's security, today, must be defined by defending its population from hunger, disease, homelessness and unemployment—not from perceived external enemies.

As we have seen, human well-being and development are particularly difficult concepts to quantify. Economists have long questioned the relevance of parameters like GNP and GDP, but only recently these have started to be widely accepted as giving us only a part of the real picture. Economic indicators are like cockpit instruments on a plane which needs to be accurate and together give a realistic idea of all the parameters so that right decisions can be made at the right time. If the indicators are wrong, planners will make wrong decisions. Today, there are not only questions about whether accepted gauges of development are right or wrong, but whether the whole concept of rich and poor needs to be redefined. Anyone who is still wondering why South Asian countries continue to lag behind the former East Asian tigers needs only to compare their respective budgets for social spending. South Korea and Malaysia, for instance, each invest about $200 per citizen on health and education. By comparison, India invests $20, Pakistan $15 and Bangladesh $8 per person.

Much of the aforementioned imbalance in media coverage has to do with the English-language media in South Asia. It is believed that local language press is even more jingoistic. If you thought the English media was bad, you should read the Urdu press in Pakistan, or some of the coverage of security and foreign policy issues in the local languages in India, Bangladesh, Sri Lanka or Nepal.

Media: Terrorism, Intolerance

The advent of internet was one ray of hope. When the internet started 20 years ago, it was finally thought of as a medium that levels the playing fields and democratises the public sphere. Since it was originally supposed to be non-profit, the wiki effect we hoped would give citizens an alternative source of information, analysis and opinion. But while the internet has connected vast populations, levelled the playing field to some extent, it is now also controlled by the same kind of corporate interest that once dominated traditional global media. Cyberspace is prone to censorship, surveillance and manipulation in ways that are even more sinister than mainstream media. It also ghettoises and fragments the audience—polarising opinion, widening the gap between beliefs, sowing intolerance and fostering anonymous hate speech. The same medium that gives space to citizen journalism and freedom of expression is also being used by terrorists to post videos of hostage beheadings, and inflammatory racist, xenophobic and extremist rhetoric.

The state's response, even in countries with long traditions of free press, is more surveillance and control in the name of countering terrorism—blogs are banned or keywords censored from search engines. The kneejerk reaction is: if there is something sensitive on YouTube, do not just disable the link but ban the YouTube.

Way Ahead

Perhaps, it is now time for the traditional press and their online editions to use their relatively better brand credibility to counter some of the volatile and dangerous content on social networking sites. Foreign policy and security issues are too important to be left to governments alone, it cannot be just left to citizen journalists and bloggers either. Here is where the moderating influence and filter mechanism of trained journalists can be pushed into play.

Openness and greater transparency is the answer, not curbing the free flow of information. Old and new media have been hijacked by those who can shout the most. It is high time that moderate, rational and tolerant voices for peace reclaim the space.

NOTES

The chapter contains excerpts from my previously published piece, "A Paradigm Shift in News", *Hope Online*, at http://hope.com.np/en/cover-story/paradigm-shift-news.

1. Deborah Tannen, "The Triumph of the Yell", *The New York Times*, January 14, 1994, at http://faculty.georgetown.edu/tannend/nyt011494.htm.
2. Ibid.
3. Ibid.

PART II
The State of Media in South Asia: Country Perspectives

6

Promotion of Jingoism in the Region by the Media: The Case of Sri Lanka

Dilrukshi Handunnetti

Background

The victory by the Sri Lankan security forces over the Liberation Tigers of Tamil Eelam (LTTE) was a defining moment in the island's history. It had been both a defining moment and one of the reckoning, when the security forces defeated the Tamil Tigers, declaring the war officially over, on May 16, 2009. This victory, predicted 'unwinnable' for decades by several former national leaders—a notion supported by the Western Bloc—instantly became the incumbent government's biggest political strength, justification for its anomalies and a convenient tool, when dealing with both national and external matters.

The defeating of the LTTE justified former President Mahinda Rajapaksa's decision to launch an all-out war in the eyes of many, at a time when the rest of the world appeared to be dealing with what were broadly classified as 'unwinnable wars'. The victory over the Tigers also propped former President Rajapaksa up, within and outside the region, as a resolute leader who could not be influenced by a combination of international opinion, a strong Tamil Diaspora and detractors at home, from single-mindedly achieving his objective—the elimination of the LTTE and bringing the war to an end.

This victory, achieved over one of the most ruthless terrorist organisations banned in many countries, also resulted in the drastic alteration of the political power play within the island nation, and with clear ramifications on relations with the rest of the world, in particular, India, Sri Lanka's closest neighbour in the South Asian region.

The most vocal of his critics may be reluctant to express criticism against the Rajapaksa administration on the issue of responding to terrorism in the manner he did. The Sri Lankan reality, however, is that the state often uses the existence of terrorism elsewhere, emphasising the need to control it—the overarching objective of the government—to the extent that defence and foreign policies are, at times, developed or adhered to, largely as a means to justify authoritarian action. In the immediate aftermath, the Sri Lankan Government moved to consolidate its political power. It brooked no opposition from any quarter; either local or foreign; adopted a no-nonsense policy on internal affairs and refused to explain itself to both the local and international communities, on matters of foreign policy and other area considered 'contentious', such as human rights. Policy making was to be guided to an extent by a brand of nationalism that had, five years since the war, taken strong root.

The government practically capitalised on the war victory by holding a snap Presidential election in January 2010, immediately followed by a Parliamentary election. Next, a vital amendment to the 1978 Constitution was passed with a two-third majority, removing the two-term restriction placed on an Executive President.

All these changes further fuelled triumphalism that continues to determine policy and practice in Sri Lanka. Civil liberties continue to be curtailed by the long arm of suppression and minority rights have become severely restricted in Sri Lanka, a country that unrepentantly caters to the interests of the majority community. It had also made the Colombo administration quite invincible, to overlook the need to further devolve power to the periphery through the 13th Amendment to the Constitution—a commitment made to the Government of India, nearly three decades ago.

If there were apologetic noises in the past for the inability to take the power sharing process forward, there was none in post-war Sri Lanka. The Sri Lankan Government had, by then, reached a level of arrogance to refuse even to consider it, except perhaps when it is an item on a bilateral agenda or a matter of pure academic interest. Any pretence at pursuing a political solution to the national question through the appointed parliamentary select committee had been relegated to the backburner. It is as if the end of the war had absolved the government from its responsibility to pursue a political solution to the national question and granted a license to ignore commitments made in the past, to address the root cause of the conflict.

Fuelling Majoritarianism

Just as much as the government rode on a wave of popularity—created by the victory over the LTTE—it also resulted in majoritarianism that sought to further the interests of the country's largest community, the Sinhalese, to the exclusion of others. Identity politics, and in this case, the re-imposition of the identity of the Sinhala majority, became the norm, with the suppression of Sri Lankan minority identities taking place.

Sri Lanka's jingoistic approach to external affairs, therefore, cannot be analysed without factoring in the prevalence of strong post-war triumphalism, a determining factor applicable to both policy and practice. Inextricably linked to the quicksand of changing social attitudes, this triumphalism remains a strong influence on the news media, which in turn, fuels majoritarianism, within and outside the shores.

The Rajapaksa administration's external affairs policy, according to former External Affairs Minister of Sri Lanka, Professor G.L. Peiris, is one that places faith in Asia, Africa and the Arab countries, based on demonstrated support and reciprocity. What is left unstated is the island's rejection of many a country that appear critical of its approach towards human and in particular, minority rights, and a willingness to cultivate only those countries considered non-critical of the state. Furthermore, Sri Lanka now speaks of a foreign policy based on the 'principle of reciprocity,' a strong contributor to the decision to cancel the on-arrival visa facility for a number of countries, including India. This decision reflected a desire to use available tools against countries that question Sri Lanka's democratic credentials.

This new approach of aggressive foreign policy has also caused Sri Lanka to veer away from its former allies—western countries -that worked closely with the United National Party (UNP) government and subsequently, with the Sri Lanka Freedom Party-led government of President Chandrika Kumaratunga.

The Rajapaksa administration looked quite uncomfortable with liberal democratic agenda-setting. Having learnt from the mistakes of the Norwegian-facilitated peace process that failed to bring the desired results to Sri Lanka, the administration as a top political priority, abrogated the Cease Fire Agreement (CFA) entered into by then (and current) Prime Minister, Ranil Wickremesinghe. This sent out a clear message to the facilitator of the island's peace process that the new administration would not hesitate to make decisions in the 'national interest' and in doing so, would not overly worry about losing some 'old friends'. It also indicated a desire to create a new agenda that was delinked from past efforts.

This unrepentant aggression towards identified western countries such as Norway, United Kingdom, Canada and the United States, strongly communicated to the world, Rajapaksa's refusal to follow others' footsteps. Besides, it also reflected an absence of finesse and diplomacy that caused it to unabashedly flex muscles, only to earn black marks for its mishandling of international affairs. This aggressive agenda openly condemned countries that questioned the human rights record, and at times, had the anti-Sri Lanka tag attached and the motive to further a separatist agenda, attributed.

The Rajapaksa regime, as a result, lost the overt support of western democracies, though financial aid continued to flow, despite strong criticism by many of these countries on its rights record. For its part, Sri Lanka has amply demonstrated its refusal to offer answers on the question of government accountability, launching counter attacks on critical countries for alleged interference in internal matters, besides being referred to as LTTE sympathisers.

Beyond its ill-concealed dislike towards the Western Bloc, the then triumphant Sri Lankan administration commenced a new routine of 'bash and shame' with India, adopting a policy of pitting China against India, to its immediate economic and strategic advantage. The Sri Lankan Government, unhappy with New Delhi for its wavering foreign policy that appeared to be strongly influenced by domestic compulsions in Tamil Nadu and often judgmental of Sri Lanka in the aftermath of the war, found China's growing interest in the island and its readily available financial aid (that came without any demand for accountability), much to its taste.

It was also refreshing to find a powerful nation showing that level of interest in the small island, helpful to send a message to New Delhi, causing the apprehensive neighbour to worry about the growing Chinese presence as well as the possibility of exerting influence in the region using Sri Lanka as a base, which goes against India's strategic interests.

As much as the demonstrated aggression towards several powerful countries was new and rash, a pro-China policy marked a clear departure in Sri Lankan foreign policy. Sri Lanka, for decades, had enjoyed strong ties with China, yet, the world's largest economy had never been the priority it had now become. However, according to the Sri Lankan Government, it was a well-considered move which was in no way a 'knee-jerk' reaction.

Sri Lanka always had, barring President J.R. Jayewardene's rule (whose foreign policy was strongly tilted towards the West and oppositional to India), consistently promoted strong relations with neighbouring India, a strategic priority in the island's foreign policy. The Sri Lanka Freedom Party (SLFP)-led government had been exceptionally pro-India in approach.

In the past few years, India's response to Sri Lanka, too, had been complex, inconsistent, and even ambiguous, fuelling mistrust. With New Delhi often appearing to be influenced by an aggressive and emotional Tamil Nadu factor, Colombo justly interpreted this as a weak Centre being dictated to by Tamil Nadu, further justifying the condemnation of New Delhi's behaviour. According to former External Affairs Minister of Sri Lanka, G.L. Peiris, there are aspects in Indian foreign policy that work against good neighbourly relations and makes Sri Lanka anxious. "It has not been possible to rely on India at crucial moments", Peiris said in an interview with the author.

While there had been many instances when Colombo had serious concerns about India's own jingoism to the detriment of the small island, the two key issues that broke the camel's back were: India's refusal to vote against the resolution on Sri Lanka before the United Nations Human Rights Council (UNHRC) on the first occasion, and the absence of then Indian Prime Minister, Dr. Manmohan Singh, when the Commonwealth Heads of Government Meeting (CHOGM) was held in Colombo in November 2013. The Indian Premier's absence was considered a serious insult by the administration that held the chairmanship of the South Asian Association for Regional Cooperation (SAARC) and needed India on its side, when Commonwealth leaders reached Colombo and conferred its chairmanship on Sri Lanka. Instead, a number of them were poised to criticise Sri Lanka severely for flouting Commonwealth principles and values. "Now that's a true crack and one that indicates India's inconsistency towards Sri Lanka", Minister Peiris remarked in an interview, a statement that reflected his government's displeasure with India's response to Colombo's invitation to have Dr. Manmohan Singh attend at least the opening session of CHOGM.

While the relationship strained, Colombo has also sidestepped the issue of power sharing, in some ways a rejection of India for its lack of reciprocity on multiple issues, which is not devoid of strong emotion. It also allowed Colombo the opportunity to portray India's own domestic compulsions as the reason for criticising the neighbour which had all to do with politics but little with minority rights. It also gave Colombo leverage to sell the idea that India was anti-Sri Lanka, with strong sympathies for the Tamil cause. This allowed the justification of a 360-degree shift in foreign policy that also influenced the decision to adopt a pro-China policy.

This strong-arm approach in diplomatic affairs was also justified on the basis of sound national interest, and also extended to the local media. The administration, well-endowed in the art of influencing domestic opinion, effectively used the war victory to demand unquestioning loyalty from the news media, quelling any possible dissent that may find space. The Sri Lankan media, both state and private-owned, had long since lost their independence. The media muzzling and the climate of fear, achieved through a spate of abductions, assaults and the murder of journalists, reflected an agenda of systemic suppression.

The International Federation of Journalists (IFJ) has rated Sri Lanka as the fourth worst place in the world for journalists to live in. The New York-based media rights organisation, the Committee to Protect Journalists (CPJ), has noted high levels of impunity in the island, reflected in the lack of investigations and justice for the murdered, as well as the large numbers of journalists driven into exile. Silenced through direct violence and other means, Sri Lanka's media practice a high degree of self-censorship, all of which had made the island's mass media extremely weak.

While it could be a part strategy to adapt to the new order and relay converged opinion—all of which favour the then ruling administration—the post-war Sri Lankan media's behaviour had often been defensive of state action and policy, while being offensively aggressive, whenever the role of the Sri Lankan administration had been questioned, particularly by the international community. As part of such converged media opinion, fair and independent journalism was replaced by self-styled, pro-government and campaign-style journalism that openly justified the government's chauvinistic responses, especially on the two critical areas of human rights and governance.

At strategic points of time, the majority of the media houses have performed the role of 'hurrah girls' and 'hurrah boys' for the incumbency, failing to differentiate between journalism and government propaganda. This role had been heightened whenever Sri Lanka's conduct became a point of discussion at the international level. More and more media houses soon fell in line, irrespective of the ownership model, to unequivocally endorse the aggressive approach of the Sri Lankan Government that reflected political arrogance, fuelled by post-war euphoria.

This reaction was partly influenced by the media's own conviction that a war-winning government deserved a measure of support. Following the victory against the LTTE, going against the western agenda on the national question was to an extent, justifiable. However, the main reason appeared to be the suppression tactics that had steamrolled media houses into passive submission. In this backdrop, the Sri Lankan media had for the large part, begun to function as an extension of the government often offering explanations or excuses for government's action—clearly reflecting poor media policy and practice but considered necessary by most media houses for survival.

Language Divide

The Sri Lankan media underwent a strong and defining negative change in the past few years. Whatever that remained plural in its character and the ability to tolerate a level of dissent was lost, with a strong convergence of opinion becoming its key post-war characteristic. While it was partly due to the application of brute force that forced media institutions into submission and individual journalists to live in fear, overriding commercial and political interests of the owners have resulted in blatant pandering to the government and following government dictates to the letter. In doing so, it had also lost the edge it enjoyed and now suffers from an unprecedented credibility crisis.

The role of propagandist, played to the hilt by some, had become significant, and in the island's context, has little to do with market dynamics that make media institutions rely on government advertising (which largely flows to state-owned media institutions) but influenced more by political and survival-related concerns.

The English media had managed to be nuanced to some extent, though not completely. Those who dared to appear to disagree also felt a strong compulsion to comply with the unwritten rule of producing content that approved jingoism as an extension of Sri Lankan nationalism. The state media, both electronic and print, continued to go all out to defend the government and tare to smithereens, countries that were critical either of the island's rights record or air concerns about other aspects of governance. The more discerning media houses—and there are only a rare few—also struggle against the current trends and worry about possible backlashes for creating space for independent viewpoints. Though considered far more discerning, the English news media that generally reflects a more globalised view, too, tend to lean towards jingoism.

A case in point is how the large majority of English media reported on the UNHRC sessions in Geneva throughout, critiquing and passing judgment on countries that called for accountability from Sri Lanka. Journalists have been instructed by media houses to 'tone down' columns and analyses, particularly when raising issues linked to Sri Lanka's response to international queries on accountability. This was based on apprehensions that such interpretation would be "against national interest" and supportive of an "international agenda", which would go against the very survival of media houses.

While the Sri Lankan media conveyed distortions as unimpeachable facts, the nosedive taken by the island's foreign policy was noted by renowned diplomat, Dr. Jayantha Dhanapala, who made a detailed commentary as to how the death of Sri Lanka's foreign policy occurred, in the context of the March 2014 UNHRC sessions. Unlike in the past, when a variety of opinions found expression, space and airtime, news media demonstrated the same jingoistic approach by condemning countries and critiquing their foreign policies on the basis that those countries sought to isolate and penalise Sri Lanka for having defeated the LTTE, thus destroying the illusion of a traditional northern homeland for the Tamils.

In this context, there had been an identifiable coterie of writers/ analysts who promoted Rajapaksa's aggressive stance towards the LTTE with zeal, during the years of war and subsequently, its aggressive refusal to indulge countries with a different view of Sri Lanka. Such contributors have collectively contributed by way of opinion, to portray western countries that called for accountability as LTTE agents, alleging their overt and covert support for a separatist agenda. Some of these opinion writers have, at times, assumed multiple identities, as in the case of a well-known Sri Lankan analyst.

A coterie of senior analysts/columnists, some whose reputation is quite linked to the state-owned media have religiously contributed to hate campaigns on countries and individuals, critiquing foreign policies. In the guise of evidence-based opinion, this was nothing but unabashed government propaganda.

The Sri Lankan state had consistently and carefully placed such opinion in the public domain promoting them through the official websites of the foreign and defence ministries as well as the military websites. This was clear indication as to whose interests were being served, causing jingoistic propaganda passing off as journalistic opinion.

Colombo's reporting had been largely consistent in its anti-India stance, often failing to differentiate between Delhi and Chennai politics. India's former Prime Minister, Dr. Manmohan Singh had been consistently targeted, both in the English and Sinhala news media and India's foreign policy suffered much condemnation.

Spewing venom had occurred repeatedly, and one of the most roundly condemned instances was the publication of a so-called political cartoon that maligned the Chief Minister of Tamil Nadu, Jayalalithaa Jayaram, who also had been a Sri Lankan media target. This cartoon, vulgar and unethical, was withdrawn and removed from the newspaper's website under strong pressure, from both Sri Lankan and Indian media and several rights groups.

The Sinhala media had largely followed the agenda set by the administration, influencing public thinking that the government deserved unquestioning loyalty for having secured the country from the scourge of war. Considerable content both in print and electronic media, directly qualified or bordered on hate speech, with only a few honourable exceptions, such as *Ravaya*, that managed to rise above the fog of propaganda and jingoism.

Defence as Key Player

In comparison with the past, the Rajapaksa regime wielded much overt and covert control over the media industry. Following the end of the war, the media had been pushed to levels of submission that the island had not witnessed before. There was no room for dissent or fair expression of differing views without having to encounter strong objections by the state. Alternative opinion was hardly tolerated and conveniently referred to as treachery.

It is also important to analyse the role and the level of influence Sri Lanka's defence establishment exerted on the island's foreign policy, which at times, ended up as an extension of the defence policy—a determining factor in the development of media content that reflected such influence. In addition to using both the state and private-owned media houses for its propagandist purposes, the defence establishment and some of its key personalities, continued to wield strong influence over privately-owned media houses. At times, they also determined media content. The official Defence Ministry website and several associated sites, too, have been used to condemn and criticise other media organisations and practitioners, labelling select journalists as traitors. The Sri Lankan defence authorities have also engaged in the promotion of nationalism, at times taking on matters of foreign policy and openly attacking countries. This aggressive pursuit of a divisive foreign policy is strongly reflected in the media, with media content being generated to further such cause.

This strong influence of the defence establishment over the media, in particular on the rights issue and the jingoistic approach to external affairs, had proved an extremely decisive factor in the recent past. This is quite visible on certain occasions such as the moving of a resolution on Sri Lanka's alleged complicity in rights abuses in Geneva.

The approach had been similar when it came to bilateral issues, particularly concerning India. Sri Lanka has noted with apprehension and dismay, the increase in Indian jingoism. Former President Rajapaksa had occasionally spoken of how restrictive this could be to a small country that does not have a massive population (convertible into mass support base) or a big economy—reasons that contribute to politically powerful nations.

As for India, there have been inevitable failures on its part—New Delhi was unsuccessful in extracting concessions from Colombo to concede greater autonomy for the Tamil-dominant areas. This induces countries like Sri Lanka, small but strategically located, to defend perceived core interests from being eroded due to external pressure. India's inconsistent and shifting foreign policy had failed to endear New Delhi to Colombo.

India's own approach towards Sri Lanka can influence its response towards the big neighbour. As documented by Raj Verma in his article to the London School of Economics publication, the top ten foreign policy priorities for India should include how it manages its relationship with the small island, also home to the Tamil Tigers.

If the Congress appeared unpalatable, jingoistic reporting reached giddy levels when it came to India's new Prime Minister, Narendra Modi. Modi's credentials of being a hardliner was touted as a positive attribute comparable with his Sri Lankan counterpart, former President Rajapaksa. In the meantime, a section of the Sri Lankan media zealously advocated closer relations with China, the justification not being China's economic strength or its ability to support development initiatives, but its willingness to accept Colombo, unlike India, that is considered by a section of the population as being sympathetic to the Tamil cause. The levels of influence that stemmed from the administration left indelible impression on the Sri Lankan media. The media ownership had long since been compromised.

Both state-owned and private media strived to fall in line, triggering off a new ownership model in Sri Lanka—business owners who purchase principle shares of private media houses on behalf of the government, resulting in further dilution of independence and the reining in of possible dissent. The Rivira Newspapers, Ceylon Newspapers and the Leader Publications make good case studies in this regard. With the government directly influencing news media's course, the Sri Lankan media has largely ended up, promoting jingoism, instead of generating critical content.

In the final analysis, jingoism has led to a foreign policy with the residual impact of effectively destroying the island's news media that now faces a massive credibility crisis. Though occasional attempts have been made to promote regional understanding and this has been demanded of former President Rajapaksa, the SAARC chair until November 2014, journalism that promotes regional cooperation and reflective of its overall social responsibility are few and far between. Instead, there is the unabashed promotion of hard core nationalism as a solution to national concerns, including national security which has become the overarching aspect of foreign policy as opposed to a variety of other factors—political, economic and socio-cultural.

In post-war Sri Lanka, jingoism had become part of Sri Lanka's unofficial foreign policy, and the media appears to be a source of misunderstanding, spewing of venom and mistrust. Yet, it is this objective that countries in South Asia must strive to achieve, with individual countries taking affirmative steps to defeat the prevalent practice of following aggressively nationalistic foreign policies that prevent peace and cooperation in the region.

REFERENCES

1. Mahindapala, H. L. D., "Judging Sri Lanka through Western lenses", Ministry of Defence, Sri Lanka, September 2015, at http://www.defence.lk/new.asp?fname=Judging_Sri_Lanka_through_Western_lenses_20121015_04.
2. Challenges to Peace and Prospects for Cooperation in South Asia by South Asians for Human Rights (SAHR) 2010.
3. Ranga Jayasuriya, "When Chickens come home to roost", *Ceylon Today*, June 6, 2014, at http://www.ceylontoday.lk/83-65670-news-detail-when-chickens-come-home-to-roost.html.
4. Bhadrakumar, M.K., "Foreign Policy and Jingoism don't go Together", *Russian & India Report*, May 13, 2013, at http://in.rbth.com/blogs/2013/05/13/foreign_policy_and_jingoism_dont_go_together_24921.html.
5. Neville de Silva, "Testing time for Lanka on world stage", 42(33), *Sunday Times*, January 13, 2008, at http://sundaytimes.lk/080113/Columns/thoughts.html.
6. Subramanian Swamy, "May 19 Should be Remembered Every Year as the Victory Day Over Despotism", Sri Lanka Army: Defenders of the Nation, September 5, 2013, at http://www.army.lk/detailed.php?NewsId=6716.
7. Rohan Gunaratna, "Creating Harmony is Paramount", *Sunday Observer*, Sri Lanka, August 24, 2014, at http://www.sundayobserver.lk/2014/08/24/fea07.asp.
8. Jude Fernando, "War Crimes Investigations in Sri Lanka: An Unpopular View", *Groundviews*, August 26, 2011, at http://groundviews.org/2011/08/26/war-crimes-investigations-in-sri-lanka-an-unpopular-view/.
9. Jayantha Dhanapala, The death of Sri Lankan diplomacy by suicide took place in Geneva on March 22, May 11, 2012, at http://dbsjeyaraj.com/dbsj/archives/6230.
10. Mahindapala, H.L.D., "No votes or peace in appeasing West and Jaffna jingoism", *Lankaweb*, July 30, 2011, at http://www.lankaweb.com/news/items/2011/07/30/no-votes-or-peace-in-appeasing-west-and-jaffna-jingoism/.
11. Samantha Power, An expert in Human Rights and Foreign Policy in the US, November 8, 2012, at http://kalpanakaranna.blogspot.com/2012/11/an-expert-in-human-rights-and-foreign.html.
12. Sanjay Kumar, "Diplomacy Trumps Jingoism at Ladakh Border", *The Diplomat*, May 9, 2013, at http://thediplomat.com/2013/05/diplomacy-trumps-jingoism-at-ladakh-border/.
13. "Narendra Modi's first foreign policy initiative shows his far-sightedness", *Deccan Chronicle*, May 29, 2014, at http://www.deccanchronicle.com/140529/commentary-op-ed/article/dc-debate-narendra-modi%E2%80%99s-first-foreign-policy-initiative-shows-his.
14. Dayan Jayatillake, "Lanka's foreign policy dictated by the Defence Ministry", *The Sunday Times*, February 23, 2014, at http://www.sundaytimes.lk/140223/business-times/lankas-foreign-policy-dictated-by-the-defence-ministryformer-diplomat-says-86284.html.
15. Nadira Gunatilleke, "TNA will bring grief, not joy to Tamils", (Courtesy *The Daily News*), December 11, 2013, at http://www.dailynews.lk/?q=features/tna-will-bring-grief-not-joy-tamils-prof-rohan-gunaratna.
16. Tridivesh Singh Maini, "Why Indian jingoism is increasing", *East Asia Forum*, January 30, 2013, at http://www.eastasiaforum.org/2013/01/30/why-indian-jingoism-is-increasing/.
17. Prashant Panday, "When jingoism gets the better of pragmatism…", *Times of India*, March 16, 2013, at http://blogs.timesofindia.indiatimes.com/the-real-truth/when-jingoism-gets-the-better-of-pragmatism/.
18. Raj Verma, "India's top 10 foreign policy challenges in 2014", *South Asia @ LSE*, December

20, 2013, at http://blogs.lse.ac.uk/indiaatlse/2013/12/20/indias-top-10-foreign-policy-challenges-in-2014/.

19. Deep Pal, "Decoding Modi's Foreign Policy", *Foreign Policy*, March 6, 2014, at http://southasia.foreignpolicy.com/posts/2014/03/06/decoding_modi_s_foreign_policy; Rohan Gunarathna, "India under Modi: A Turning Point in Indo-Lanka Relations", News.lk, the Official Government News Portal of Sri Lanka, August 21, 2014, at http://www.news.lk/news/sri-lanka/item/2473-india-under-modi-a-turning-point-in-indo-lanka-relations-prof-rohan-gunarathna.
20. Jaliya Wijeyekoon, "Tamil Nadu politicians not concerned about Tamils in Sri Lanka", *Sunday Observer*, April 14, 2013, at http://www.sundayobserver.lk/2013/04/14/pol04.asp.
21. Lynn Ockersz, "Regional policy considerations and President Rajapaksa's re-election", *The Island Online*, January 29, 2010, at http://www.island.lk/2010/01/29/features8.html.
22. Suba Chandran, D., "Indian regional aspirations vs national interests", *Ceylon Today*, November 18, 2013, at http://www.ceylontoday.lk/59-47809-news-detail-indian-regional-aspirations-vs-national-interests.html.

7

Maldivian Media: Ownership, Orientation and Trends

Ibrahim Waheed

Maldives: History, Geo-political Significance

Archaeological and historical evidence indicates that the Maldives had a socially-organised and viable permanent population as far as 2500 years ago. Even though the details surrounding the finer aspects of the livelihood of these people are shrouded in the mists of time, all indications are that they travelled among approximately 1,100 islands, used a Sanskrit-derived language that, if not universal, comprised a group of largely mutually intelligible dialects. Prior to 1153 A.D., the islands subscribed predominantly to the Buddhist faith, and prior to that, some historians are of the opinion, to Hinduism, and perhaps even forms of animism. In 1153 A.D., the people of Maldives converted to Islam and remain so to this day.

The archipelago of the Maldives is situated in a north-south alignment of coral atolls separated by channels, each atoll comprising a multitude of islands of differing sizes. In the South, the Maldives actually straddles the equator. Time immemorial saw the Maldives directly on the maritime crossroads of vessels which plied the Indian Ocean on routes to and from the various trading points on the East African seaboard, the Arabian Peninsula, the Indian subcontinent and what is today Sri Lanka, and the erstwhile

Malayan Peninsula and the East Indies. These trading points, most of them to formally become named ports of designated countries at later points in history, served, in turn, their own areas of outreach and influence. In this scenario, various points in the Maldives not only served as convenient ports for stopover and victualling but also as the supplier of the *Cypreamoneta* cowrie which was often used as money throughout these regions and beyond.

It goes without saying that the socio-cultural influence of the regions the Maldives dealt with in aforementioned fashion, had a significant effect in shaping all aspects of life even during that historically brief but otherwise significant hiatus in the freedom to move, communicate and trade in the region—the colonial period. Post-colonial, post-independent, and today, the Maldives continues to play the role as a point of passage to maritime traffic, with major internationally sanctioned commercial shipping lanes of the Indian Ocean traversing the country. It has also become a major high-end tourist attraction. Its history as a classified and strategic British base during and after the World War II is relegated to the annals of history. Less is mentioned in the public arena about the strategic location of the Maldives. However, once again, some media reports appear to exhibit a certain interest in this direction.

Maldivian Media: Brief History and Contemporary Modes of Usage

Printed public media officially came into existence in the Maldives in 1943. A newspaper printed in the local and official language, Dhivehi, appropriately named "*Sarukaaruge Khabaru*" (translation: News of the Government) carried news of officialdom and public announcements. On rare occasions, it also published news about town or entertainment which was at first, a novelty. The paper was printed on the capital island Male—with immediate circulation limited to subscribers in Male itself while copies taking weeks to reach the outer islands. The novelty soon wore off and other dailies and periodicals, state-owned and privately owned, became the vogue. Today, most of the print media is privately owned, with their highly dynamic web manifestations as well.

Radio as public media started in the Maldives in 1962 with a station called "Male Radio". Interestingly, this was not an entirely state-owned enterprise in the beginning; it became the official state radio station only in 1966, re-branded as "Maldives Islands Broadcasting Service" and later as "Voice of Maldives". The station continues to be in service, having undergone various changes in nomenclature, frequencies and modes of administration, both in the AM (Amplitude Modulated) and FM (Frequency Modulation) modes in addition to web streaming. Private radio stations in the FM and web streaming modes have also come up in recent years.

Television started in the Maldives in 1978 with a full-colour PAL (Phase Alternating Line) service. Initially covering the Male area only, the state-owned channel, Television Maldives now covers the entire republic. Privately-owned television channels also operate with varying degrees of success in the Maldives. Some supplement their outreach via cable and the internet.

Cable television started in the Maldives at the turn of the century. Though there were two or three privately-owned companies to start with, they quickly merged into a monopoly called Media Net, which is the only cable television service provider in the Maldives and provides many options including local television channels as well as a myriad of international channels to cater to demand.

Reference must also be made of the internet (service commenced in the Maldives in 1996), and the mobile phone network (mobile phone service started in the Maldives in 1997). With near-universal coverage of the archipelago, both media serve as highly versatile platforms for static and dynamic websites, streaming media, video on demand, etc. for the dissemination of information, news and pseudo-news of all followings.

Use of the Vernacular vs. English and Other Foreign Languages

The official language of the Maldives is called Dhivehi. It is a Sanskrit-based language with elements of other Asian, Oriental, Middle-Eastern, Western and even African influences in it. Dhivehi is the official language of the Maldives and has a few dialects, predominantly noticed for the most significant variance from the standard formal version of the middle Maldives in the South. All dialects, however, are highly mutually intelligible. Largely, the mid-Maldives dialect/tone is used in the schools for education, in the media, and for official communication and record-keeping. Since Dhivehi is also the language of communication within the family ('mother tongue' as it was), the language remains not only a language with more than 2000 years of written history but also a very lively and dynamic language. As such, the local print, radio, television and non-traditional media almost exclusively carries content in the Dhivehi language. A section of writing or radio-television program is rare than the norm.

Foreign languages are more common in the non-traditional media and in the foreign-origin programmes carried by the internet and cable service providers. In this area (apart from Dhivehi, of course), English and Hindi would appear to be the most popular languages.

Traditional and Non-Traditional Media: Current Status

The following section delineates several types of media and forces influencing the ownership of media in the Maldives, including political issues, reporting trends, etc.

(a) Types of Media

(i) Print Media: Even though the 1950s saw the advent of privately-owned dailies and periodicals in the Maldives, with no real state-owned organ (except the "Gazette", which was a carrier of legislation), the reality on the ground was that most of the dailies and periodicals in circulation, almost at the turn of the century, were owned by individuals or groups of individuals who held strong positions in the government, and were often run with subsidies or grants from state treasuries. As expected, these organs carried much news of the government and its activities and policies, the state, and key personages. Differences of opinion, not to mention any form of dissent, were unheard of. Legislation which existed at the time was hardly conducive to what later came to be known as "freedom of speech".

En passant, it must be mentioned that the late 1990s (excluding a few prior instances) saw the advent of a few clandestine papers of dissent, often issued anonymously, and definitely unregistered. These, however, often disappeared after some time.

A new legislation was introduced with the ratification of the new Constitution of the Republic of Maldives in 2008. The ensuing freedom of speech brought in more possibilities for the print media, with one poignant after-effect unrelated to the legal dynamic—economic and technological factors coupled with lifestyle changes had made print media almost obsolete in the Maldives in real-life terms. All the print media now have online versions which carry serious readership.

(ii) Radio and Television: From the time public radio started in the Maldives as a quasi-private enterprise in the early 1960s, radio soon became and remained a state enterprise until the early 2000s.(In the 1980s, an enterprising individual did start a private FM radio station in Male, but had to quickly shut down for various 'official' reasons).

As mentioned before, state-owned Television Maldives remained the only TV station in the Maldives from 1978 up to the early 2000s.

Officially in 2007, but in reality a little while before that, private radio stations, all FM stations with the inevitable line-of-sight transmission capability, began to operate in the Maldives. Initially covering only the Male region, most have now expanded into the outer atolls as well. Television channels, often coupled with visual radio (with a hazy line separating the two), followed suit, often run by the same owners.

(iii) **The Internet:** The internet has become the most vibrant platform in the Maldives. The print media in the Maldives has largely become online. History shows that the voices of dissent of the early 2000s ran on the internet. Many radio stations are using the web streaming, and also, there are some registered, unregistered and even owner-unknown sites of virtuous following in the Maldives. All these factors indicate that the internet has become a considerable platform for non-conventional media in the Maldives.

(b) Forces Influencing the Types/Forms of Media in the Maldives

(i) **The Importance and Role of Political Parties in Maldivian Media:** In 2005, when political parties first officially came into existence in the Maldives (some having declared themselves into existence out of the country prior to that), it quickly became apparent that most of these parties wanted media outlets to propagate their points of view to the general public to garner support. Thus, it was inevitable that the ground realities, even to this day, remain thus: most organs of the public press and media, be in print mode or registered online versions thereof, be they private radio or television, are overtly or covertly controlled by either of the political parties. Similarly, major individual political players heavily influence all contents carried out by these outlets.

Regarding most of the political parties in the Maldives, it is observed that: most political parties, even though they would, or should, have clearly publicised and published manifestos, are viewed by the general public as parties 'of so-and-so', indicating politically powerful or economically advantaged individuals. It is, therefore, no coincidence that sometimes there exist only a few hazy lines in published content on these organs and media between and among the political manifestos, the organ or station agendas, and the socio-politico-economic visions and aspirations of these individuals—a reality that manifests itself more in varying degrees of overtness and covertness in the case of different channels under observation.

It is believed that some of the regulatory bodies either do not have the necessary clout, legislative power, initiative, expertise, or the resources to ensure that there is a more equitable, sensible and professional approach to constructively regulate the media industry. However, at the risk of sounding blasé to a point on the one hand, and trivial on the other, and even subject to future public retaliation, one would like to ask two questions: of what relevance are the personal opinions, grudges, take-me-down and commercial aspirations of an economically well-endowed individual as prime report on the prime-time news slot on a television channel that declares itself to be a public broadcaster? Can/should any regulator take notice?[1]

Maldivian Media: Role in Regional Dynamics, Harmony, Peace and Accord

Here are few observations on Maldivian culture, language and faith issues from a regional point of view. As mentioned before, the geographical placement of the Maldives in the Indian Ocean, firmly in the middle of historical and even current shipping lanes that criss-cross the Indian Ocean has influenced the culture of its inhabitants. The necessities of having to make life viable with the meagre resources available to very small coral islands has made the culture one of constant and fast adaptation to whatever comes its way. Thus, while most Maldivians would still subscribe to the identity of being uniquely Maldivian, this capacity to adapt fast remains one of the most salient facets of Maldivian life.

Coupled with this adaptability comes a language which has strong roots in the Sanskrit. This is an anomaly in geo-linguistic observations since the languages of proximity, except for Sinhala in Sri Lanka, appear to be more Dravidian in the north, and extremely varied to the east and the west. The language acts not only as a strong uniting factor among Maldivians but carries with it a rich and centuries-old heritage. It is also a proud asset that is in dynamic use throughout the land (in this case 'islands' would be a more appropriate word).

The faith of the Maldives comes from the Arabian Peninsula—Islam. This brings with it not only the religion and its beliefs but also the traditions associated with the lands it came from—larger Arabia in the beginning, to be quickly supplemented by the scholars who came from as far and wide as what used to be greater North Indian lands, the erstwhile Persia and even the East Indies. These influences continue to come, sources and types invariably varied if not different. And the mix remains dynamic.

The 'Nation' vs. 'Our World' Conundrum

As we have seen, the Maldives comprises, in summary, a mixture of regional realities. It has a population of mixed race, a culture derived from the countries around it and built on a strong near-neighbour sub-stratum language with a backbone of Sanskrit, a religion born of the Middle East and refined in Asia.

Contemporary realities also place the Maldives firmly in the global arena. It has now become a world-renowned high-end tourism destination which caters to the needs of tourists from the Americas, Europe and the Orient. This, according to some sociologists, has placed the Maldivian culture under tremendous stress. However, the adaptability factor of Maldivian culture appears to be winning. Needless to say, even Islam, one of the great uniting pillars of Maldivian society, also appears to be undergoing sustenance of some form with new thought from young Maldivian scholars coming in from the Arab world and elsewhere.

The Maldives continues to be at the crossroads of maritime and other trade routes over and across the Indian Ocean; it also has a vote at the United Nations, equal to any non-veto-empowered large country.

However, a few pertinent questions remain: a) Are there any ground realities in, around, or about the Maldives, perhaps mentioned frankly or phrased more delicately in euphemisms that concern its regional neighbours? If so, how many of these are media-related? b) Do the reality of Maldivian media ownership, as it currently stands, lend itself to constructive and more responsible media efforts to actively participate in the promotion of regional harmony and/or greater integration? c) Does these two above-mentioned questions pre-suppose any assumptions that could be made about media in the Maldives?

Conclusion

Today, the world faces many challenges. Geo-political forces, including the world economy, democratic and other forms of governance, are undergoing wilful and unwilling, willed and unwitting, and perhaps, unforeseen, if not unnoticed, changes at a pace the world has never seen before. Our region is no exception. In fact, some of these changes would affect our region, in years to come, will face more of these changes than some of the more 'developed' regions of the world.

A reality that one must face in today's world is also this: the moving force behind change today is information—how much or how little, how real or ersatz, how independently acquired or forcefully given, how free or agenda-driven the information is? And the media, both in its traditional forms and more so in the so-called unconventional forms, are the vessels that bear this information. And the cup becomes the Holy Grail!

It is our duty to ensure that we remain our own free masters, both of our current welfare and our destinies. And to do that, we need to be fully cognizant of where, how, why, and with what strings attached, if any, our information comes from, media forming a significant purveyor thereof. However, the question remains: Can we do anything at a regional level to address this from a wide-picture perspective?

Disclaimer: The points of view presented, questions asked, and suggestions made in this paper are solely those of the author who does not formally represent any state, government, political party or other organisation.

NOTES

1. For details, please see: UNICEF: http://www.unicef.org/maldives/Press_Freedom_Maldives.pdf.

8

Regional Understanding: Does Media Ownership Really Matter?

Kaberi Gayen

Introduction

Wrapping up media within any distinct theory has become almost impossible these days. It has become harder to predict and/or measure the role of media in ensuring peace, understanding and human rights across the world now more than ever. As the structure of media has been passing through a massive and continuous flow of change in form, content and ownership pattern, more challenges are accumulating to understand how public discourse, especially within the media, can be handled towards enabling a transparent, well-informed policy response with positive human rights outcome, within the country and across nations. This is even more challenging in South Asian countries, given the historic and contemporary realities of this region, as mentioned in the Kathmandu Roundtable Report on *Conflict, Media and Human Rights in South Asia 2010*. The reality of this region has been identified in the roundtable as:

> "...the post-conflict situation in Sri-Lanka, insurgence in Jammu and Kashmir and the North East of India; the turmoil in Pakistan over the blasphemy law and other issues; the political tensions in Nepal; and the struggle in Bangladesh to deepen democracy" (p. ii).

All of this is happening in a context where the media has become increasingly commercialised and simultaneously subject to not only state controls of various kinds, but also of the flow of 'neo-liberal' capital. So, to understand how media may promote regional understanding, it may be useful to understand 'the nature of the state, media ownership and civil society interactions and dynamics in the region', which actually shapes the public discourse and policy about neighbouring countries of the region.

As post-colonial nation states in South Asia, there are some similarities in the pattern of nationhood and constitutional and politico-legal frameworks between these countries. Resources, territory and identity are at the core of conflicts among the countries in this region, embedded in a complex historical context with the addition of changing contemporary contexts. In the historical context, like other social and political institutions, the media in South Asia also carries a legacy of pivotal events, such as the partition of colonial South Asia. On the other hand, the rise of identity politics, mainly religious and linguistic, and neo-liberal globalisation since the 1990s, created new multi-layered politics in the region.

Whenever any conflict situation arises between countries, the state-owned media for certain, along with other media, construct the image of that situation, keeping national interest as their focus. The use of media in the construction of ideas of 'national interest' and 'manufacturing citizens' consent' is a common practice across states. According to the theory of representation, there is nothing we can call real—what exists is the construction of reality, and the process of constructing it. However real they may seem, all texts actually represent a 'constructed reality'. With time and repeated usage, the constructed reality appears to be real. Even the frame of judgement to interpret the representation is constructed. The dominant economic-social-political-cultural power structure constructs the standardised yardstick of judgement, which Marx (1845) commented on in his *German Ideology* as follows—*The ideas of the ruling class are in every epoch the ruling ideas.* Thus, representation of any event or issue is essentially a selective process. In both structural and post-structural theories, the 'reality' and/or 'truth' have been considered as the construct of a particular way of representation. Any representation is, thus, motivated by ideology. So how the 'reality' of regional conflict (or issues of disputes) is represented and constructed in media, and how that construction shapes the mind-set of the people and creates their attitude towards neighbouring countries in South Asia, is impossible to generalise. This is largely owing to the huge diversity of channels, newspapers, and new media sources. Here comes the importance of the political economy of mass media institutions in the construction of news on conflicts, as well as news that might promote mutual understanding across countries of the region.

Media Ownership and its Impact: Theoretical Concerns

Though the 'hypodermic needle' model of media impact on its audience has long been abandoned, mass media in the form of newspapers, radio, television, and now increasingly represented by internet content still has a powerful impact on shaping society (Perse, 2001). This impact can be seen in bolstering existing institutions and maintaining the status quo in terms of power relations in society. New technology has increased the perviousness of the media. There is now a constant flow of real time global news. Robinson argues, this has impacted how governments form foreign policy as the scope for calm deliberation is reduced and policy-makers are forced to respond to whatever media houses focus on.

Croteau and Hoynes refer to two models of media development so far: 'the market sphere model' and 'the public sphere model'. In the market model, the content and distribution of the media is seen as a product and the media owners' purpose is to make profit. The idea is that the competition between media companies will ensure that public interests are served. However, studies of Hollifield and Park, for example, show that the media market does not always lead to diversity and high levels of competition may result in decreasing diversity. McChesney observes, "In commercial media, owners hire, fire, set budgets and determine the overarching aims of the enterprise. Journalists, editors and media professionals who rise to the top of the hierarchy tend to internalise the values, both commercial and political, of media owners".

On the contrary, Croteau and Hoynes perceive that the public sphere model works on a macro level, as a social discourse that enables the circulation of ideas and knowledge, thereby, ensuring the successful socialisation of individuals into society. The public sphere model argues that the media market is regulated in order to address the different interests of different people, form social (cultural and national) identity and protect audiences from harmful content. Depending on the sphere adopted, content is influenced in different ways.

Needless to say, world media today is mainly dominated by the market sphere model. Also, there is increased concentration of media ownership across the globe. Commercial enterprises via media ownership act to influence and control society in a way that the interests of corporations come before those of society. As a consequence of worldwide deregulation and mergers, the media is increasingly entering into the possession of a certain few. For example, according to *Media Reform Coalition 2014* report, in the United Kingdom, 70 per cent of the national market is controlled by just three companies (*News UK, Daily Mail* and *General Trust,* and *Trinity Mirror*), the public broadcaster BBC accounts for 55 per cent of radio listeners, and majority of commercial radio stations are owned by Sky News. The situation is even shoddier for the USA; Lutz points out that six corporations control over 90 per cent of the US media. The increasing corporatisation of media ownership has resulted in a greater adoption of the market sphere approach. This in turn, has fuelled further consolidation. For example, in 2006, the US media was dominated by Disney, AOL-time Warner, Viacom, General Electric, News Corporation, Yahoo, Microsoft and Google.

In India, Mukesh Ambani's Reliance Industries Limited took over one of India's largest media companies—Network18 Media and Investments Limited, which comprised TV channels (including CNBC TV18, CNN-IBN, CNBC Awaaz), websites (firstpost.com, moneycontrol.com), magazines (including the license for Forbes India), entertainment channel (Colors, MTV and Homeshop Entertainment) among other businesses. Forbes/Business columnist Megha Bahree observes on this take-over: "once combined with RIL's telecom business, makes the combined group likely bigger than media baron Rupert Murdoch's empire in India and bigger than any other media group in India".

Media pundits warn media conglomeration to have some serious consequences—the main concern is the compromising of media independence. A major concern is that journalistic freedom and autonomy is restricted and corporate pressures push trivia rather than analytic and investigative journalism. Wright and Rogers point to the procedure through which the freedom of media gets compromised as a result of media concentration:

(i) The free press is identified with the free market and as newsgathering and dissemination is very expensive and requires large organisation and employment—reliance is place on advertising. Hence, corporate control emerges and news, now in the corporate interest, gets restricted or corrupted. As newsgathering becomes global and expensive, public sector broadcasters, such as the BBC, find it increasingly difficult to compete.

(ii) Though commercial ownership of the media should work where there is competition and different stances in debate are taken, sometimes, media becomes concentrated and even becomes monopolistic. Then, the existence of competition becomes questionable.

(iii) Corporate control of the media means that in order to satisfy shareholders there must be a commitment to the bottom line, done by cutting costs and driving up revenue. The effect is a reduction in expensive critical content and a growth of uncritical content such as press releases and celebrity trivia. McChesney observes: "to do effective journalism is expensive and corporate managers realise that the surest way to fatten profits is to fire editors and reporters and fill the news hole with inexpensive syndicated material and fluff. The result has been a sharp polarisation among journalists with salaries and benefits climbing for celebrity and privileged journalists at the elite news media while conditions have deteriorated for the balance of the working press".

Wright and Rogers conclude that these processes: "undermine the autonomy and effectiveness of the news media as the 'fourth estate' of the political system serving the public interest by helping to create an informed citizenry. Reporters and editors, even when they personally believe in the professional ethics of neutrality and objectivity, are severely constrained by the interests and orientations of the owners and business executives of media corporations and the commercial advertisers that are their main source of profits".

Guha Thakurta raises a similar question in the context of India, "If India's biggest corporate conglomerate is also India's biggest media company, what it does to diversity of opinion, plurality of opinion, what it does to unfavourable news coverage?" Guha Thakurta points to the outcome of when big business interests get into media business as, "they influence what comes out into public, what is heard and read…The greater the monopolisation and corporatisation of media, the less the space for smaller voices, differing voices, dissenting voices".

When media turns into a mere business conglomerate, news is nothing but a commodity. Selling the commodity to its clients gets the main priority in maximising *the triumph of invested capital* of the owners. So, rather than presenting issues of neighbouring country's general populace and their lives, their culture and struggles, more focus is given on the news of the glamour industry, heavy conflicts and preaching of hate-news in the name of 'national interest'.

Media Trends in Covering Conflicting Issues in South Asia

Traditionally, either the government or the market has controlled the media in South Asia. Public or state-owned media has a colonial history and the ministries of information try to use these as state propaganda apparatus. The impact of neo-liberal economic reforms and the wave of deregulation across South Asian countries in the late 1980s led the expansion of media—both print and broadcast—and the end of state monopoly over television and the advent of cable television in the 1990s have given rise to an explosion of news and entertainment television across the region. As the business side has become the major focus of these info-entertainment industries, there has been more focus on turning news into political theatre in 2010 and a way of earning money. In this perspective, the debates about regional conflict issues are no less than business commodities. The presentation packages focus on selling the news items to their concerned audiences. Rather than carry out a deep analysis of any event, perpetuating the existing standardised view about those issues has been the priority.

While compiling the tendencies of representing conflict news in South Asian media, the experts of Kathmandu Roundtable 2010 mentioned 10 trends:

1) An episodic treatment of conflict and human rights issues;
   Media coverage tends to lack a historical perspective and uncritically invokes dominant, taken-for-granted imaginaries in framing and narrating events.
2) An instrumentalisation of human rights concerns and their subordination to so-called larger concerns; in this, media tends to reproduce larger social consensus, such as 'national interest', 'state security', etc.
3) A fragmenting of issues and a focus on the spectacular;
   Particularly in broadcast media, to address the huge competition among media houses, production of an incessant flow of 'breaking news' ends up with 'sound bites' journalism. This requires constant

'polarisation and political theatre' in TV journalism to turn news and current affairs into 'drama' to increase TRP.

4) Simplistic categorisations based on 'common sense' and a black and white interpretation of events. Oversimplifying or over-contextualising are the components here of simplistic categorisation.
5) Uncritical framing of events by use of terms and labels in ways that are often reductionists or foregrounding reality selectively.
6) Ideological biases on class and other power relations that determine what constitute 'news'.
7) Systematic silence and exclusion that relate to the situations and voices of marginalised zones of conflict; the media in South Asia exercises a high degree of self-censorship.
8) Media narratives challenging democratic values.
9) Linguistic hegemonies, biases and associated class interests.
10) A growing tendency of the major news media moving from the role of reporting events towards becoming an 'interested player'. The role of media as an interested player raises the spectre of altering news itself.

While the mainstream media has been constrained with some set criterion of state policy and/or created market demand, advancement of internet technology is emerging as a source of nourishing alternative views and opinions of the citizens. Since 2000, the number of internet users in Asia has multiplied over 1000 per cent and broadband penetration rates are 31.7 per cent. Asia now accounts for 45.1 per cent of world internet usage, (http://www.internetworldstats.com/stats.htm). In Figure 1, the rise in internet penetration in South East Asia is depicted.

Facebook, Twitter, blogs and various news portals are being used to mobilise society's alternative views. Free from policy regulations as well as market demand (if wished), citizens express their views through blogs, e-groups, social networking sites, e-campaigns, event pages, thereby, creating their own public sphere. Two of such glaring examples from the recent past are: young protestors in Kashmir valley used Facebook and Twitter to speak up against military intervention in 2010, and young online activists in Bangladesh utilised similar social networking techniques in the Shahbag movement of 2013. The emergence of digital media and new technologies have democratised the technology of production and distribution. On the flipside, there is the vicé of anonymity, by abusing which many websites and blogs are preaching hate messages about religious and ethnic minorities, women, and people of different political views, and of course, about the historic rivalry of neighbouring countries. In almost all the countries of the South Asian region, there are some policies to curtail the voices of dissent on the internet. The Information Technology Act of 2000 and the Information Technology Act, 2008 in India, the Information and Communication Technology Act, 2006 in Bangladesh are some of those acts. In Bangladesh, under the ICT (Information and Communication Technology) Act, 2006, online bloggers were arrested by the government for writing allegedly anti-religious (Islam) speech, whereas there are many sites continuously conveying hate speech about other religions, faiths and atheists in the region. In fact it is hard to stop the malignant attempts of these netizens.

Media Ownership in Bangladesh and Politicised Journalism

Bangladesh carries almost the same post-colonial media history as other countries of South Asia. Indian researcher Tarapada Paul notes that the history of the newspaper in India is parallel to its political history. Similar was the statement of a veteran journalist of Bangladesh, Santosh Gupta, who wrote that the history of the newspaper in Bangladesh is parallel to the political history of Bangladesh. In both cases, common is the specific relationship between politics and the media. When Bangladesh became independent in 1971 from West Pakistan, it had only a few newspapers. As India helped Bangladesh extensively in the war, the political atmosphere was friendly towards India in the early days, as reflected in the then print and broadcast media. However, within a year or so, when some bilateral issues started to pop up—the distribution of enclaves, Berubari-South Talpatti-Tin Bigha Corridor[1] followed by Farakka dam, border smuggling and killing, wired fence, and so on and so forth in later years, the amity started to fade away and a trend of anti-Indian politics emerged. This was reflected in the mainstream newspapers. Broadcasting media, both radio and television, were government owned. In fact, television's status as a public corporation came to an end in Sheikh Mujibur Rahman's era, which was previously a public corporation. The state-owned newspapers, and the state-owned radio and television represented the then India-Bangladesh relationship as a sharp mirror image. Needless to say that, the India-Bangladesh relationship was friendly at state levels till 1975. The relationship with Pakistan was tense, and the relationship with other countries of the region was friendly, but not visible.

Figure 1: Internet users per 100 people (Source: World Bank, 2014)

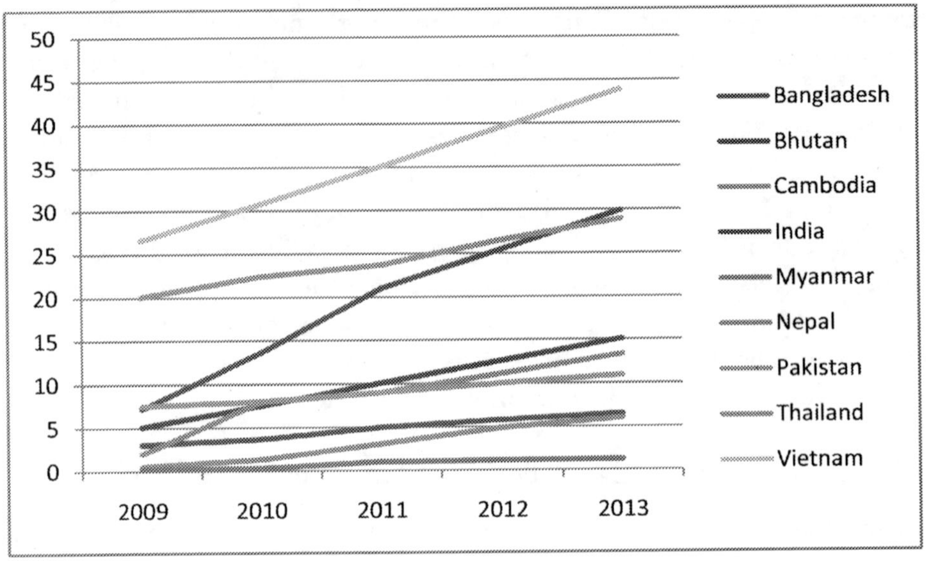

After the brutal assassination of the first Prime Minister and the leader of the Bangladesh's War of Independence, Sheikh Mujibur Rahman and his family in 1975, Bangladesh experienced a long passé of military rule. It started with General Zia ur Rahman in 1975 and continued till the fall of General Hossain Mohammad Ershad in December 1990 following a popular uprising. Both Generals came into power via coups d'état, formed political parties, played the religion card largely for political ends, and took up an anti-Indian and pro-Islamic stance. They played the religion card tagging Awami League as pro-Indian and anti-Islamic, and this politics still prevails. This division was visible sharply in the media. During this period, both the state radio and the television were used to further political agendas and acted as propaganda machinery.

However, the print media played a role of resistance; Even under the strict control of the two generals and amidst the pan-Islamic and anti-Indian atmosphere, newspapers like *Daily Sangbad* and *The Observer* created less 'anti-Indian' and 'pro-Pakistan' frenzy in the name of 'national security', 'autonomy' and 'regional cooperation'. After the fall of President General H.M. Ershad in December 1990, the then caretaker government took the de-regularisation attempt, following which the number of newspapers increased suddenly.

Bangladesh launched its first satellite channels ATN Bangla in 1997, which was soon followed by Channel-I in 1999. However, it was Ekushey Television (ETV), the first private terrestrial channel aired in 2000, which made a clear difference with BTV in respect of news treatment and its inventive programmes. People welcomed the channels because they replaced the '*saheb-bibi-golam* box' news of BTV with more authentic news. The success of ETV influenced businesspeople cum politicians of the country to invest in private television channels. However, the BNP-Jamaat allied government closed ETV for 'licensing problems' and thus "an anarchy envelops the television licensing process. Political loyalty is the only criterion to get licenses". The country saw the boom of private television channels in a short span of time of the BNP-led four party alliance government of Begum Khaleda Zia (2001-2005).

The whole licensing process is now politicised. It is almost impossible to get a private television license without the 'blessing' of the ruling party. Both the major political parties BNP (Bangladesh Nationalist Party) and the AL (Awami League) want to have a greater influence on the private television channels of the country for the sake of power and politics. Now Bangladesh has 26 private television channels. But if we analyse the content of these private channels, it seems regional news is near absent unless a major incident occurs, like elections in India and Pakistan, terrorist attacks, or state visits by premiers. Television channels, though private, are extra cautious not to not produce any regional news of their own, normally depending on agency news instead. The tendency of covering regional conflict issues is not different from the South Asian media trend, as identified by the Kathmandu Roundtable 2010. Superficial news of only the biggest events is represented, that too, without any follow-up or analysis. News of Bhutan, Maldives, Sri Lanka and Nepal is almost absent (unless it is an event also being covered by the big media agencies of the world, for example, the earthquake in Nepal in 2014). India happens to be a mighty neighbour that cannot be ignored. But nonetheless, the coverage received by India and Pakistan is also dependent on agency news, in which case it is hard to trace the news channels' own views. In this regard, print media tends to offer greater diversity in opinions.

From the 1990s, as mentioned earlier, there was a boom in the newspaper industry. We get three models of newspaper ownership: liberal capital (*Prothom Alo, The Daily Star, Samakal, Jugantor,* and recently *Dhaka Tribune*), liberal capital+ highly partisan (*Janakantha, Vorer Kagoj, Amar Desh*), and Pan-Islamic (*Sangram, Inquilab*). We can actually see the impact of ownership in print media. Covering regional news is mainly dependent on news agencies and the trend is, undoubtedly, commercial and superficial as in most of South Asia; yet there is an added component—the religion card. Though Bangladesh achieved independence by negating the 'two-nation' theory on which the partition of 1947 was based, the army generals who came in power through coups d'état in the post-1975 era played the religion card and anti-Indian sentiment was at the core of their views and actions. First, General Zia Ur Rahman changed the constitution and replaced secularism with *Bismillahir Rahmanur Rahim* in 1976. General H.M. Ershad further amended the constitution declaring Islam as the state religion. Therefore, gradually the politics of Bangladesh became polarised: on the one hand, the AL-led secular force, also known as '*muktizuddher pokkher shokti*' (the force that upholds the spirit of the War of Independence) and on the other, the BNP-Jamaat alliance (popularly known as '*jatiyotabadi shokti*') and other Islamic forces. The sense of polarisation is also vivid in media. The whole industry is divided into these two camps, which are manifested in the all-pervading partisan journalism.

Almost all the big newspaper houses are dependent on corporate business and in a way are serving corporate interest. The party politics in journalism is so strong that media researcher Khan puts forward as: "...the journalists are also divided in line with two major political parties—the Bangladesh Awami League (AL) and the Bangladesh Nationalist Party (BNP). Even the Bangladesh Federal Union of Journalists (BFUJ) is divided into two groups by this political line. Journalists' trade union bodies like BFUJ and Dhaka Union Journalists (DUJ) and journalists' unions of other towns and cities in the country cannot protect vulnerable journalists' right".

The polarised media even distorts news, publish false news for fulfilling the political agenda of their owners, and not face any punitive measures.

To understand how this partisan journalism has destroyed professionalism, a few examples may be helpful. Long before the demolition of Babri Mosque in India, *The Daily Inquilab* spread the first lead in 1989 that the holy mosque had been demolished; this caused huge communal frenzy throughout the country. Newspapers like *The Sangram, The Daily Inquilab, The Daily Amar Desh* frequently publish provocative news, which help in spreading hate against neighbouring countries, mainly India and Myanmar. *The Daily Inquilab* published one such news item in January 2014 when the country was facing continuous attacks from the Jamat-Hefajot force and experiencing post-election violence. *The Daily Inquilab's* lead item on January 16, 2014 was how the Indian Army helped the joint force operation in Satkkhira.

Picture 1: 'Help of Indian Army in the Joint Force Operation in Satkkhira!' *The Daily Inquilab* January 16, 2014. *The Daily Inquilab* cited certain Facebook posts as the source of the news.

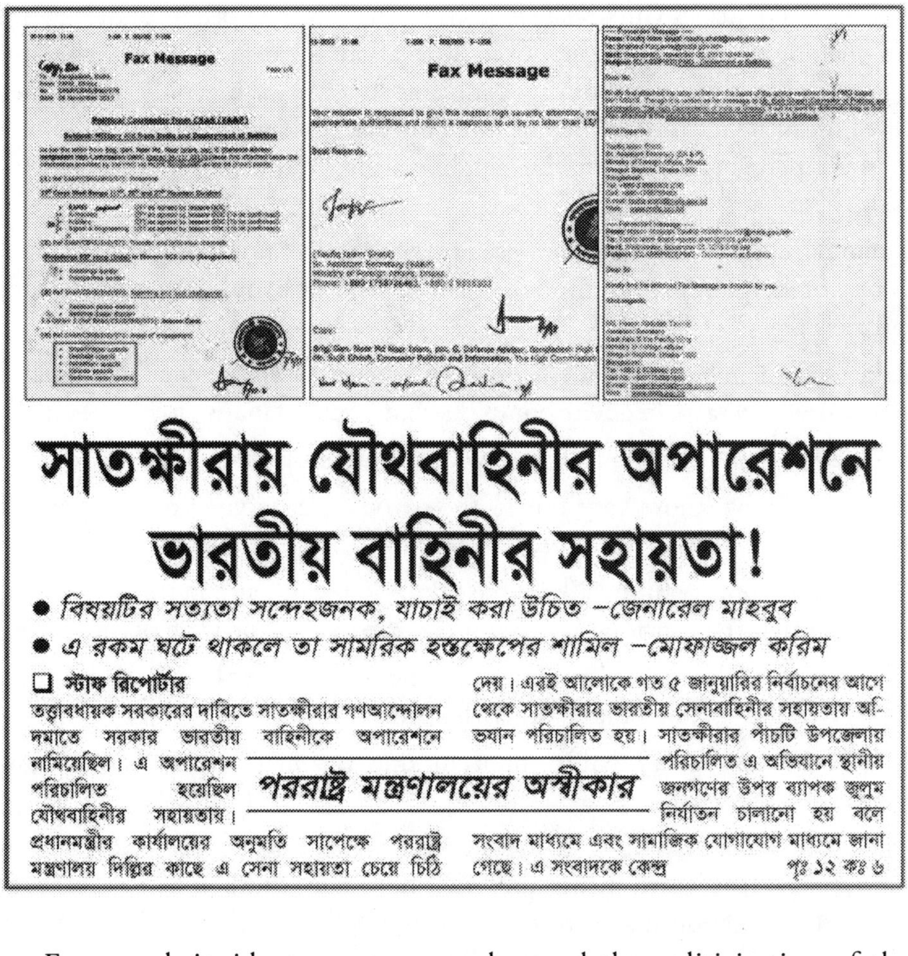

Fax Message

Fax Message

সাতক্ষীরায় যৌথবাহিনীর অপারেশনে ভারতীয় বাহিনীর সহায়তা!

- *বিষয়টির সত্যতা সন্দেহজনক, যাচাই করা উচিত –জেনারেল মাহবুব*
- *এ রকম ঘটে থাকলে তা সামরিক হস্তক্ষেপের শামিল –মোফাজ্জল করিম*

❑ **স্টাফ রিপোর্টার**

তত্ত্বাবধায়ক সরকারের দাবিতে সাতক্ষীরার গণআন্দোলন দমাতে সরকার ভারতীয় বাহিনীকে অপারেশনে নামিয়েছিল। এ অপারেশন পরিচালিত হয়েছিল যৌথবাহিনীর সহায়তায়। প্রধানমন্ত্রীর কার্যালয়ের অনুমতি সাপেক্ষে পররাষ্ট্র মন্ত্রণালয় দিল্লির কাছে এ সেনা সহায়তা চেয়ে চিঠি দেয়। এরই আলোকে গত ৫ জানুয়ারির নির্বাচনের আগে থেকে সাতক্ষীরায় ভারতীয় সেনাবাহিনীর সহায়তায় অভিযান পরিচালিত হয়। সাতক্ষীরার পাঁচটি উপজেলায় পরিচালিত এ অভিযানে স্থানীয় জনগণের উপর ব্যাপক জুলুম নির্যাতন চালানো হয় বলে সংবাদ মাধ্যমে এবং সামাজিক যোগাযোগ মাধ্যমে জানা গেছে। এ সংবাদকে কেন্দ্র পৃঃ ১২ কঃ ৬

পররাষ্ট্র মন্ত্রণালয়ের অস্বীকার

From such incidents, one can understand the politicisation of the profession of journalism and the media industry, as well as the immense power of online media activists. On one hand, activists spread false, fabricated news while another section of activists prove that the whole matter was false and fabricated. Thus, the ideology of the owners is very important.

Absent Neighbourhood

As already mentioned, except for India and Pakistan, the media of Bangladesh is almost silent about other neighbouring countries. In Bangladeshi media, there is no news of Bhutan, Maldives, Sri Lanka (unless any political mishap takes place), and Nepal (unless any big accident takes place like the massive earthquake in 2014); no follow-up, analysis, contextualising, and individual reporting is done; also no update is given on the common people of the region. An ongoing research by the author in 2015 about the perception of secondary school children on neighbouring countries shows that they only have either very little or no idea about their region. However, following are some examples of their perceptions about the neighbouring countries, mainly SAARC countries:

India: Big country, emerging power of the world, does not care about disputed issues of neighbouring countries, the Bollywood industry and cricket fanaticism;

Pakistan: Enemy of Bangladesh as a consequence of 1971 genocide, military rule, no democracy, frequent bombing, and cricket fanaticism;

Sri Lanka: Conflict zone (only a few could mention that), no clear idea;

Bhutan: 'Don't know very much' (however, 11 interviewee talked about Bhutan being a beautiful and scenic country since they had travelled there);

Nepal: The country of the Himalayas, 'don't know other than this'; (it should be noted that the earthquake had not occurred yet at the time of interview);

Afghanistan: Taliban rule, present government is in power by US intervention (23 mentioned), 'don't know other than this';

Maldives: The country that is important due to climate change, 'don't know other than this'.

There was a variation in the answers depending on the readership of newspapers. It is worth mentioning that not many children had a clear idea about the neighbouring countries. A sample of the varying cultures of the SAARC countries appeared only in 1985, when the artists of different countries performed in the first SAARC summit held in Dhaka on BTV (Bangladesh Television). Those performances featuring in the media opened doors into the yet unknown lives and cultures of the neighbouring countries.

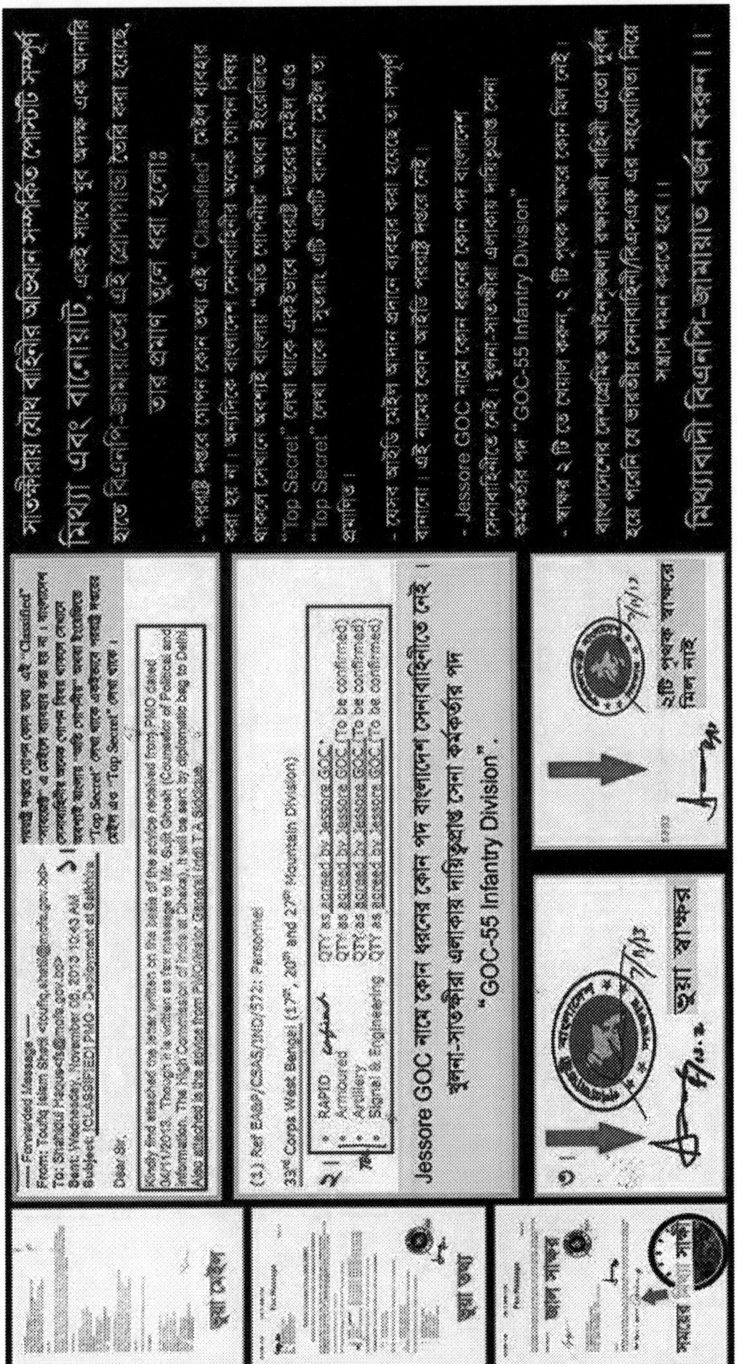

Picture 2: Online activists proved that the posts regarding the news in *Inquilab* were false and fictitious. They managed to prove that the email accounts and faxed emails used as the basis of the news were all fake. The signatures used in the mails were also fake. And finally, there was no rank named 'Jessore GOC' within the Bangladesh Army.

Picture 3: *The Daily Inquilab* sought apology for their news of January 16, 2014. Under the headline 'We are sorry', the *Inquilab* stated on behalf of the editor that the news was not authentic and that they would be careful in future before publishing any such news item.

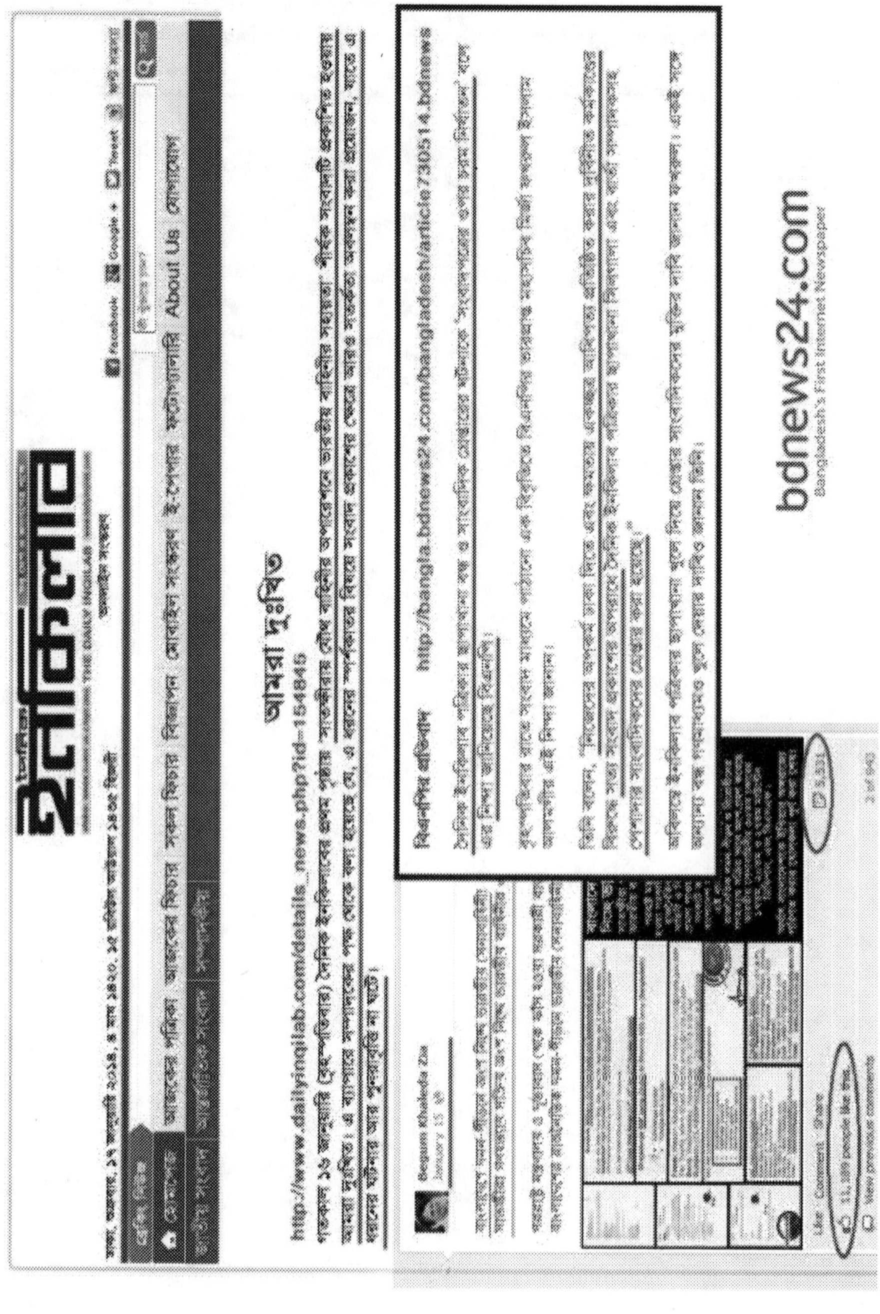

Ways to Overcome

Theoretically, the media can play an important role in improving regional understanding—it has the scope for promoting tolerance and dialogue among cultures and people of neighbouring countries. The media can share the knowledge of different value systems and build respect among nations and cultures. The news coverage and programmes—showing commonalities, shared values, and cultures which exist across regional boundaries—may encourage people to comprehend, respect and appreciate the uniqueness of different cultures in their region. Media, thus, can empower people through information that may help them to understand the local and regional perspectives of many common developmental issues and how they can work together to build a better future for all.

But the question is, will the media do so? The answer to this question has a synergetic relationship with the political economy of media ownership.

For the media to be effective in its role of improving regional understanding by resolving conflicts, it needs to be free, independent, professionally sound and credible. Where these conditions are absent, there remains the risk that the media will instigate skirmishes through biased and even propagandistic reporting that can exacerbate tensions. Media censorship is an integral part of many South Asian countries—added to state censorships in the name of Special Powers Act and so on, business-media-conglomerates monopolistic invisible market censorships are increasingly becoming threats for the media practitioners to be free and work independently.

Then, for the media to work as a change agent for regional understanding is only possible if "media are taken seriously from the point of regional development, a part of the world's new and emergent development framework, which is being built upon three main axes: sustainable development, poverty eradication and peace".

As the 'market sphere model' of media growth is dominating the 'public sphere model' worldwide, the South-Asian countries being no exception to that, it will be hard to get the media across the region to work for improving regional understanding. The scholars and practitioners from the SAARC countries generally agree that in today's neo-liberal scenario, media in their countries are mainly dominated by the market sphere model, where 'triumph of invested capital' is the aim and is manifested in TRP (Television Rating Point) journalism.

Also, as the media mostly publishes or broadcasts regional news that is gathered from the same agency sources, only standardised and stereotypical news filtered through the media industry is served to the audience. Thus, space for regional understanding gets clogged. This is one side of the obstacle. The other side is that partisan journalism serves only in line with the owners' political and economic aspirations. In both cases, regional understanding is at stake. In this situation, an alternative may be to promote the 'Public Sphere Model' of media growth. Within this model, attempts towards reducing the knowledge gap of 'social culture' and 'political culture' amongst the nations of the South-Asian region may improve regional understanding.

Who will do this? Journalists' forums across the region may be an option. The South Asian Free Media Association (SAFMA) was launched to make the association between media across the region more effective. A social network approach among the media of different countries of this region may strengthen the embedded social capital of trust, commitment and development, and thus outsmart that media which works against this spirit. Networks of journalists in the South Asian region may take initiative and rely on their professionalism to put forward the agenda of regional understanding. However, the skill and capacities of the journalists across the region are not equal. For this, two things are essential: First, proper research on media practices about regional news treatment, as we do not have a clear picture about the representation scenario; Second, proper training of media professionals on regional understanding—a training that will give emphasis on a humane approach while covering regional issues instead of opting to take up a competitive outlook.

Democratic governments may promote the idea of regional understanding through their political practices and regional cooperation, which will then be reflected in the media. This is the time for governments of this region to find out why the SAARC could not be effective. Resolving bilateral disputes among neighbouring countries, in particular, can be a good gesture from the governments' sides to initiate better regional understanding. However, the media may create the right atmosphere to foster dialogue to resolve the bilateral disputes.

To play the role of a facilitator, the media network across the countries may consider taking several immediate initiatives:

(i) Exchange programmes among media practitioners, artists, writers, and producers—this will enable them to have a better understanding of neighbouring countries. It will ultimately help identifying common interests, issues of disputes, and the ways to overcome such problems.

(ii) Exchange of media content—this may allow media consumers to have direct exposure to regional issues.

(iii) Initiative of joint productions of media content—for instance, some important regional issues may be addressed jointly by media professionals of different countries, and published or broadcast simultaneously by the media of concerned countries.

However, to attain a more sustainable effect, further attention needs to be accorded to the ownership model. The BBC experience may be a wakeup call for the free-will agent journalists across the region to think more about the ownership pattern that will curtail the domination of the market on media by few corporations. Strengthening the public sector of mass media ownership i.e., public subsidies that are free of government influence, and public control to promote wider media ownership—can be a better solution for public interest in the region. This could be hard to attain, so only a limited role can be aspired to by the mass media to promote regional understanding. A strong alternative may be online platforms of journalists and media practitioners.

NOTES

1. Bangladesh and India sealed a historic land pact on the June 6, 2015 to swap territories, which will finally allow tens of thousands of people living in border enclaves to choose their nationality after decades of stateless limbo.

REFERENCES

1. T. W. Adorno and M. Horkheimer, *The Dialectic of Enlightenment*, English edition, Herder & Herder, New York, 1972.
2. M. Bahree, "Reliance Takes Over Network18: Is This The Death Of Media Independence?", *Forbes* /*Business*, May 30, 2014, at http://www.forbes.com/sites/meghabahree/2014/05/30/reliance-takes-over-network18-is-this-the-death-of-media-independence/ (Accessed July 2015).
3. "Conflict, Media and Human Rights in South Asia: Report from Round Table", 2011, International Council on Human Rights Policy, Panos South Asia, and the Tata Institute of Social Sciences, at http://web3.apiu.edu/researchfile/Research%20Materials/Social%20Issues%20In%20Asia/Conflict%20Media%20and%20humnan%20rights%20in%20 south%20asia.pdf (Accessed September 12, 2014).
4. D. Croteau and W. Hoynes, *The Business of Media: Corporate Media and the Public Interest,* Sage, Thousand Oaks, CA.
5. T. Islam and K. Gayen, "Perception of Neighbouring Countries among the Higher Secondary School Children in Dhaka City", 2014 (unpublished).

6. S. Gupta, "The Milieu of Muktizuddha: The Liberation Struggle of the Press (Muktizuddher Prochchhodpot: Songbadpotrer Swadheenota Songram)", pp. 152-186 in Md Muniruzzaman (Ed.) *Blood-stained Bangla* (*Raktakto Bangla*), Muktodhara: Dhaka, 1971.
7. S. Hall, "Cultural Identity and Cinematic Representation", pp. 704-714 in Robert Stam and Roby Miller (Eds.) *Film & Theory*, Blackwell, Oxford, 2000.
8. E. S. Herman and N. Chomsky, *Manufacturing Consent: The Political Economy of the Mass Media*, Pantheon Books, New York, 1998 and 2002.
9. C. Hollifield, "News Media Performance in Hypercompetitive Markets: An Extended Model of Effects", *International Journal on Media Management*, 8(2), 2006, pp. 60-69.
10. M. A. R. Khan, "Private television ownership in Bangladesh: a critical qualitative inquiry", PhD Thesis, University of Hong Kong, 2013, at http://hdl.handle.net/10722/195981 (Accessed July 13, 2015).
11. P. Lazarsfeld, B. Berelson and H. Gaudet, *The People's Choice*, Columbia University Press, New York,1944 and 1968.
12. A. Lutz, "These 6 Corporations Control 90 per cent of the Media in America", *Business Insider*, June 14, 2012, at http://www.businessinsider.com/these-6-corporations-control-90-of-the-media-in-america-2012-6 (Accessed October 2014).
13. K. Marx, *The German Ideology*, Marx-Engels Collected Works, Volume 5, International Publishers, London, 1976.
14. R. McChesney, *Corporate Media and the Threat to Democracy*, Seven Stories Press, New York, 1997.
15. Media Reform Coalition, "The elephant in the room: a survey of media ownership and plurality in the United Kingdom", April 28, 2014, at http://www.mediareform.org.uk/wpcontent/uploads/2014/04/ElephantintheroomFinalfinal.pdf (Accessed October 2014).
16. S. Park, "Competition's Effects on Programming Diversity of Different Program Types", *International Journal on Media Management*, 7 (1-2), 2005, pp.39-54.
17. T. Paul, *The Newspapers of India*, Arora Printers, Kolkata, 1972.
18. E. M. Perse, *Media Effects and Society*, Lawrence Erlbaum Associates, Hillsdale, NJ, 2001.
19. P. Robinson, "The CNN effect: Can the new media drive foreign policy", *Review of International Studies*, 25, 1999, pp. 301-309.
20. UNESCO, Media in Support of Sustainable Development and a Culture of Peace, UNESCO, Jakarta, 2015.
21. World Bank, at http://data.worldbank.org/indicator (Accessed October 2014).
22. E. O. Wright and J. Rogers, "Democracy and Corporate Control of the Media", in *American Society: how it really works*, Chapter 19, W. W. Norton & Company, New York, 2011, pp.1-13.

9

The Role of the Bhutanese Media in Bhutan's Democratic Evolution and Governance

Tenzing Lamsang

Background and Evolution of the Bhutanese Media

Media, in a modern sense of the word, started only from 1970s onwards in Bhutan. Media, like much else, took off as a part of Bhutan's process of planned development and modernization that started post 1962 with the country's five-year plans. The Bhutanese media's initial role, similar to many small developing countries, was primarily to act as a tool for development and keeping citizens informed of the government's plans and activities. The media in Bhutan could have continued to perform such role as it happens in many countries of the world. However, in case of Bhutan, His Majesty the Fourth King Jigme Singye Wangchuck also got involved and empowered the Bhutanese media as a part of his process of decentralization and gradual transition from an absolute monarchy to a democracy. This process was further taken forward by His Majesty the King Jigme Khesar Namgyel Wangchuck, under whose reign Bhutan saw the advent of a very vocal and active private media, a tremendous growth of media, both in quantity and variety. Therefore, the free and vibrant media in Bhutan is also a major part of the democratic process and decentralization of power. It was on this premise that the Bhutanese media really took off and became a player in governance and state after the introduction of democracy.

The State-owned Media

The development of media in Bhutan started with the national paper, *Kuensel,* and the national broadcaster, *Bhutan Broadcasting Service* (BBS). *Kuensel* began in 1965 as a government circular that was meant mainly for government officials as a source of basic information on the government's activities which had just finished its first five-year plan. Starting from 1986, *Kuensel* started publication of a weekly paper managed by the Department of Information under the Ministry of Communications. In a sign of the changing times and decentralization process in 1992, *Kuensel,* by a Royal Edict was made independent from the government ministry that used to run the paper. However, it remained as a government-owned media. In 1998, it stopped receiving government subsidy, and in 2006, the paper sold 49 percent of its shares to the public. BBS was started in 1973, initially known as *Radio NYAB* and managed by the National Youth Association of Bhutan (NYAB). In 1979, *Radio NYAB* was put under the Ministry of Communication and it became a national broadcaster providing news for the masses, apart from the national paper, *Kuensel.* BBS was delinked from the government on October 1, 1992 through a Royal Edict allowing it to function as an autonomous broadcaster. In 1999, with the introduction of television in Bhutan, BBS also launched its national television station. Currently, the national broadcaster has two channels, BBS 1 focusing on news and current affairs, and BBS 2 focusing on education and entertainment. BBS also has two radio channels: the 1st Radio Channel carries news and programs in local dialects, Sharchop and Lhotsam, and in English. The 2nd Radio Channel is broadcast in the national language, Dzongkha.

The development of the state media is interesting, in that, it brought about the introduction of professional journalism in a relatively closed society, and it showed the prominent role that media can play in the development and evolution of the Bhutanese society and polity. At the same time, the state media, in many ways, reflected the evolving Bhutanese society, polity and economy. *Kuensel* began its life as a government circular that followed the government announcements and developments as a reflection of the times, both economically and politically. However, with increasing economic development and political reforms initiated from the throne, *Kuensel* evolved into a professional newspaper run by professional journalists and editorial board. The delinking from the government brought in visible changes, as one could see more critical writings, and even the odd investigative journalism, which would have been considered as explosive by Bhutanese standards at the time. The unthinkable also started happening when *Kuensel* started criticizing the failures of the government and highlighting audit and corruption reports.

The state media played an important role in forging together the idea of a modern and cohesive Bhutan of today. At an early period of Bhutan's development, the state media also played an invaluable role in the development process of the country, educating the people about issues in the areas of health, education, agriculture, etc. It was also an active participant, along with the state, in the gradual process of democratization of Bhutan culminating in the 2008 Parliamentary elections.

The state media, in its early days, was criticized for being government-owned and toeing the government line. It has come a long way from that phase, becoming more independent, but what truly set the cat among the pigeons was the advent of the private media in Bhutan.

The Private Media

The media revolution in Bhutan started from 2006, with the advent of Bhutan's first private newspaper, *Bhutan Times* in 2006 and followed a few months later, by another private newspaper, *Bhutan Observer*. A spate of other private newspaper launch, in English and Dzongkha, began in 2008. *Bhutan Today* in 2008, Bhutan's first business paper, *Business Bhutan* in 2009, *The Journalist* in 2009 and *The Bhutanese* in 2012. Afterwards, private Dzongkha papers, like *Druk Neytshuel* was launched in 2010, *Druk Yoedzer* in 2011, *Gyalchi Sarshog* in 2012 and *Druk Melong* in 2012. In the same period, a news magazine, *Drukpa*, and entertainment magazines, *Trowa* and *Yeewong* were also started. Not to be left behind were the private radio stations, like *Kuzoo FM* launched in 2006, *Radio Valley* in 2007, *Centennial Radio* in 2008 and *Radio Waves* in 2010. These radio stations are mainly focused on entertainment given the licensing conditions.

The advent of the private media was a game changer, not only for the Bhutanese media, but also in terms of the media's impact on democratic evolution and governance. The first major impact of the private media was not only breaking the monopoly of the state media over news, but introducing a more critical and investigative journalism, or what one in Bhutan likes to call "controversial articles". The private media also gave a strong sense of competition to *Kuensel* and BBS. The state-owned media upgraded its editorial quality and also started doing a higher number of investigative and critical stories. *Kuensel*, free from government funding and separated from government control through the Royal Edict, was particularly active, and on many occasions, even outdid its nearest rival *Bhutan Times* from 2008 to 2010 in the number of investigative and critical stories. The private media combined with younger and more exposed journalists in *Kuensel* and BBS did not make it just out of the ordinary to criticize the government, but in fact, made it a norm.

The private media also strengthened the critical media and brought about new and independent players in the form of private individuals or corporate houses owning newspapers. Though both the government ownership of media and private ownership has its own well-known flaws, but in the bigger picture, there was a healthy balance.

Media and the Democratic Process

The media really took off during March 2008 Parliamentary elections, as for the first time a gruelling election process between the Druk Phuensum Tshogpa (DPT) and the People's Democratic Party (PDP) saw the once mighty pre-democracy ministers going around in the most humble homes and villages begging for votes—a common sight in other South Asian countries but in Bhutan—this was extraordinary. The power equations had changed overnight, and the people realized that they could vote for leaders of their choice. The media was an important factor in this equation as it played the key role of informing the people about the candidates and parties so that people could make correct choices.

The 2008 election was also an important turning point for the government which had traditionally relied on a top-down system, with the King at the top. Now suddenly, the government realized that it had to function in the bottom up system of democracy and elections. Since none of the ministers were in power, and the interim government functioned with limited powers, the media, under the watchful eyes of the Election Commission of Bhutan, came into its own and started to play an active role.

The elections further enhanced the critical and independent role of the media as a whole. It was for the first time that political parties criticized each other, not sparing the party presidents and candidates. The media, in carrying out the criticism and charges being traded, started to find a deeper and stronger voice. In a society where ministers were not used to hearing criticism, the media played the role of not only a reporter, but also that of a critic and analyser. Soon, it was not uncommon to see editorials lecturing and chiding both parties and their leaders.

The 2008 election was crucial in bringing the three key and relatively new components of a young democracy together—the empowered voters, the new politicians and the media. Each played a part and found a role for themselves in Bhutan's new democracy. This was also in the context of a situation where the ministers and bureaucratic figures, on an average, were double the age of their much younger and inexperienced journalist counterparts.

All in all, the media that emerged after the 2008 elections was more familiar with the politicians, more experienced and politically aware, and much self-assured. This was useful, especially, in a democratic era where various democratic institutions were also finding their own space, power and responsibilities within the larger system.

Media and Policy

With the democratic government in power from 2008 onwards, the young but confident and increasingly powerful Bhutanese media plays an important role in informing the people, criticizing the government, and in forming policy. In Bhutan, given the stage of development, the main intelligentsia and movers and shakers still work in the government as a civil servant. The government continues to employ a large majority of people, around 25,000 out of a population of around 700,000.

Governments in the past had the power to fix the pay scale and revision of civil servants and then announce it. However, the media coverage of the pay hike proposals, giving higher raise for senior officials and politicians, in 2009, virtually replaced the pay commission as irate civil servants responded to the news. Based on the media's feedback, the government was forced to reject the report of the pay commission and come up with separate provision based on feedback from the media and public. Such events may seem normal for countries that have been a democracy for a long time, but in Bhutan's case, it was one of the first cases, generated by media and public opinion, that directly affected government policy.

The media in 2008 also highlighted an attempt by the then ruling party to get state funding for political parties. This agenda was hidden in the national budget being discussed in the Parliament at the time. The media exposé lead to a public debate and repeal of the proposal. In 2010, the government was on the verge of taxing junk food like soft drinks, chips, chocolate and other packaged snacks as a part of larger taxation measures. However, when the plan was exposed by the media, it became a major issue for small shops and price sensitive consumers, forcing policy makers to repel the tax.

The public opinion against other provisions of the taxes also led to the opposition party, the PDP, taking up Bhutan's first constitutional case on the issue that taxation measures had to be approved by the lower house as part of a Money Bill and not be imposed ad-hoc by the Executive arm. The Opposition won the case, which has become a landmark case in Bhutanese democracy of someone taking the government to court and eventually winning.

Subsequently, even after making record profits, Bhutan's monopoly and state-owned power utility companies proposed doubling of electricity charges. The media's leaking of the proposal prompted outrage, and the better sense prevailed as the government rejected the high raises, and instead levied more realistic power charges. The draconian Tobacco Act that criminalized a bad habit and saw scores of people going to prison was also amended after significant media pressure and activism on the issue.

The media was well used by tour operators in conveying their opposition over the consultancy company McKinsey's recommendation to lower tourism tariff leading to higher tariff rates. The government on June 5, 2012 introduced the Pedestrian Day on the World Environment Day, whereby every Tuesday, people were not allowed to use vehicles with only very limited vehicle movement allowed. This was seen as a draconian step, and the media, while conveying people's unhappiness, again managed to convince the then government to reduce it to one Sunday per month. The new PDP government has altogether done away with it.

A key role played by the media was in bringing about the Right to Information Bill, which is currently in the upper house of the Parliament after being passed by the lower house. The media raised awareness on RTI ever since 2008, just after a new democratic government came into place. The media pressure forced the previous government to promise an RTI Act. However, faced with bureaucratic resistance and scams, the former DPT government could not get through with it. The media then made it an election issue in 2013 and all parties promised to bring about the RTI. The new PDP government had lived up to that promise by introducing a not so perfect but still fairly liberal version of the bill in Parliament. Like in India and other parts of the world, the media hopes that RTI will be a positive game changer for transparency and good governance.

The media's increasingly critical tone has made the government more aware of deficiencies in government services and governance, and it has led to many more cases where rectification measures, big and small, have been undertaken. A strong example is what some rural folk say about the media. They say that earlier when they faced problems they only had His Majesty the King to go to, but now they first come to the media.

Media's Role in Fighting Corruption

Bhutan's ranking in the Transparency International Corruption Perception Index in 2008 was 45 out of 180 countries and number one in the SAARC region. Bhutan improved its ranking to 33 in 2012, and finally in 2013, it stood 31 out of 175 countries, and is still at number one in the SAARC region. There is corruption in Bhutan, but unlike other countries, it is not pervasive. For instance, traffic police or the other police in Bhutan will never ask for bribe to let somebody off. The credit for such a good ranking goes to a variety of factors—key among them is the role of the media.

One leading institution which has had great success in fighting corruption to the extent of even prosecuting and convicting ministers is the Anti-Corruption Commission. Its chairman in a 2013 interview on BBS stated that the media has played a significant role in fighting corruption in Bhutan and making even the most powerful people accountable.

This is also widely acknowledged by the intelligentsia and, public in general, in Bhutan. As explained above in detail, the media became bolder and stronger with the evolution of the democratic process and the introduction of the private media. After elections, a democratic environment and a constitution, that guaranteed freedom for media and freedom of expression as fundamental rights, further emboldened the media.

It also gave several people the privilege of coming back and practicing investigative journalism in Bhutan. Upon knowing that Bhutan's only international airport was running a grave risk due to the substandard work done by an unauthorized sub-contractor, the media took serious note of it. This early exposé in a young democracy caused a fair amount of controversy, especially, in a society that was not used to investigative journalism. The impact was that the whole airport was resurfaced with quality material, and therefore, minimizing the risk to the lives of the people.

The Bhutanese media has conducted several investigative and critical stories on illegal mining to unethical mining practices across the country. Such practices causing environmental violations led to ACC investigations and, later court prosecutions. It also resulted in better awareness, transparency and accountability in the allocation and running of mines and quarries by the government agencies.

The Ministry of Health is the fourth largest recipient of government budget as it provides free medical care to the citizens in hospitals and basic health units spread across the country. There are no private hospitals in Bhutan as the rules do not permit it. A huge chunk of the budget in the ministry goes into the procurement of drugs and medical equipment every year. A five-part investigative report series published in 2009 uncovered that over a period of many years, a system of institutional corruption had been forged between the international companies and their middlemen that supplied drugs and medical equipment, and corrupt senior bureaucrats in the ministry and even health professionals. It resulted in a public outcry, leading to detailed investigations by the Anti-Corruption Commission and Royal Audit Authority upon verifying the report. More damning findings followed that led to prosecution of the guilty and resignation of the then Health Secretary. An important outcome was the revamping and restricting of the entire Bhutan health procurement process, making it more transparent and healthy.

The media also exposed several irregularities in the procurement of goods or services by other ministries and agencies. This has contributed to Bhutan adopting a more stringent norm and international best practices in tendering norms. In many ways, the media has led to improved systems and procurement rules that reduce legal loopholes and discretionary powers of procurement committees and individuals.

Another major impact of the media was in exposing cross border corruption in Bhutan Lottery, mainly on the Indian side, at a scale running into hundreds of crores. Bhutan Lottery is a government of Bhutan lottery, which was one of the most popular lotteries sold in some states in India, like Kerala, West Bengal, etc. Based on more than 20 investigative articles, the government did a special audit on Bhutan Lottery and decided to shut it down.

In a third world country, land is the prime source of wealth and capital. At the same time, it also attracts a lot of corrupt activities, particularly by the powerful. The media exposed some major land scams revealing grave issues of accountability and transparency in the distribution of prime land in Bhutan. This has, more than any other corruption issue, struck a chord with the people. Some investigative stories on plot allotments in a commercial town lead to the conviction of two ministers and a legal ban on them from the political office. Around 60 plots were seized from high profile bureaucrats, judges, and three other ministers and handed back for re-allotment to the real beneficiaries—the common people.

After the land scam stories, it is not uncommon to find farmers and ordinary citizens regularly calling the media to cover land-related issues. The media has been active in exposing major and minor corruption cases and bringing the powerful to account. Overall, the relentless coverage of corruption by a few dedicated media houses and journalists have made people aware of corruption. As a result, people have become less tolerant on the issue. Corruption has become a part of the national dialogue as across the board, from newspapers to politicians, it is being widely debated.

The 2013 National elections saw the political parties raising concerns on several corruption scams reported by the media in their speeches to the voters. Many election observers felt that the corruption issues and critical stories brought out by the media played a major role in the election outcome, where the world's smallest opposition party of two members came to power with a landslide victory of 32 members in the lower house of Bhutanese Parliament.

Media and a Democratic Culture

Apart from the obvious influence and impact of media on policies and fighting corruption, it has also had a subtle but strong influence in strengthening the democratic culture of Bhutan. Today, Bhutan is a different place after democracy and a stronger media. In past, leaders and decision makers, at many levels, did not accept criticism. Even at the societal level, people refrained from saying anything critical to each other. The media has played a major role in changing this pattern, by not only publishing critical stories, but also giving more voice to the common people. People today, from farmers to civil servants, are not afraid to question and demand accountability from their leaders and also vis-a-vis each other. In the absence of a strong civil society in Bhutan, the media has also been the champion of various constitutional rights of the people.

Apart from dissent and criticism, the varieties of views, ideas and expressions in the media have made Bhutanese democracy richer and stronger. The media, as it keeps a check on the government, is also a source of intellectual content and dialogue on a host of issues. The media has been an active supporter and proponent of democratic rights and practices in Bhutan, like fundamental rights, human rights, and more. The media in Bhutan, therefore, has encouraged a vibrant national dialogue. Though electoral democracy came into being in 2008, a 'democratic culture' and 'democratic attitude' had yet to take strong roots. The free and vibrant press, in that sense, considerably strengthened the discourse and practice of democracy by asking tough questions to the powerful, going after the corrupt, encouraging people to speak up, and making powerful institutions accountable to ordinary citizens. In doing so, it strengthened the Bhutanese democracy and has also contributed to internal stability and well-being of the nation.

The Global Peace Index for 2014 has ranked Bhutan at 16 out of 162 countries. Bhutan's successful and peaceful transition to a democracy has made such a ranking possible. This would, by itself, highlight the positive role played by the media.

Challenges for the Bhutanese Media

While the Bhutanese media has achieved much, however, it has been suffering since the last three to four years, primarily due to financial reasons. Given the media's role in fighting corruption and exploring new boundaries, there has also been some backlash, especially from the previous government. The Bhutanese media, which consisted of three papers in 2006, mushroomed into 12 papers by 2012, allowing the much needed diversity of views. However, it also increased the competition for limited advertisement resources. The majority of the advertisement revenue comes from the government, given Bhutan's relatively undeveloped private sector.

Due to cost cutting and austerity measures, the government spending on advertisement started dipping from 2010 onwards. However, the big crunch came in 2012 with the onset of an economic crisis that forced the government to tighten its belt. As a result, the lack of advertisement, being the main source of revenue, forced papers and other media outlets to lay off staff and carry out other cost cutting measures. Given the tough times, Bhutan's second private paper, *Bhutan Observer*, had to fold up its newspaper in 2013. There are other newspapers on the brink of closure. There has been a general trend of senior journalists taking up other professions.

The former government responded to critical and investigative stories that exposed corruption by using the economic stick of withholding advertisements. At the same time, there were also cases of sycophantic media houses and journalists siding up with the former government for political reasons, going as far as requesting the former government to crack down on the media. During the 2013 general elections, one of the major election issues was freedom of press raised by the opposition and other parties in the fray.

A Journalists Association of Bhutan (JAB) study on the situational assessment of journalists in Bhutan showed that the media situation in the country was not very good. The survey covered 90 journalists working in 16 media organizations and 29 former journalists. The majority (71 per cent) of working journalists felt that journalism has lost its attraction. About 58 per cent of working journalists felt 'unsafe' to cover critical stories fearing reprisal. They felt uneasy practicing journalism in a small close-knit society due to lack of adequate skills and objections from their management. About 66 per cent of working journalists stated it is 'difficult' to access public information. In fact, 11 per cent of them mentioned it as being 'very difficult'. 58 per cent of working journalists mentioned the existing media legislations and policies failed to ensure media development.

Media's Role in Foreign Policy, Defence and Nationalism

Foreign policy and defence in any country is largely driven by the government. However, since the media impacts populist and flag waving nationalism in any country, it also has some indirect role, as populist nationalism plays a major role in foreign policy and defence. Though no self-respecting government in the world will admit to any influence from the media in its foreign policy and defence, there is no doubt that the media plays a role, indirect as it maybe. The government also finds it useful to use the media as a tool to justify its foreign policy and defence goals.

A good example is the invasion of Iraq by the United States of America, where some of the world's most credible journalists and news outlets were riding at the front of tanks and troop transport vehicles as part of an invading force. However, when no weapons of mass destruction were found, the same media houses and journalists changed sides. In the case of South Asia, the media traditionally functions as a flag waving citizen first and then as a journalist second syndrome. The South Asian media is also, too often, accused of nationalistic jingoism which gets good TRP ratings, and goes down well with the audience. However, of late, there are some positive changes—journalists and media houses are increasingly demonstrating maturity and understanding in covering foreign policy, defence and geo-strategic issues.

Journalists across borders have been trying to connect and understand each other better. The Indian media, which is in line with the political mood, is trying to understand its neighborhood better. The detailed coverage of Prime Minister Narendra Modi's first ever foreign visit to Bhutan is a good example. At the same time, people often make the mistake that the media coverage on foreign policy, national and defence issues is organized and planned. Like any other news coverage, the media has its own dynamics which cannot really be controlled or directed in a particular way. The media, in many ways, reflects the politics, national mood and popular perception. Generally, the media is driven by the nation's politics and popular mood in any country. We have only seen the differing coverage on the same issue by countries in South Asia.

In the case of Bhutan, like elsewhere, the media coverage on foreign policy, nationalism and defence is driven by the nation's own politics and popular perception. Bhutan, as a small country surrounded by giants, has always been conscious about sovereignty. The media coverage in Bhutan on issues of national interest, like foreign policy and defence, is very restrained and driven primarily by the practical foreign and security policies practiced in the country.

With the constitution and democracy established in 2008, the Bhutanese media has had more say and impact, in terms of the nation's politics, and coverage of other countries, and by that extension, on foreign policy and perception of countries. The Bhutanese politics and media have not yet followed its neighbours as elections and issues are primarily domestic in nature. The media, at the same time, has been highlighting issues of national interest in a rational manner.

Bhutan, especially after democracy, has been very active on the international stage establishing diplomatic ties with several countries and playing a more active role at multilateral institutions, like the UN. However, the Bhutanese media felt more was needed to be done at the home front. The media severely criticized the previous government for being far too interested in international events and tours when there were dire issues and problems at home yet to be resolved, like the rupee crisis. Such criticism put the government on the defensive, leading it towards a climb down in international events and focus more on domestic issues.

In an unprecedented trend, an increasingly mature and assertive media also started advising the government on foreign policy matters through editorials, articles and opinion pieces. The media is also no longer satisfied with press releases and has started asking probing questions to the government on sensitive matters like boundary negotiations with China. This trend has facilitated better flow of information and transparency on pertinent issues.

The Bhutanese media has started writing extensively on the various facets and implications of relations with our neighbours and the wider world. There is more discussion and awareness on geo-strategic issues. These are exciting times in the Bhutanese media, when it comes to our interaction with the world.

In comparison to our neighbours, the Bhutanese media is not jingoistic, but it is definitely sensitive and responsive to Bhutan's core national interests. The people of Bhutan, including the media, value our sovereignty. This sentiment is neither jingoism nor a siege mentality, but a very practical, determined and disciplined nationalism originally created by the Monarchy that has served Bhutan so well for decades.

Bhutanese Media and India

Bhutan may be the only South Asian country where there is no anti-India politics and anti-India media in the mainstream. As a small country, it is convenient and tempting for political players to blame a bigger neighbour for domestic woes, and also substitute populist nationalism for practical and matured politics. Bhutan's politics and media have not fallen into this trap due to the rational nature of its leadership, embodied in our Kings, and also the overall practical behaviour of Bhutanese people.

Bhutan, from a position of confidence, has been able to cultivate and benefit from its special relationship with India over the decades. The mutually beneficial ties have resulted in many partnerships, like harnessing clean energy through hydropower. Much before Bhutan was even in the picture, a combination of mistrust and misunderstanding fuelled by anti-India politics and anti-India media in Nepal closed the curtains on hydropower development. As a result, Nepal today barely has around 680 MW. Under the leadership of a wise and practical Monarchy, Bhutan took the opportunity to develop hydropower with India. Bhutan has around 1400 MW of power already. The goal is to achieve 10000 MW with around 3000 MW under active construction.

However, there have been some problems as far as media coverage of Bhutan in India is concerned. Bhutan successfully removed all NDFB (National Democratic Front of Bodoland), ULFA (United Liberation Front of Assam) and KLO (Kamtapur Liberation Organisation) militant camps from Bhutan during the 2003 'Operation All Clear' led by His Majesty the Fourth King Jigme Singye Wangchuck. Still, there are occasional reports in sections of the Indian media on the possible presence of camps. Such reports are far from the truth as evidenced by the testimony of local people and villagers travelling in those areas. Then there is problem of militants camped in India that have been occasionally kidnapping Bhutanese people along the Bhutan-India border and few living near the border being taken into Assam for ransom. Prior to 2003, Bhutan never denied that there were camps, and instead, informed India of the steps it was taking to deal with the militants.

Similarly, the local media in West Bengal has also been inaccurate and unfair in regularly blaming downstream floods on a small run of the river dam in Bhutan called Kurichu.

Media's Role in Promoting Regional Harmony and Cooperation

When it comes to the media's role in promoting regional harmony and cooperation, the onus lies mainly on the governments and people of the region. The media, while being a factor in regional harmony, primarily reflects and responds to what is already happening. However, the media does have an important role in ensuring better regional understanding by primarily practicing good and ethical journalism. The first step in this direction would be getting credible facts and information before media in a particular country reports on issues about another country. The story should be objective and balanced by bringing in both sides of the story. In Bhutan's case, coverage by the media in some neighbouring countries on Bhutan has been totally off the mark and, hence, promoted more confusion than clarity on issues. For instance, there is a feeling in Bhutan that the Kathmandu press has been less than fair to Bhutan in the past on various issues.

The media of all SAARC countries should do their research and follow basic ethical practices in reporting on cross border developments or broader issues that affect relations with other countries.

The respective government and agencies, on their own part, should ensure that they have set up mechanisms to provide accurate information to journalists from other countries. At the professional level, more interaction among journalists of the region would also be important in understanding each other. There are existing bodies, like SAFMA, but more such forums can be developed.

Media and journalists of different countries can work together to tackle and report common issues, like climate change, trade, poaching, corruption, transport, energy, etc. An example is the Bhutan lottery scam, where the Bhutanese media had an opportunity to work with Indian journalists and shared information.

The South Asian media, instead of settling for jingoism or fear mongering, should carry in-depth research on regional issues and report the facts. The media, at the end of the day, still has a major role in influencing public perceptions, and should encourage conflict resolution, peace and understanding over conflict and mass hysteria. The press can play an important role in promoting greater people-to-people understanding by knocking down the walls of prejudice and misunderstanding. Rather than flaming narrow prejudices, the media should play a calming and responsible role.

A huge problem in the South Asian media is the lack of good media models and professionalism which results in bad journalism. Countries with better experience and resources should help their counterparts develop a stronger professional media environment. The media in partnership with the respective governments could also have exchange programs and visits for journalists to promote greater understanding between various countries. With South Asia being a cauldron of religious, ethnic and regional strife, not only between the countries, but also within those countries, the media should be even more sensitive and responsible in reporting on issues as a whole. The media should downplay, or if possible avoid, content that is purposefully designed to create disharmony and instability between communities and countries.

REFERENCES

1. Various articles, opinions and editorials from the *The Bhutanese*, *Kuensel* and *Business Bhutan* newspapers.
2. "Situational Assessment of Journalism in Bhutan", Journalists Association of Bhutan, February 2015, at http://jabbhutan.com/wp-content/uploads/2015/02/Situation Assessment_final.pdf.
3. Annual Reports of The Anti-Corruption Commission of Bhutan (2011, 2012, 2013).
4. Media in Bhutan, Bhutan Media Foundation, at http://www.bmf.bt/media-in-bhutan/.
5. Bhutan Information, Communications and Media Act 2006, at http://www.asianlii.org/bt/legis/laws/bicama2006402/.
6. Media Development Assessment 2010, Department of Information and Media, Ministry of Information and Communications, Royal Government of Bhutan, at http://www.mediasupport.org/wp-content/uploads/2012/11/ims-bhutan-mdi-assessment-2010.pdf.
7. Information and Media Policy of the Royal Government of Bhutan, Ministry of Information and Communications, at http://www.moic.gov.bt/daden/uploads/2014/04/Information_and_media_policy.pdf.
8. Global Peace Index 2014: Measuring Peace and Assessing Country Risk, Institute for Economics and Peace, at http://economicsandpeace.org/wp-content/uploads/2015/06/2014-Global-Peace-Index-REPORT_0-1.pdf.

10

The Role of Media in Myanmar

Myo Lwin

Background: The State of Media in Myanmar

With 51.4 million population, Myanmar has about 400 periodicals—weeklies, monthlies and 12 dailies. It has about 10 private and government FM radio stations and also 4 TV channels. The ownership of the print media in Myanmar belongs to different interest groups. Some of them are ex-generals, some are ex-ministers from previous military government while some media houses have the backing of political parties. Media in Myanmar can be roughly divided into three categories—journalism that is pure, professional and unbiased, then there are those who treat journalism as a money minting business and, lastly, those who manipulate media merely for political gains. The publications that have a fair share of readership and are profitable are mostly weeklies. Interestingly, in Myanmar, about 12 dailies appeared around the year 2014.

Most of the private dailies have been making loss due to unavailability of commercials or advertisements and some of them are published only in local language. Popular dailies include: *The Eleven*, *The 7-Day*, *The Voice*, *The Mizzima*, *The Standard Time*, *Pyi-Htaung Su Daily*, and *The Pyi Myanmar*. There is no daily newspaper in English language that is run by the private sector. Myanmar has only one English daily and it is the government-owned

The New Light of Myanmar. Most of the newspapers in Myanmar have a daily print run ranging from 20,000 to 1,00,000 copies.

Most readers accept newspapers' editorial contents but show less interest for the advertisers who spend their money on weeklies. The media houses keep publishing weeklies, which have been their first publications prior to the issue of licenses. Normally, a 24-page private daily is sold at K200 and a 50-page weekly is K500 in retail market.

Government Media

The government in Myanmar has three dailies—two in Myanmar language and one in English language. The military has its own newspaper. All are selling well at K100 a copy in retail and K2500 for monthly subscribers. The two government dailies in Myanmar language have a print run of 3,00,000 (*The Myanma Ahlin*—1,30,000 and *The Kye Hmon*—1,70,000) while the English daily has a circulation of about 20,000 copies. Running an independent media organisation is not an easy thing in Myanmar, especially, when one has to compete not only with its private counterparts but also the much subsidised government media.

While most private dailies are losing and some have decided to stop entirely, the government has proudly announced that its dailies, which constitute 50 per cent of the nation's total print-run of 6,00,000, are making profits, as quoted by the Myanmar Marketing Research and Development in 2014 in the *The Myanmar Times*. There has been increased expenditure on media advertising, mostly from external sources. Those expenses have increased from US$ 11.7 million to $ 152 million between 2001 and 2013 and it is expected to reach $200 million in 2014, according to the research firm.

Constitutional Provisions

Safeguards on Freedom of Expression: In the Section 354 of the Myanmar Constitution (2008), it is mentioned—Every citizen shall be at liberty in the exercise of the following rights, if not contrary to the laws, enacted for Union security, prevalence of law and order, community peace and tranquillity or public order and morality: (a) to express and publish freely their convictions and opinions; (b) to assemble peacefully without arms and holding procession; (c) to form associations and organisations; (d) to develop their language, literature, culture they cherish, religion they profess, and customs without prejudice to the relations between one national race and another or among national races and to other faiths.

Restrictions on Media: However, there are certain restrictions under the Criminal Law relevant to media.

Under Section 500 of the Criminal Law, the sentence is up to two years if someone is convicted of defamation. Section 124 a notes: Whoever by words, either spoken or written, or by signs, or by visible representation, or otherwise, bring or attempts to bring into hatred or contempt, or excites or attempts to excite disaffection towards [the Government established by law for the Union or for the constituent units thereof,] shall be punished with transportation for life or a shorter term, to which fine may be added, or with imprisonment which may extend to three years, to which fine may be added, or with only fine.[1]

Section 505 states: Whoever makes, publishes or circulates any statement, rumour or report,—(a) with intent to—cause, or which is likely to cause, any officer, soldier, sailor or airman, in the Army, Navy or Air Force to mutiny or otherwise disregard or fail in his duty as such; or (b) with intent to cause, or which is likely to cause, fear or alarm to the public or to any section of the public whereby any person may be induced to commit an offence against the State or against the public tranquillity; or (c) with intent to incite, or which is likely to incite, any class or community of persons to commit any offence against any other class or community, shall be punished with imprisonment which may extend to two years, or with fine, or with both.[2]

Myanmar Printing and Publishing Enterprise Law 2014: Enacted in March 2014, those who wish to publish are expected to abide by this particular law. They need to register with the Ministry of Information and the license has a five year validity. The law repealed 'The Press (Emergency Powers) Act' and 'The Printers and Publishers Registration Law' of 1962.

Media in Myanmar: Limitations

When *The Myanmar Times* English was launched 15 years ago, there were only few weeklies in Myanmar language. There were as few as 10 reporters in the newsroom and they used to try hard to find out and learn about developments in their own area so as to cover and file the news on time. Under professional expatriate journalists, the local journalists who were very few, used to be serious and responsible. As the media expanded over a period of 2-3 years, other weeklies emerged and media owners appointed young reporters without much experience and training. The number of weeklies increased over the following years and so did the number of journalists. The current number of active journalists in Myanmar stands at almost 4,400 according to a joint survey conducted by the Myanmar Press Council and the Ministry of Information. A member of Myanmar Press Council Interim noted that less than 10 per cent of the journalists are aware of relevant laws and ethics concerning media. This implies that the majority of journalists work without being well informed on the do's and don'ts in journalism. This has complicated the situation and created problems for both the sources and the government officials. There has been growing distrust between the concerned sources and the media, especially in the domain of print media.

While sources realise the significance of engaging with the media, they become reluctant due to errors committed and partially due to misquotations. There have been several cases of arrests, demotions and dismissals of sources who spoke to the media due to misquotation and wrong attributions. For instance, at a media development conference in Yangon in September 2014, there was a case where the media noted "Mr. so and so said off the record". This elicited laughter from the audience but, ironically, reflected the reality of print media.

Another issue regarding most journalists in Myanmar is that they are underpaid or get low salaries. Despite the fact that certain journalists represent media houses, some of them can be easily approached for commercial, political or personal interests. With the rampant increase in the number of media houses, there are people who manipulate media to fulfil desired objectives. There have been instances where young reporters were enticed, bribed in some way or the other, knowingly or unknowingly.

Conference on Media Development

Core issues such as election reporting, media ethics and public service broadcasting were on the agenda at the third conference on media development held at Yangon on September 18-19, 2014. The theme was 'Moving Towards a Sustainable Media Environment'. In the concluding remarks, Myanmar Minister of Information, U Ye Htut, endorsed greater access to information for journalists and noted that there was need to professionalise the media as the way out.[3] In this conference, a cross section of media editors, media workers from private and state media, civil society, the Ministry of Information and international media experts deliberated in some of the most constructive and dynamic discussions. They debated the current state of the media environment in Myanmar three years after the first media reforms were set in motion in 2011.

Media reform in Myanmar has come a long way in three years with a Media Law adopted earlier in 2014 and a Code of Conduct for journalists recently published by the Myanmar Press Council Interim. However, speakers during the conference noted that that there are laws that still infringe on the freedom of expression and that these must be repealed. Also, lack of professionalism amongst journalists' community is one of the major challenges, participants emphasised. Lack of professionalism must be addressed, it was noted, particularly at a time when media is playing an important role by covering developments in a conflict situation and also in view of upcoming elections in 2015.

As a matter of fact, there have been numerous mistakes committed by the local media. Due to this problem, the government or external sources have become reluctant to interact with the media and provide key information. As a result, the communication gap between the two sides has widened even as the number of media organisations has been growing recklessly.

The overall capacity and calibre of journalists and the efficiency in the business management of media organisation owners are other important factors. As a result of stiff competition in print media, some are relying on over sensationalising their stories. There is no clear line/differentiation between advertising and editorial contents policy. There have been instances in which publishers or the media owners pass orders to the editors to compromise their editorial policies. The media becomes totally oriented towards the advertisers forgetting the interest of masses or the large sections of readers. After more than two years of press relaxation, the number of media related disputes have actually increased. That situation has been acknowledged by the government, judiciary, legislature and the media and they are making efforts to change it. In this regard, the role of Myanmar Press Council Interim has become pivotal.

Press Council Interim

The formation of the Press Council Interim was enacted on March 14, 2014 by Pyidaungsu Hluttaw (Parliament). The News Media Law has three important functions: pursue freedom of press, mediation for media related disputes and capacity building of the media persons at the media houses. President U Thein Sein, Speakers of both Houses and the Commander-in-Chief of Defence Services met with Myanmar Press Council Interim. The meeting underscored the significance of media's role. There is growing realisation that there is need to engage with the media unlike in past during the previous military government. The News Media Law drawn by the Press Council and amended and approved by Parliament has some salient points.

Formation of Council: Function and Duties (as stated in the News Media Law)

The council shall be a single organisation for freely operating under the provision of this law as regard news media men. The State President shall form Myanmar News Media Council under the notification comprising the person of the following organisation to carry out the objective, function and duties of this law. The term of the council member is three years as on the date of being elected. Amongst the key functions and duties of the council, some are as follows:

(a) Enhancement of the quality and observation to news media;
(b) Coordination with the relevant government departments for the minimisation of taxes in exporting paper, stationary and machines in relation with the news media enterprise;
(c) Organisation of holding workshop and talks in relation to news media;
(d) Coordination with periodical organisation for awarding outstanding people of the news;
(e) Setting up projects for the progress of the news media enterprise;
(f) Issuance of news as and when necessary;
(g) Coordination with the council for acquiring true news to the public and stipulation of the accountable person for the release of the press in the government department, organisation and civil societies;
(h) Reporting on the state of the performances of work and process of roadmap to the State President without delay once per year.

Media in Myanmar: An Assessment

In Myanmar, presently, only the print media appears liberal and more neutral. The broadcast and electronic media concentrate more on the entertainment than on information. Media landscape in Myanmar has been changing quite dramatically in the past few years. That happened along with the democratic transition the country has been going through. The print media, which had been under constricted centralised control for nearly 50 years, became more open after the newly elected government lifted the pre-publication censorship in August 2012. The licenses to print and publish still need to be approved by the Ministry of Information but as stated above, there seems to be more publications coming up than ever.

The government still has three dailies and several other publications but the role of the private sector in the print media is growing exponentially in the last couple of years. Most of the publications are still based in Yangon, the commercial capital, and a few in Mandalay, the second biggest city and the seat of the last Myanmar King. Recent years have seen a few publications appearing in the ethnic areas. Shan, Kachin, Mon and Chin states now have a few weekly publications in their provinces in both Myanmar and their own ethnic languages.

Due to greater freedom, media is running stories many of which are sensational and emotive. This trend could be interpreted as good but in some cases, it also has negative impacts. One major hurdle has been the lack of skill and capacity amongst journalists. Then, there are numerous disputes between the concerned sources and media. While there have been dramatic shift and more freedom in the print media, it is still more about entertainment in the broadcast and electronic media. Nonetheless, people in Myanmar can access international TV channels like CNN, BBC, VOA, Al Jazeera, etc.

Despite the thwarting on part of the government, it is now trying to compromise by allowing greater flexibility especially with regard to the print media. Many say the government has been trying to appear indulgent while dealing with the private media. The meeting of President U Thein Sein with Myanmar Press Council Interim on August 1, 2014 followed by the meetings with Hluttaw Speaker and the Commander-in-Chief of Defence Services, Senior General Min Aung Hlaing in mid-October 2014 are significant developments in this direction.

Media persons have often expressed concerns that actions could be taken against them while they continue their pursuits for freedom of press. There are some laws which are obsolete and need to be cancelled, amended or redrawn by the legislature. The actions that have continued to be taken against the media by the administration is not in sync with the spirit of democratisation process. It is rather reminiscent of the practices during the dictatorship era in Myanmar. Even if the media people are required to be closely watched and monitored, some of the procedures and practices adopted by the administration while taking actions are not suitable during this phase of democratisation process.

The media council made another important observation on cases filed by the administration against the media. Such cases have been handled by the judiciary but under the influence of the administration which does not abide much to the rights of freedom of expression as mentioned in the Constitution. The fact that these arguments are broadcast further underscores the need for professionalism to be exercised by all the stakeholders in Myanmar's politics. As noted earlier, in an unprecedented move, the Commander-in-Chief of Defence services, Senior General Min Aung Hlaing and a few generals met with the Press Council on October14, 2014. Several critiques attempted to downplay the meeting thinking it would be just a casual meeting which the military commander would conduct following the meeting between the Press Council and the President and also with the Amyothar Hluttaw (Lower House) Speaker.

According to U Thiha Saw, a Press Council Member, the Press Council members were surprised to see the level of interest shown by the military chief and how the military was seeking to engage with media. The meeting took place for much longer than many had expected, he noted. In order to be transparent about the activities of the military, the Commander-in-Chief assigned a Major General from Psychological Warfare Bureau and two Brigadier Generals as spokespersons of the military, according to the State newspaper, the *Myanma Ahlin.*

Vice chairman of the Press Council Interim, U Khin Maung Lay, noted that the appointment of the military spokespersons is in response to a request from the Press Council. It is required for the media people to be ethical while writing stories, the paper quoted U Khin Maung Lay, as saying. He cautioned that it is necessary for the media to be impartial and not to become a public relation tool of the military. Overall, the Press Council members were positive after meeting those in power, according to U Thiha Saw. About a month later, the Commander-in-Chief of Defence Services, Senior General Min Aung Hlaing met with the Press Council Interim yet again and discussed media's access to information from the military. A workshop between the media organisations and military representatives was proposed to be held in Yangon in early December 2014 to deal with the issue of access to information.

Though the access to information will still remain limited, several sources in media industry saw the developments as a positive step ahead. Myanmar's standing on the freedom of press has improved from the 170th country out of 172 countries two years ago to 145 in 2014, according to a freedom of press index study conducted by the Reporters Without Borders (RWB) or *Reporters Sans Frontières (RSF).*[4] In short, one can say, generally the role of media in Myanmar has become stronger than before especially in the domain of print media. However, we still need to wait and watch the evolving role of broadcast and electronic media in Myanmar.

The other three main pillars-judiciary, legislature and executive—are realising that the four pillars of state need to be acting appropriately and with checks and balances. With this trend continuing for some time, the political scene is likely to follow suit. The process and timing should neither be too swift nor slow. In the meantime, media owners are expected to consider enhancing the capacity of their journalists as an essential prerequisite to improve the state of media in Myanmar. While much blame has been laid on three pillars-legislature, executive and judiciary, it is the media that needs to continue striving towards quality and excellence.

Conclusion

It is hoped there will be comprehensive improvement in all four pillars in Myanmar state and society. Change is required not only in the media organisations but also at the level of media ownership. They should try and improve their standards of management and business operations in order to ensure that their target audience becomes the masses and not the market. It is believed that the print media landscape in Myanmar will improve in times to come and the democratisation process will be speedier. As the state of media in Myanmar is still evolving at the moment, it cannot be expected to play an effective role in promoting regional understanding in South Asia. However, considerable section of senior media personnel in Myanmar is aware of such responsibilities and could be more than willing to participate in any initiative towards better regional integration.

NOTES

1. Briefing Paper on the Situation of Human Rights in Burma/Myanmar, *Forum Asia*, March 12, 2015, at https://www.forum-asia.org/?p=18520.
2. Burma/Myanmar: New Forms of Control and Threats to Freedoms of Expression, Assembly and Association amidst Reforms Fanfare, International Fact-Finding Mission, *Forum Asia*, October 24-30, 2012, at http://www.forum-asia.org/uploads/books/2013/March/FA-FFM-Burma-2013March.pdf, p.2.
3. 3rd Conference on Media Development in Myanmar, September 2014, at http://www.myanmarmediadevelopment.org/.
4. 2015 World Press Freedom Index, *Reporters Without Borders*, at https://index.rsf.org/#!/.

11

Evolution of Afghan Media: Role in Promoting Regional Understanding

Danish Karokhel

After decades of violence, Afghanistan is reaping the fruits of development and the nation-building process. The rebuilding of government institutions has begun, the foundations of economic progress have been laid and a vibrant civil society is emerging. Despite continued violence we have seen an upward trend towards modernisation and democratisation. Afghan people are eschewing violence and want stability and order. The ballot culture is steadily replacing the bullet culture. Still, a lot needs to be done.

Media Development in Afghanistan

Before discussing the main issue, it is useful to provide a brief overview on the development of media in Afghanistan. Civil society, in general and the media in particular, has experienced unprecedented growth; the importance and role of the media is acknowledged by all quarters. If on the one hand, the phenomenal growth of the media is creating opportunities, on the other hand it is posing some challenges, as a vibrant media and its activism is inviting the displeasure of various governmental and non-governmental actors.

For discussing the media's role in Afghanistan, we must understand the phenomenon of its recent growth and its characteristics. Being the Centre-stage of the so-called war on terror and given its strategic importance, the region has attracted the attention of internal as well as external actors in the media.

Apart from an increase in duration of programmes and the start of new radio and TV channels in main Afghan languages abroad, there was keen interest in developing local media in Afghanistan. Not only was the state-run media rebuilt but there was also a mushrooming growth of outlets and media-related organisations in the private sector. Today, there are 170 TV channels, 174 Radio stations, and more than 300 registered newspapers and periodicals in Afghanistan. The Afghan media can be categorised in four parts—state-run media, private media, foreign media and Jihadi media.

The Afghan media has three characteristics which distinguish it from the media in other countries of the region. Firstly, its growth is not due to its natural socio-economic development and is not market-driven; rather it is facilitated and supported by external agencies.

Secondly, since this growth is mainly facilitated and supported by external actors, it is heavily dependent on foreign funds. Day-by-day, it is getting strengthened and starting to generate its own resources from the corporate sector and other sources, but at the same time, it is still financially dependent largely on external sources.

Thirdly, its dependence on external resources makes it vulnerable to external pressures for pursuing the donors' agenda; particularly those outlets established and run by politicians or political parties which are highly politicised and further their agendas.

Role in Promoting Regional Understanding

Having discussed its growth and characteristics, the role of Afghan media in promoting regional understanding needs to be highlighted. Due to its geographic location, Afghanistan is a member of various regional forums/ blocks such as the Economic Cooperation Organisation (ECO), South Asian Association for Regional Cooperation (SAARC), the Shanghai Cooperation Organisation (SCO), etc.

Since the focus is the South Asian region, the paper is limited to Afghanistan's role in South Asia only. Though Afghanistan joined SAARC quite late, still Afghanistan gives due importance to the organisation. There is great potential for cooperation and joint work in areas such as terrorism, drug smuggling, proliferation of small arms, human trafficking, regional trade, environment, etc. Mutual respect, trust and confidence are important pre-requisites for promoting regional understanding. The regional rivalries, conflicts, disrespect for each other's sovereignty and diversity, lingering disputes and competition for influence by some regional powers, besides the presence of jingoistic and extremist tendencies and groups, cause mistrust and tension in South Asia.

It is unfortunate to see that most of the media space is devoted to material promoting hatred, tension and violence among communities rather than mutual respect and trust. This trend ought to be reversed and changed and more space given to matter and material promoting regional understanding.

Being a powerful tool of change, media can play an important role in not only countering such tendencies but also promoting mutual understanding, respect, confidence and cooperation. The Afghan media's role as watchdog-generating debates on public and private accountability and transparency by exposing corruption and raising and highlighting issues of good governance, is laudable.

The media has so far failed to explore the commonalities and bring the communities closer for fostering historical and cultural bonds and ties among people of the region. At times, it became a tool for spreading mistrust, hatred and violence. There is a need for a serious audit or self-criticism of media's role in the region.

As far as the Afghan media's role in promoting regional understanding is concerned, unfortunately, due to certain reasons, its role has not been up to expectations. Due to its internal political and security problems, Afghan media in general, did not take much interest in other countries' issues; the Afghan media was mainly pre-occupied with domestic issues. Also, due to lack of resources and capacities, it cannot play its rightful role. Due to India-Pakistan and Iran-Saudi Arabia proxy wars in Afghanistan, sometimes the Afghan media, particularly media supported by regional powers, is taking sides and is relentlessly spreading the propaganda of hatred.

There is a need for close cooperation, collaboration and networking among media outlets and journalists from different countries of the region. The following recommendations can be considered:

- Regional initiatives for bringing regional media together (the on-going initiatives are project-based, limited).
  - Governmental-level (SAARC) initiatives: SAARC Information Centre (SIC)—SIC focused on popularising the activities and achievements of SAARC among the wider audience within and outside the region. The SIC works towards creating a strong network of communications, both within the SAARC region and beyond.
  - Non-Governmental—SAARC level (SAFMA) and two-country level initiatives—IMS (International Media Support), FES (Freidrich Ebert Stiftung), Mediotek, etc.—Pakistan and India, Pakistan and Afghanistan.
- Networking/cooperation among leading media houses/news agencies: offices in each other's countries, regular meeting of the heads of leading media houses/news agencies of member countries for closer cooperation; professional training.
- Collaborative projects among regional media groups (*Aman ki Asha* by Jang Group of Pakistan and Times Group of India, Jang Group and Tolo TV) for highlighting common issues and taking common positions for promoting understanding and bringing the people in South Asia closer. This would also discourage negative trends fanning/causing hatred and enmity among people in the region and endangering regional peace. If allowed to operate independently, the media can also play an effective role in unearthing South Asia's huge trade potential. Regional trade, in turn, can go a long way in addressing longstanding issues between different countries. With the growth of regional trade links, peoples' living standards will improve a great deal. If alleviated out of poverty, the teeming masses can contribute a great deal to efforts towards economic stability and prosperity in their respective countries.

People-to-people ties, which could be immensely strengthened by the media, could lead to regional proximity and collaboration in different areas, including the social sector. However, this depends to a large extent on constant support and encouragement from the government. Besides espousing social causes, a vibrant media can ensure continued dialogue on issues of peace and security in the region—home to one-fifth of humanity. Regrettably, an overwhelming majority of our people are living in poverty. If its problems are enormous, South Asia's resources are also immense.

A change of mind-set on the part of stakeholders is urgently needed. The media can play a proactive role in this regard and in bringing down the huge spending on armaments, rationalising defence budgets and diverting more funds to education, health, etc.

Raising awareness about the benefits of durable peace and eradication of extremism through enhanced trade and ending hate propaganda is a job that can be best done by the media. The media, through its support to high-quality, thoughtful comments and debates on public issues, has a key role to play in supporting good policies and building decent societies.

Update on Afghan Media's Role

The complex election process, the new political scenario and the uncertain future led some main players within the independent media to reflect on its responsibility and role. Its managers have deliberated that while the current situation reflects Afghanistan's political reality in a way that cannot but be acknowledged, they are also witnessing among people a growing confusion and loss of hope regarding the democratic exercise in which they have been encouraged to participate. This affects, notably, the majority of the youth within the population.

While the media has not contributed to reactivate ethnic rivalries, neither could it "condemn" a process that has harmed democracy. The risk is, going backwards 20 years and to be within 20 years, at the same point as today. Instead, and unlike earlier, the country now counts on legal tools and a media sector that can actively contribute to develop democratic practices and restore public confidence, working together with civil society in fostering accountability and transparency. The independent media also believes that the new institutional and political context would not trust an independently structured opposition that could contribute to good governance.

There is the need for sharing these concerns and considering potential developmental collaboration with the European Union, the UN as the inter-governmental body, with the highest understanding of the role media can play, and with policy frameworks that could enhance its fulfilment. These concerns were experienced throughout the electoral process, notably during the run-off crisis (in 2014 Afghan Presidential elections) when some media groups were biased in a way that contributed to the uncertain situation being created, showing lack of responsibility or sensitivity about the probable impact on the Afghan population. This practice should be addressed or at least counter-balanced, through the implementation of well-measured editorial policies.

A meeting between European Union's highest level functionaries and those of main independent media organisations, can be suggested, in which the latter could explain their vision and analysis of the current national situation, and editorial policies and aims.

The organisations that would participate in such a meeting have created the Independent Media Consortium (IMC), integrated with the main national news agency (*Pajhwok Afghan News*, which serves all domestic media), the main print media with national outreach (daily *Hasht-e-Subh*, weeklies *Killid* and *Morsal*), a network of over 60 radio stations covering the entire country (*Killid*, *Nawa* and Community Radios), a TV channel reaching 14 provinces, two printing houses, websites and social media, and 400 professional staff. Altogether, these represent unprecedented outreach, hitherto under-utilised.

Vehicle of Change

All too often, the role that journalists play in the region in challenging existing policies and promoting reforms, is risky. There are many instances of journalists taking huge personal risks, and sometimes paying a heavy price for conveying the news as it is.

Governments could use the media to help defuse crises, as the Kennedy administration did during the Cuban missile crisis. If there is any chance to make the world a more peaceful place, then the most important human value that one should promote is tolerance.

Afghanistan's fledgling media, that has a wide reach, especially radio and TV, could be an engine of change. They are following the footsteps of their global counterparts in weakening the control of authoritarian regimes over dissemination of information and its content. Afghan social media has also encouraged universal values such as security of the people, political participation, human rights, including women's rights, and free trade economies.

During the presidential election, budding journalists in Afghanistan made their presence felt, but mainstream media tended to ignore their commendable work. The election was seen as a revolutionary development being underplayed in the press. In particular, radio has played a vital role in political and social awakening in remote areas of the country. Afghan media professionals, including women, contributed as efficient watchdogs and educated the people about elections and democratic norms. They stressed that the credibility, inclusivity and transparency of the presidential elections was critical to the future stability of Afghanistan.

Journalists and media leaders developed a series of recommendations and presented them to the Independent Election Commission (IEC) looking into regulations governing reporting, as well as standards for self-regulation, or codes of practice. Media networks deserve credit for their work in monitoring the elections.

Social Media's Influence

After years of controlling internet access in the country, the Taliban themselves are now turning to Twitter and Facebook to promote their agenda, including recruitment of new members. On the other hand, Afghani web denizens are also leveraging social media as a tool for progress in the war-torn country.

We can safely assume that the media is connecting Afghanistan to the rest of the world. A big social media get-together called Paiwand began a day after the International Peace Day, to help improve the country's global image and show Afghanistan in a positive light. Increasingly, artists and activists are switching to Facebook to gain an online presence, and promote their work through social networking channels. The Paiwand summit featured panels from creative entrepreneurs and leaders. One panel, "Skype diplomacy" promoted a start-up that connects Afghans and people from other countries with similar background for a discussion on global issues.

One renowned artist spoke about how to use Afghan street art to connect the country with the wider world. "Kabul Street" is an Art for Peace initiative that hopes to spread tolerance and compassion throughout Afghanistan, and also raise awareness beyond the country's borders that there is a movement for peace. A founder of the initiative notes: "Kabul is dark, so no matter how small the light, it will shine". The government also had a strong presence at the summit, anticipating the role that Twitter and Facebook play. Officials welcomed start-ups like Baztab, a new social network for reporting on elections.

Organisers of the social enterprise start-up—Impassion Afghanistan—seek to recruit young people to join the movement and make a civic contribution. There have been discussions on how the web can be used to keep government officials and criminals in check and boost transparency, the challenges for women in technology, how to use social media for disaster relief, how it can enable citizen journalism, and a workshop on how to make Google Maps.

Mushrooming Growth

All this is happening in a country, where the fundamentalist Taliban regime allowed only a single state-run outlet—Radio Sharia—on air. With music banned and an independent press non-existent until 2002, the broadcasts were essentially propaganda. After the Taliban's ouster, American government agencies and international aid organisations have poured hundreds of millions of dollars into building the media industry– a sector that now boasts over 75 television channels, 175 FM radio stations, hundreds of print publications, including more than a dozen dailies, and several news agencies. Around 10,000 journalists are working for the media outlets.

There is a clear reason for governments and aid organisations to support Afghan media: a burgeoning democratic country not only deserves, but needs a functioning and free press. Given that the US officials have long spoken of the need to win "hearts and minds" amid warfare, funding for media outlets—offering not just news, but entertainment and music options—is one way to try doing so.

By supporting Afghan media, the US also helped ensure that its policy positions were not missing from the coverage of and debate over, the war and continued presence of troops in the country. The US has funded foreign media before, most notably in broadcasting Radio Free Europe and Radio Liberty into the former Soviet Union-occupied states during the Cold War.

Since 2002, USAID and the State Department have supported numerous media projects in Afghanistan, such as the Salam Watandar radio network, which includes 53 independent FM radio stations, and Tolo TV and Arman FM, the most popular TV and radio stations. They have supported initiatives to expand cellular, TV and radio accessibility. International aid organisations and NGOs from other countries have also supported news outlets, radio and TV stations in Afghanistan. A 2012 BBC Media Action report described the role of donors in supporting media in Afghanistan as "probably greater than in any other country at any time".

Struggle for Survival

Due to the Afghan government's reputation for corruption, there are understandable fears that international aid would not reach the intended recipients. Yet, in *Pajhwok's* case, donations have not gone missing. The news agency is widely regarded as a journalistic success. But the situation for many news outlets looks bleak. It is not only warlords who fund publications to promote their viewpoints. Iran and Pakistan are looking for opportunities to fund news outlets in Afghanistan, presumably to give their own spin to the news, which some argue the US is doing through its funding. Some have turned down Iranian offers to provide financial support, but others may accept that kind of offering.

While print outlets struggle to find a workable business model post-2014, television channels and radio stations may have a better chance of survival. There is more advertising money in TV and radio and those mediums are not negatively affected by high levels of illiteracy and lack of widespread internet access.

One of Afghan media's biggest success stories in recent years has been on the broadcast side. In 2010, *The New Yorker* described Saad Mohseni, chairman of The Moby Group, as "Afghanistan's first media mogul". In addition to Afghan TV and radio holdings, Moby owns a record company, an ad agency and production company, and it partnered with News Corp. on the Farsi 1 satellite network beamed into Iran.

Post-2014 Situation

After an end to NATO's combat mission in Afghanistan in 2014, local media is bound to face significant cash constraints, which would undermine their ability to contribute to efforts at stabilising the country. Vibrant news organisations are central to a stable Afghanistan. With the support of the Afghan media, Afghanistan, China, Pakistan and India could fast-track the implementation of the TAPI (Turkmenistan-Afghanistan-Pakistan-India) gas pipeline as well as the CASA 1000 (Central Asia South Asia Electricity and Trade projects).

With local media support, China, Pakistan and India have several incentives to develop Afghanistan as a regional trade and energy hub. The country is a gateway that connects Central Asia to South Asia and Southeast Asia and occupies a location of great strategic significance. The neighbours must back a stable Afghanistan for sustaining their long-term economic/ security interests for both the countries and the Central Asian region as a whole.

Media Collaboration

Some years back, a quiet but significantly important step was taken to promote better engagement, understanding and collaboration between the media in Afghanistan and Pakistan as a means to improving perceptions, approaches and engagement between the people and governments of both countries.

The Pakistan Institute for Peace Studies (PIPS) launched an initiative aimed at enhancing bilateral media contacts and cooperation between Afghan and Pakistani journalists and media organisations by holding an Afghanistan-Pakistan Media Dialogue in Kabul. PIPS partnered with The Killid Group (TKG) to improve cooperation between the electronic and print media of Pakistan and Afghanistan and arrange training for journalists to improve the media's capacity to cover complex issues with a view to enhance qualitative/ quantitative reporting on regional problems. The initiative was aimed at using influence of the print and the electronic media in the region to shape narratives of peace and develop discourses. It was also aimed at improving coverage and understanding of Afghanistan and issues of common interest in Pakistan by bringing on board the mainstream media.

Multi-year Funding

To be able to foster regional understanding and help transform nation-building from a zero-sum conflict to a positive-sum process, in which disagreements are resolved peacefully, the Afghan media direly needs long-term international support. International donor support has two primary goals: the short-term objective has been to counter the effects of communication fuelled by insurgency in order to win the hearts and minds of the Afghan people. The long-term goal has been to create a free and independent media that will continue to function after donor support has ended. Although millions of dollars have been invested in the development of the Afghan media since 2001, neither of these goals has been met conclusively. Donor support has led to the growth of radio and television channels that are almost entirely dependent on foreign funding—direct and indirect.

Donors should invest primarily in the Afghan media's production and dissemination of socially constructive content rather than in building media institutions or infrastructure that the Afghan economy cannot support. For such content to be received as authentic and credible, they must reflect the vulnerabilities and priorities that Afghans themselves have identified as vital.

Donors should make a multi-year funding commitment to the media in Afghanistan. Support should be allocated to both terrestrial and wireless media through a transparent and competitive process developed jointly by donors and Afghan media experts. Aggressively supporting the dissemination of socially constructive contents through new outlets will permit access to both geographic and demographic segments of the population which is not adequately served by current media outlets.

Donors should support media institutions and infrastructure provided that support facilitates the production and dissemination of socially constructive content, and without the expectation that these institutions or structures will become self-sustaining.

As often and as intensively as possible, media interventions should be accompanied by face-to-face community outreach activities that provide Afghans an opportunity to put into practice ideas and options that the media have brought to their attention.

Commitment to Press Freedom

On the campaign trail, both President Ashraf Ghani Ahmadzai and Chief Executive Officer Dr. Abdullah Abdullah endorsed a statement supporting freedom of press for the beleaguered Afghan journalists. The endorsement of the 12-Article statement came as the media experienced one of the most violent periods in recent years. Both vowed respect for the freedom of speech and that of the press. They pledged to spare no legal measures to promote and protect the ideal endorsed by the statement. The said statement was drafted by a broad coalition of journalist groups: Afghanistan's National Journalists' Union, Nai, the Afghan Independent Journalists' Association as well as the Afghan Journalists' Safety Committee (AJSC).

Although the commitment to support press freedom is significant, the situation for local media remains fundamentally insecure. Violence against Afghan journalists increased by 40 per cent in the first six months of 2014 compared to the same in 2013. Nearly two-thirds of incidents of violence were perpetrated by the government and security forces.

Oath of Responsibility

A resolution setting guidelines for how media should cover post-election events was thus drafted and intensely debated by media managers and experts for two days. All stakeholders acknowledged that Afghanistan is at a vulnerable juncture of history and there is a need for media and media stakeholders to act responsibly. The Afghan Election Commission and representatives of both presidential candidates unanimously approved the resolution that was drafted by the media support organisations and media managers.

Credibility

Many Afghans praise the state-run network, Radio Television Authority, despite its pro-government bias, partly because the privately-run stations are considered too uncontrollable. This is largely due to the importance people accord to respect for local culture, as well as their distaste for divisive politics. Ultimately, though, the roles many Afghans want their media to play—that of a watchdog, agenda-setter, and provider of relevant information—coincides with the ideal role of the media.

Self-restraint

Since 2001, extremely lax licensing laws have meant that almost anyone with the means has been able to start a media outlet. The state RTA (Radio Television Afghanistan), today, competes with hundreds of radio and TV stations, print publications and online outlets. Regrettably, the authorities have also used official channels to silence the media whose views they do not agree with. The attorney general's office has often been called on to harass or even arrest reporters behind unfavourable coverage.

In 2012, the Karzai administration attempted to push through a widely criticised Mass Media Law. The law would have granted the Ministry of Information and Culture comprehensive powers to set laws governing the media, as well as criminalise a long list of vaguely defined "media violations". Tabled after almost no consultation with media professionals or civil society, the law caused an outcry and has yet to be enacted. Repeated calls from media rights groups for a freedom of information bill have also fallen on deaf ears.

The less tangible threat to media freedom is the self-censorship that many reporters feel is necessary to protect themselves. The risks of publishing a critical story often outweigh the rewards, in particular on issues around corruption or human rights abuses. An example from this year's election campaign is the lack of discussion about transitional justice. Addressing war crimes is still taboo in Afghanistan, not least because so many individuals who face serious accusations of human rights violations still occupy influential government positions.

Media Programming

The country's 174 radio stations are prime vehicles for conveying messages, information, and entertainment, particularly across rural Afghanistan. An estimated 27 million Afghans say that radio is their primary source for obtaining news and information. Television outdoes radio in urban areas, but radio remains the primary source of information and entertainment. The Afghan media airs programmes that models, messages, and mimics. Radio Azadi's "One Village, A Thousand Voices" models a culture in which Afghan youth can claim a stronger voice in family and community affairs. LEMAR TV's "Innocent Hearts"—called the "soap of hope",—follows the story of a 12-year old boy who returns home to Afghanistan following the death of his father and falls in with the Taliban, telegraphing poignant messages about the harms of choosing the wrong path. Tolo TV's "Afghan Star", now in its 10th season and "The Voice of Afghanistan", mimic their successful musical talent show forebears in America.

BBC's "New Home, New Life" celebrated its 20th year on air in 2014, first broadcast from Peshawar to Afghans in Pakistan refugee camps in 1994. The Afghan soap is set in two fictitious hamlets where villagers grapple with real-life situations through entertaining radio programming. "One Village, A Thousand Voices", airs on Voice of America's Radio Azadi twice weekly in both Dari and Pashto languages, followed by a live call-in show following Friday's broadcast. The rule-of-law themed drama features fictionalised stories of young Afghans and their elders, as they deal with family and community conflicts. The show has 7 million listeners.

The Moby Group whose media stable includes TOLO TV, TOLO NEWS (Afghanistan's first 24-hour news station), LEMAR TV, FARSI1, ARMAN FM, and ARAKOZIA FM started in 2003 with the country's first private radio station and has, in one decade, grown into "a diversified portfolio of 16 businesses and six markets… serving over 300 million people from Central Asia to North Africa". TOLO TV claims 59 per cent market share in Afghanistan's media market. The Killid Group, led by award-winning journalist

Najiba Ayubi, opened its first radio station in Herat in 2005. Today, the Radio Killid Network manages 11 radio stations in 17 provinces with a reach across the country of 12 million listeners.

In 2012, BBC Media Action pioneered a live discussion public affairs programme called "Open Jirga" that brings ordinary Afghans together to engage in debate with government leaders and policymakers. The show highlights the importance of accountability of high standards for all office-bearers. "Salaam Watandar", produced by Inter news, airs news and entertainment four hours daily, often mixing the country's two main languages, Dari and Pashto, in the same sentence in an effort to promote national unity. Radio Azadi's human interest programme, "In Search of Missing People", reunites families with loved ones lost to war or violence. The show draws an average of 9 million listeners weekly. Since 2012, Radio Nawa and its affiliate FM stations across the country have broadcast *Baghch-e-Simsim*, Afghanistan's own "Sesame Street".

The prominence of the media in the 2004 presidential election inspired a new media genre referred to as "warlord media", so-called because all were founded by renowned military and political leaders and *mujahideen* fighters who led the struggle to rid the country of the Soviet occupiers. Such media outlets include Ayna TV owned by Uzbek military leader, now first Vice President to President Ghani, Abdul Rashid Dostum, Balkh Governor Atta Mahommed Noor's Arzu TV and radio, and the former President late Burhanuddin Rabbani's Noor TV. Much of the programming on these stations promotes ethnic or political agendas. Observers are divided on the value of these outlets. Some believe they contribute to ethnic divisiveness and promote disunity. Others believe they promote ethnic and cultural diversity.

The Fourth Pillar

In the run-up to the second round of voting in the 2014 presidential election, media associations signed a Code of Good Conduct calling for "ethical coverage of events without inciting hatred", and advocating "serious investigative reporting to inform the public about any irregularities or fraud".

At the same time, candidates Ashraf Ghani and Abdullah Abdullah signed campaign pledges committing "to spare no legal measures to promote and protect press freedom and freedom of speech". Such a commitment to protect and preserve an independent Afghan media that can keep the public informed without fear of reprisal or violence is essential for the country's transition into an open society.

But keeping the public informed comes at a great risk for the Afghan media. Incidents of violence against journalists increased in 2014 with 125 recorded cases of violence against them, including 8 deaths, 9 cases of injuries, 20 arrests, 38 beatings, and 50 cases of threats and insults. Murdered journalist 23 year-old Zubair Haatami was injured in the December 11, 2014 attack on Kabul's Istiqlal High School and died in hospital a week later. He was filming a performance of "Heartbeat: Silence After the Explosion", a musical play condemning suicide attacks.

Access to Information Law and Mass Media Law

The 2004 Afghan Constitution guarantees the right of freedom of expression and access to information. The 2009 Mass Media Law "promote[s] and support[s] the right of freedom of thought and speech, defend[s] the rights of journalists, and ensure[s] the ground for their free operation".

The 2009 law "could be counted one of the best in the region, but the problem is the implementation of this law by government", notes Mujeeb Khalvatgar, Managing Director of Nai-Supporting Open Media in Afghanistan, the country's media watchdog. Nai trains journalists, tracks and publishes data on violence against journalists, and concentrates in five areas: media law, access to information, defamation law, media ethics, and journalists' security.

The most serious problem with the law, according to Khalvatgar, is the status of the Commission designed to monitor media. The 2009 law calls for a Mass Media Commission to replace the existing Media Violations Investigation Committee, a vestige of the 2006 Media Law (one of four such laws since 2002) which vests authority for monitoring alleged media violations in the Minister of Culture and Information and 9 Commission members, none of whom represent the media. Khalvatgar and his colleagues call it the long arm of the government encroaching on freedom of expression.

As reported in *Human Rights Watch's* January 2015 report on "Threats to Media Freedom in Afghanistan", Former Minister of Information and Culture, Sayed Makhdoom Raheen, stated that one of his main responsibilities in response "to complaints from officials about critical coverage" in such cases was to ensure that journalists apologised to the relevant government officials and agencies".[1]

In December 2014, President Ashraf Ghani signed the Access to Information law, over the misgivings of the media sector; the bill is flawed. A major sticking point with the media is Article 15 of the Access to Information law, with its sweeping prohibition on content that "endangers independence, sovereignty, territorial integrity, national security, and national interests" or "violates the privacy of a person". This broad brush approach limits significantly the independence of Afghanistan's media.[2] It has been recommended that Article 15 be amended to allow for disclosure of information on issues such as corruption, crime, human rights violations, and danger to the public security as long as such disclosure can be shown to be in public interest. They also want a provision designed to protect the identity of sources.

The success of the National Unity Government depends on buy-in from civil society, and that buy-in depends on the free flow of information between the government and the public. Media must be able to investigate and expose corruption in a responsible manner and to share this information with the populace. Such a free flow can only be achieved if the current pall of fear that hangs over the media is lifted.

Conclusion

A vast majority of journalists agree that Afghanistan cannot afford to remain isolated on the global stage. Likewise, media leaders and employers list removing the trust deficit between Afghanistan, its neighbours—notably Pakistan and Iran—and other countries, as their principal priority. Many journalists were sent abroad in recent years for professional capacity-building training courses. On their return home, the reporters and editors have underlined the imperative for regional cooperation on issues of common interest. They have also been espousing a host of social causes, including human rights, women's education, good governance, gender equality, freedom of speech and democratisation of the state. Their mission to influence government policies is gradually coming to fruition.

The Afghan media's role in increasing trade links among countries and amicable resolution of disputes has been acknowledged in the country as well as internationally. For this positive trend to continue, the new Afghan government and the world at large will have to support the news outlets in the long term. One is confident that the new president, being a world-renowned economist and educationist, is fully aware of how well free media can contribute to Afghanistan's struggle for global recognition as a country with an enlightened and progressive worldview. Therefore, the Ashraf Ghani administration is expected to further improve the existing level of media freedom at a time when the country has successfully achieved security and political transitions. There may be problems, but these have to be converted into opportunities.

NOTES

1. "Stop Reporting or We'll Kill Your Family: Threats to Media Freedom in Afghanistan", Report by *Human Rights Watch*, January 21, 2015, at https://www.hrw.org/report/2015/01/21/stop-reporting-or-well-kill-your-family/threats-media-freedom-afghanistan.
2. Abasin Zaheer, "Access to information law be amended: Journalists", *Pajhwok Afghan News*, February 19, 2015, at http://www.pajhwok.com/en/2015/03/10/access-information-law-be-amended-journalists.

12

Truth vs Hype: Media, Hyper-nationalism and Impact on Perceptions in India-South Asia Relations

Shruti Pandalai

Introduction

In an ideal world—the photo-op at PM Modi's historic swearing-in ceremony on May 26, 2014 with all SAARC leaders joining hands pledging improved relations in South Asia, would be equivalent of a clean slate for a region fraught with tense and historically burdened relationships. The symbolism was not lost to the world. The message ticked all the right boxes, reflecting the new government's commitment to its neighbourhood and was reciprocated in kind. The media frenzy as expected was unprecedented. Even before Mr. Modi had been officially appointed as Prime Minister, English news anchors on Indian Television were expressing faith in Mr. Modi's ability of moving the "India-Pak relationship beyond the zero-sum game".[1] They, of course, changed their mind soon and the optimism was short-lived.

Cut to August 2014, the decision of Mr. Modi's government to cancel Indo-Pak Foreign Secretary level talks after Pakistan's High Commissioner to India met with Kashmiri Separatist leaders, was supported by enraged chest-thumping by the same set of journalists as a "befitting response to Pakistan's open aggression". Prime-time was abuzz with discussions with shouting matches from guests on both sides of the border debating why "Pakistan had it coming" since "Mr. Modi was clearly walking the talk".[2] The increased tension along the LoC (Line of Control) in the recent past have seen similar discussions often accompanied by the hashtag #PakDaresIndia #BorderBetrayal on the Indian side.[3] Sections of the Pakistani media too followed suit, with twitter reporting #cowardmodi[4] as a top trending hashtag across the border. At the risk of sounding both cynical and over-simplistic, for sections of the electronic media at least, it was back to business as usual on both sides. It is also explains why the role of media in polarising public opinion and fanning hyper-nationalism in matters impacting foreign policy are gaining credence in official circles. However, media and its representation of reality often reinforce stated positions, so is it fair in entirety to shoot the messenger?

The inferences from the Indo-Pak episode are telling but not new. Despite a consensus among most nations in South Asia on the merits of a unified and prosperous neighbourhood, framing of relationships in the mass media have not moved beyond the threat-security paradigm and are often confined to narrow nationalist constructs. Considering the historic baggage of embittered relationships, unresolved conflicts of territory, resources and identity, the frames of reference have remained unchanged. This, despite technology opening up and allowing for greater access and exchange of information for people in the subcontinent. So how does one explain the rise of hyper nationalism—even if spurred on by some sections of the electronic media—when access to multiple resources of information are available in the internet age? The answer lies perhaps in the fact that generations of South Asians have grown up with these perceptions and stereotypes, which have been appropriated and reinforced in the national discourse over decades and popularised in the mass media. They remain the 'natural' prisms through which issues of the present realpolitik are viewed; which means objectivity and factual reportage are often undermined.

A caveat is necessary at this point to say that there exist media houses in India and its neighbourhood which remain true to their craft and offer objective analysis on issues of foreign policy (especially the print media) and this paper is not making any broad-brush generalisations. However, in the era of 'breaking news' and competitive markets vying for viewership/readership, they are more the exception than the norm.

Given this context, can media in South Asia (practically) ever act independent of national discourse and its framing of national interest? When do the lines blur between national interest and jingoism and how has the Indian state responded to the rise of hyper-nationalism? While there is no dispute on the role of the media in mobilising opinion on matters of national interest, why is it suddenly being perceived as an agenda setter on matters of foreign policy? Is this influence being overestimated given the often episodic nature of coverage and lack of public interest beyond events? Is this impact or influence independent or contingent upon conditions? Many within the media have questioned the assessment that they bear the responsibility of carrying bilateral or neighbourhood relations forward. How do we deal with this dilemma? Regional media initiatives have rung hollow despite the good intentions they were conceived with—what are the limitations these platforms face? Finally, can we really expect the media in South Asia to provide alternative narratives when attempts to go beyond established frameworks run the risk of being seen as 'anti-national', 'soft' or 'seditious'? The intolerance of dissent is a new reality of media in South Asia which is increasingly corporatized and burdened with vested interests.

This paper attempts to navigate through many of these issues and argues that mass media impact on foreign policy is short term and episodic and dependent upon specific conditions, but runs the risk of polarising public opinion in an attempt to homogenise the framing of national interest. Since most often electronic media are accused for fanning hyper nationalism, the coverage of Indian English media television news networks on matters of Indian foreign policy vis-a-vis South Asia will be investigated and the normative and systemic challenges to reportage will be discussed. This is also being done to limit the scope of the paper and make it more focussed. The shortcomings of both the media and the past Indian governments in handling the rise of hyper-nationalism will be discussed.

Analysis of the state of the Indian media and its prevalent attitudes have been drawn largely through primary interviews and observations from serving and former diplomats, foreign office spokespersons, retired media advisors and editors and foreign affairs correspondents of leading Indian English media houses. The paper is introspective, as it looks at the Indian media's approach towards South Asia and does not claim expertise or attempt comparison with neighbourhood media.

It aims to offer no instant solutions but makes a case for more in-depth reporting and increased government transparency and access to facilitate narratives that go beyond the stereotypes of security dilemmas and historical baggage, to reflect the commonalities in aspiration of the new generation of South Asians. The new government in New Delhi has managed to usher in, at least symbolically, a renewed sense of hope for better relations in South Asia. Can the Indian media while cheering from the side-lines, also offer critique and follow up on the deliverables constructively in each of these relationships, remains to be seen.

Mass Media, Public Opinion and Impact on Foreign Policy

The agenda setting function of the media and its agency vis-a-vis foreign policy issues is a subject researched previously[5], by drawing on western academic literature—which provides a conceptual rubric to link cause and effect of the role played by the media in decision making and policy reception process and makes use of variables to map its influence. Bernard Cohen, in a landmark study on media and foreign policy in 1963, famously noted that press may not be able to convince people how to think, but it succeeds in telling them what to think about.[6] So, by the process of story selection (gate-keeping), contextualisation (framing of news) and prioritisation (indexing or high-lighting), the media was able to flag issues (media agendas). The issues discussed were salient to public interest (public agenda). Public opinion generated would finally translate into these issues being viewed as being important to policy makers (policy agenda).[7]

Media, hence, establishes itself as an actor in the process of policy formulation by creating an environment, first, by working as the "input channel" for the policymaker; and, second, as a feedback mechanism where decisions are tested by gauging of public opinion and garnering legitimacy for action.[8] It is used for "trials" of policies through press conferences and leaks, and as a "de facto hotline" when all lines of communication are severed during a crisis. It essays the roles of a 'pressure group', a 'critical observer' as also a 'participant' in the policy process.[9] Yet this influence is not independent.

It has been observed that agenda setting by the media is contingent upon a number of conditions. The input variables include the type of issues covered (e.g., obtrusive vs. unobtrusive), the specific media outlets (television vs. print/online), and the sort of coverage (e.g., negative vs. positive). Political context variables like "the time period (election vs. non-election), the type of political actors and institutional norms in their interaction with input variables produce outputs that range from no political adoption to fast and substantial adoption of media (highlighted) issues".[10]

Most scholars agree that conditions of *policy clarity, issue salience* and *sensitivity*, *type* and *duration of coverage*, and *clear political responsibility* weigh greatly in exerting media influence in foreign policy.[11] For instance, if the government of the day is seen as soft or undecided/divided over a policy decision, the media becomes independent and critical, often acting as a pressure group. The type of issue being flagged and *its bearing on pre-existing sensitivities* of both the public and the policymakers also has an impact. *Negative and continuous coverage* introduces the time factor and urgency. It identifies clear political responsibility and speeds up the decision making process.[12]

Technology has proved to be a dangerous game changer in the media-policy relationship. Television and now, new media technologies have imposed real time coverage constraints on the policy making process. This has meant shortened reaction time, expectations of immediate responses to crises, avenues for diplomatic manipulations and the delivery of instant judgments.[13] Foreign policy, which often lends itself to negotiations behind closed doors, has had to adjust to this insatiable thirst for information and, in many cases, has lost out on the short term perception battles.

So, while there is little evidence to suggest that media has an impact on the long term process of policy formulation in diplomacy, it does hijack agendas in the short term and disrupts the decision making process influencing immediate decisions. It does so, because irrespective of the regime type, "The exercise of power and authority and hence reputation is grounded on the executive's unique capability to speak for the nation. If the media positions or portrays the executive's actions as incompetent or immoral, then the elite consensus and power coalition will be disturbed. This creates the pressure on the executive to act".[14]

Shared and contested national narratives, conflicts over identity, resources and borders, threat perceptions of terrorism emanating from the neighbourhood all qualify and have a bearing on conditions of pre-existing sensitivities, issue salience, type and nature of coverage, which contribute to influencing public opinion. The media can, hence, act as a pressure group having a direct/indirect or perhaps even a symbolic impact on matters of foreign policy in the neighbourhood, especially during times of crisis. This argument will be further explored in the sections ahead where a few case studies will be discussed.

Tectonic Shift: 'Modi'-fied Foreign Policy, Public Interest and Media Frenzy

During an interaction with the author (on a research project investigating the role of the media in the India-China relationship), the MEA Foreign Spokesperson had lamented on the lack of substantive/quality media coverage and public interest in matters of foreign policy. The statistics[15] shared were: India has 93,985 print publications, of which only 300 look at foreign policy and the world beyond our borders. An estimated 413 out of 821 television channels cover news and current affairs excluding the 30 odd state channels. Of these, hardly 5 have dedicated programmes on foreign affairs. While India is home to about 192 foreign correspondents from 113 news organisations, only a meagre 30 Indian correspondents report for eight organisations in 9 countries.

Even in terms of coverage, the Indian media's map of the world seemed myopic if numbers (data from end of 2013) were taken on face value. Three countries stayed in focus: the United States, Pakistan and China. Here 70 per cent news related to the US, 15 per cent to Pakistan and 10 per cent to China. The rest of the world, all countries taken together, got 5 per cent coverage.[16] This was seen as a direct reflection of audience interests. Given the statistics, sustaining interest in foreign policy reportage is an uphill task—is the regular justification given by most media houses.

Foreign affairs were seen as only priority in times of crises. Media in the UPA II government was accused of amplifying cleavages—playing up statements from different arms of the government and speculating in the absence of clear official communication on India's strategic affairs. The fact that UPA II reeling from a series of domestic scandals, was not popular with the people, meant the media's criticism often veered on the extreme and pushed the government to take up rigid postures on previously flexible positions.

A year on the tides have changed. India, has just emerged from an era of coalition politics with the Narendra Modi-led government enjoying an absolute majority. PM Modi's emphasis on re-energising neighbourhood relationships has seen a series of high profile bilateral visits in a span of few months and, hence, the neighbourhood has jumped back into the media's frenzied radar. Private news networks which often limited coverage of official bilateral visits to an odd discussion in the past (unless it was Pakistan), now broadcast LIVE for hours the entire duration of the Prime Minister's speech. The coverage of many of these events is almost door to door. The Prime Minister famous for oratory skills, draws very high viewership and many beat journalists feel "it's not so much as a spike in interest in foreign affairs, but Mr. Modi and how he is projecting India to the world"[17] that is drawing interest. He has managed to "blur the lines",[18] says Suhasini Haidar, Diplomatic Editor with *The Hindu* and former Anchor of the *World 360*, on CNN-IBN. "Under Mr. Modi, the lines between domestic and international are thinning […] now you are seeing a domestic (state) election campaign being fought on an international plank. Even the PM's foreign trips are a pitch back home. He is going to each of these visits with a very clear view of how it's playing back home. Everyone (in the media) is caught up in the optics and a critical assessment of the pros and cons of the visits, the deliverables etc. are lost in this saturation coverage", she adds.[19] Mr. Modi's visit to Nepal and Bhutan and the huge traction they drew, both in our media and the hosts media, validate this claim.

De-facto, Mr. Modi's popularity has fuelled interest in India's foreign policy initiatives. The MEA Spokesperson has been quoted saying that since Mr. Modi's government came in, there has been "enhanced interest in the MEA's website" while social media interest has "increased by 400 per cent".[20] Many of the journalists felt that peak in public interest in the government and its activities are rise in expectations since the historic election. "We are now in the honeymoon phase with the government. After all, India has just emerged from having seen the worst of coalition era politics. The Modi government is making all the right noises and obviously being given the benefit of time. Whether this will be the case a year from now remains to be seen,"[21] stated a news editor with one of India's leading private news broadcasters.

The private news media, clear from the registered protest of The Editor's Guild, have not found a foot in the door with the new government.[22] If the last government in New Delhi was accused of not being able to speak in one voice, this government has put in place a very strict protocol for any engagement with the media. The PM speaks for the government and speaks only to central and state media agencies or through public discourse.[23] There has been no appointment to the post of media advisor to the PMO, and "for all practical purposes the Spokesperson of the Ministry of External Affairs is the only active spokesperson for the entire government", says Suhasini Haidar.[24]

The PM and his government are active on social media—Facebook and Twitter, where he has over 7 million followers. The strategy to "bypass traditional media" has "spurred editors to complain about a lack of two-way communication and debate".[25] No other ministries hold any meetings and access to bureaucrats has been restricted so sources of information/leaks are drying up.[26] PM's flights on international visits no longer take private media journalists along, and they are not part of any events where they could get unhindered access to the PM.[27] While many journalists welcomed this move, saying sometimes these trips were junkets that "came at the cost of the tax payer's money" all of them were concerned at the loss of an opportunity—"the on-board press briefings become an opportunity for the media to subject the government's chief executive to scrutiny on policy issues".[28] It is a "very controlled and consistent message which is being projected and hence the government is looking very cogent".[29]

Given that this is the new reality of the Indian media, how much leeway does it really have in the realm of reportage on foreign policy—a beat for which Indian journalists traditionally have depended solely on the government as a source of information? Case in point says Suhasini, "Are the tensions along the LoC with Pakistan? A year ago when ceasefire violations happened, the media's targeting of the government was incessant and the portrayal of it was soft and weak. Today the targeting is of the opposition for not getting united behind the government".[30] The tone and tenor of the coverage vis-a-vis tensions with Pakistan has not really changed, it is the government's response which is being seen as direct with clear read lines. In such scenarios how does one define the lines between when certain coverage is seen as jingoistic and when it is deemed to be in national interest? We clearly need more deliberation on how and what the media-national security relationship needs to look like.

Ideological and Systemic Challenges to Indian Media's Reportage on South Asia

We have established that certain sections of the media being investigated in this paper in the past have succumbed to amplifying hyper-nationalist views in times of crises and creating an environment where emotions trump objectivity (especially vis-a-vis Pakistan). However, it is also a fact that media is not an independent actor in terms of influence on perceptions and gets traction only during times of conflict—which turn into media spectacles. Here coverage is largely negative, there is a play on pre-existing sensitivities and narrow national constructs. Media narratives attempt to homogenise select framing of national interest which are reproduced, highlighted and amplified. But these also die down once the episode is over. Television interest is largely episodic, foreign policy construct is not.

So, do we run the danger of over-estimating media's influence in polarising public opinion on matters of foreign policy? "Yes", says Indrani Bagchi, Senior Diplomatic Editor of the *Times of India*, the country's most widely circulated English Daily.[31] "Look, everyone knows private news media is a commercial enterprise. Television does get over excited and theatrics take centre-stage, but it feeds into the rage of middle India and the viewer always has the option to switch off the channel. Now social media is taking up this space. The fact is, unfortunately, the readership interest in the neighbourhood is very minimal aside of Pakistan. So it is only select episodes of bilateral cooperation or conflict that get highlighted. Rest of the time India is too busy in its internal dynamics",[32] she adds. The following section identifies some of these challenges to in-depth objective reportage on the neighbourhood.

1a) Strategic Focus, Fixed Mind-sets and the Indo-Pak Hyperbole: Media will naturally reflect the strategic realities of the region and the troubled India-Pakistan relationship, hence, occupies the lion's share of focus. Two nuclear powers, having fought three wars, with active disputes over territory, resources and state-sponsored terror and whose national identities/consciousness are rooted in imagining the 'other' as the 'enemy' over generations—is a tough discourse to overhaul. It is also a relationship which has seen the maximum number of ups and downs and international interest. So it draws a lot more copy/on air time vis-a-vis other South Asian neighbours.

Journalists argue that while the charge of "over-the-top theatrics, on the brink of war-mongering in the aftermath of the beheading incident of two Indian soldiers by Pakistan along the LoC in January 2013 was accepted" and led to introspection among Indian broadcast media,[33] sometimes it is also caught in the cross-fire while just playing to gallery. If one were to briefly analyse flash points of Indo-Pak relations coinciding with the advent of 24x7 news media, it becomes clear that media of both nations have been fighting a proxy war, which has been appropriated by the state from time to time to manage public opinion, especially in times of crisis.

A comprehensive study of contemporary Indo-Pak media, for the Reuters Journalism Institute maps how many "televised media wars" (Kargil 1999, Agra Summit 2001, 26/11 Mumbai attacks) have been fought and used by the troubled neighbours in an aim to legitimise their point of view.[34]

The Kargil Conflict was India's first televised war and left an indelible mark on the national psyche. Images of body bags of soldiers, stories of their grieving families, briefings by government officials on casualties of war including a televised press conference releasing government recordings of intercepted messages between the then Pakistan army chief and his deputy, proving Pakistan's complicity in guerrilla activities, were images that India lived on for 60 days.[35] The media united the country in its hour of grief. "Kargil was a watershed mark in the militarisation of the Indian mind", commented a strategic affairs expert for a leading Indian English news network.[36]

The image of our brave soldiers holding up the Indian flag after recapturing Tiger Hill, is etched permanently in the Indian mind. This has been reproduced time and again, both in television and popular mass culture—symbolic of the sacrifice of the Indian soldier and the treachery of a scheming 'enemy'. The Pakistani media's impact was not felt as much, say experts, since they had to support the official version that it was not the Pakistani military but the *Mujahideen* that had instigated the conflict.[37] The Indian soldiers had won the war, but for many within the Indian media, they too had emerged victorious from it. There really has been no looking back since.

Tragically, November 26, 2008 was Indian television's biggest story. The terrorist attacks on Mumbai, a 72-hour siege on India's financial capital left 179 people dead and a nation terrorised. Newsrooms did not stop beaming and India did not sleep. From the first pictures of the captured Pakistani terrorist Ajmal Kasab, to the final dossier of evidence that was sent to Pakistan—all the pieces of the jigsaw were put together by the media for the Indian public.[38] Media persons were present throughout before the historic Taj Mahal Hotel which was up in flames, hearing gun shots being fired and reporting LIVE on a hostage situation for over 40 hours. This was India's 9/11 and that is how it was reported. Media was, once again, at war.

Sample this episode[39]. Initially Pakistan disowned captured terrorist Ajmal Kasab as its citizen demanding concrete evidence from India. On December 22, 2008, an MEA press release informed the media that Kasab had written to the Pakistani High Commissioner demanding legal assistance, thus, proving his nationality. Pakistani Interior Minister, Rehman Malik, called the reports false. Within 24 hours, CNN-IBN had put out a report citing public anger over inaction and graphically represented what "India's possible military options" were in case of a clash with Pakistan. Both NDTV 24x7 and TIMES

NOW were debating on "prime time" whether "a surgical strike option on Pakistan's terror havens" would be a viable option. The discussion involved panelists from both sides of the border; who ultimately argued against the aggressive posturing. The drama escalated when Pakistan's then National Security Advisor, Mahmud Ali Durrani spoke to CNN-IBN and accepted Kasab's nationality. Within hours he was sacked by a livid Pakistani PM Yousuf Raza Gilani for breach of protocol. Gilani in his statement finally accepted Kasab's citizenship. As much as there was no defence of television media's sensationalist coverage of 26/11, there was also a grudging acknowledgement of the media handing New Delhi a diplomatic victory on LIVE television in making its case against Pakistan.

We have seen numerous episodes ever since where animosity, mistrust and suspicion have laid siege to any rapprochement in India-Pakistan relations. Television images burned into collective memories have become linked to national identities. India's former Prime Minister Manmohan Singh's ambition of normalising relations in 2009 suffered as a consequence, in what is infamous as the "the Sharm-el-Sheikh fiasco".[40] The then Indian Prime Minister met his Pakistani counterpart on the side-lines of the NAM (Non-Aligned Movement) summit in Egypt in July 2009. In the joint statement issued, former Prime Minister Singh looking to calm tensions sought to quell Pakistan's concerns of India's involvement in the troubled Balochistan region, even as Pakistan made no new commitments on the 26/11 probe. The backlash was severe. CNN-IBN's discussion was entitled "Is the PM facing nation's trust deficit?" with the PM's speech running and a window showing images of the 26/11 attacks.[41] Newspaper headlines screamed "Abject surrender at Sharm-el-Sheikh"[42] and, hence, on his return the former Prime Minister sought to repair the damage. In a televised statement in Parliament he clarified: "I wish to reiterate that the President and the PM of Pakistan know, after our recent meetings, that we can have a meaningful dialogue with Pakistan only if they fulfil their commitment, in letter and spirit, not to allow their territory to be used in any manner for terrorist activities against India".[43] The composite dialogue stood suspended.

As former Indian Foreign Secretary, Salman Haidar wrote in *The Hindu* in 2009, "Sharm-el-Sheikh has become shorthand for cardinal diplomatic error. The media has gone to town on the communiqué, endlessly turning it over and trumpeting adverse findings. The 'strategic community,' has jumped in, as has the parliamentary opposition. Even usually sober observers have been swayed by the clamour and are inclined to blame the Prime Minister for putting his name to the document. On his return, he was left conspicuously alone, with nobody in the government showing much inclination to stand by him as the criticism mounted".[44]

The above anecdotes are meant to illustrate how strongly the media has asserted its agency in the India-Pakistan relationship, having gauged the public sentiment. Even the cherished Agra Summit held at the height of bonhomie in 2001 ended inconclusively when New Delhi got upset with the former President of Pakistan, Pervez Musharraf, for holding a surprise breakfast meet with select editors. The last straw was its telecast on NDTV and Pakistan Television.[45] Here, the General in a "clear pitch back home", harped on the centrality of Kashmir to Indo-Pak ties and refused to acknowledge cross-border terrorism or any remorse for Kargil in his speech.[46] While the saturation coverage of the Agra Summit was being seen by the Indian government as facilitating a thaw post Kargil, many experts in India blamed the media for the summits failure, as the mood had soured post the telecast.[47] The General's surprise meet with the editors was called a 'propaganda coup' to ensure a hero's welcome back home.[48]

There are countless other examples—including the emerging bonhomie post the Modi-Sharif meet which grew cold when tensions along the LoC flared up. They prove how media in both countries drive and are driven by public obsession with the vicious cycle of the India-Pakistan equation. With such baggage and an all-consuming nature of a volatile relationship, it is little surprise then that rest of the neighbourhood is neglected by the Indian media.

1b) China, the Elephant in the Room: If the Indian media is not obsessing over Pakistan, its attention is generally taken up by China's presence in South Asia. It is an open secret that India sees itself being vulnerable to a war on two fronts—with Pakistan on the west and China on the east. China's sharing of nuclear technology with Pakistan and their much talked about 'all weather friendship' have always made India uncomfortable. Over the last decade, China's foray into South Asia has only heightened India's unease. The media, too, reflects this mind-set. An analysis of most coverage of the neighbourhood, shows strategic competition with China in what the media describes as "India's backyard", driving most reportage.[49]

China's building of ports in Pakistan and developing of alternate trade and energy corridors, Free Trade Agreement with oil exploration rights in Bangladesh along with naval access to Chittagong Port, Energy and

Infrastructure investment in Myanmar, development aid, oil exploration rights and building of energy, port and bunker facilities on the southern coast of Hambantota in Sri Lanka, investment in infrastructure along the China-Nepal border, etc. are all reported in the Indian media as a "strategic loss for India" or neighbours playing "the China card with India".[50] The analysis of bilateral relationships on their individual merit hardly find play nor do analysis of delivery of signed agreements.[51] Television mostly follows print leads in such stories, using the facts broken down by the print media to report on the incident, because without pictures there is no spectacle in the story.[52] Indrani Bagchi notes: "Without China and Pakistan—unless there is a coup in Bangladesh or the Royal massacre in Nepal or the killing of LTTE chief Prabhakaran and routing of the Tigers in Sri Lanka", both media and public interest is episodic and often "such news never makes it to page one of the paper"[53] or a television headline. In television especially, often reports on the neighbourhood outside of a crisis, find their way in one minute news-wraps which are a round-up of news events from across the globe.

1c) Good Neighbourhood Relations not the Mandate of the Indian Media: "It is not a journalist's job to be an upholder of relationships; the job is to report a story accurately and the relationship is to be handled by south block".[54] This seems to be the overwhelming opinion of journalists across private networks in India interviewed for this paper. Budget cuts, staff being spread out too thin, fighting with editors to keep a foreign affairs story alive on a news page/bulletin, minimal audience interest, lack of visas and access, etc. are the very real obstacles journalists face on a day to day basis in newsrooms. Given the expanding corporate ownership of the media space, commercial interests loom large and grabbing viewer attention to attract advertising revenue in the absence of a subscription system, come at a certain cost. The ugly truth is that while the media is supposed to inform and educate the audience, commercial considerations drive story selection in private media and resources allocated will be subject to audience interest. The US, China and Pakistan—seem to hold the attention span of the Indian audience and, hence, the media focuses on stories from the region.

It must be pointed out that the Indian policy experts as well as practitioners interviewed for this paper, agreed on principle, that the media in India was not expected to uphold a bilateral relationships and noted that reporting in most cases reflected strategic realities. However, the propensity of 24x7 media to oversimplify complicated matters, and opinion shows amplifying extreme views as the mood of the nation were seen as problematic, but not reflective of the entire media space.

Adding to the *ideological* obstacles, following are the *systemic* challenges in the Indian media that impact overall reportage:

2a) Issues of Access/Visas: Apart from Nepal and Bhutan, access to South Asia becomes the biggest stumbling block in creating news reports and content that break stereotypical coverage of the region. When they were granted visas many journalists noted they felt they were on "patronage tours" often 'feeling obliged to a good story' and this has restricted more in-depth reporting on the region. The problem is compounded for television journalists, since a story cannot make a compelling case without images, hence, the interest in crisis coverage.

2b) Lack of South Asia Correspondents: Indian television networks find it difficult to station journalists in the region due to budget constraints. In the absence of easy access and freedom of coverage, they find it easier to fly in a reporter when required. So the building up of ground-up country knowledge and expertise is non-existent.

2c) Crisis Coverage and Competitive Pressures: Domestic politics in India consumes the audiences and, hence, the interest in international affairs only peaks at the time of crises. Mostly, the coverage of conflict means more time spent on negative news which while driving up readership/television ratings also impacts public opinion negatively. In such scenarios, sections of the media have often been accused of resorting to sensationalism and television theatrics.

2d) Lack of Expertise and Analysis: Television has become a prisoner to its own medium. Even if there is an editorial interest to pursue or analyse a story, the next episode or event is often an ad-break away. This translates into superficial coverage. In addition, on mass media like television, the popular debates get oversimplified and reduced to binaries. This is due to the absence of journalists who have field experience from the region to bring out those stories to defy stereotypes. Such discussions get reduced to a battle between the supposed "hawks" and "peace-niks", with no space for substantial discussions amidst shouting matches.

2e) Lack of Reportage on Trade in Neighbourhood: Despite intra-regional trade growing at less than 5 per cent [55] owing to many non-trade barriers in the region and the focus on China's growing investments in South Asia, reportage on trade hardly finds traction in the news media. In fact, a study by the Indian Council for Research on International Economic Relations (ICRIER) documents meticulously the under-reporting on trade-related activity between India and Pakistan, and makes a case for the media's selective reporting as an important impediment to trade normalisation between the two neighbouring countries.[56] So, stories of trade from the neighbourhood are often restricted to tables in business newspapers if at all.

2f) Social Media and Online Nationalism Driving Coverage: The rise of social media and online nationalism has never been more conspicuous. In India, one sees the convergence of traditional and online media where increasingly 24x7 media is relying heavily on social media for breaking the news content as well as direction of coverage. This also means social media is left vulnerable to manipulation. Sometimes, online populist opinion on issues gets reflected on traditional media without any filters, amplifying issues which would seem not cut teeth in an editorially vetted story. Social media is two steps ahead of television in impact, immediacy and reach and, hence, finds itself increasingly driving coverage.

Former television journalist and strategic affairs expert, Nitin Gokhale, has recounted in a clear timeline, how through his twitter handle, he first heard the news of the beheading of Indian soldiers by Pakistan along the LoC in January 2013.[57] Before he could confirm the story from official sources, "soldiers, families, ex-servicemen, all piled pressure on the media and discussed the government's soft response".[58] He adds, "No one is able to control the information flow. While some mainstream media outlets wait for official confirmation before breaking news, social media has no such compulsion. Mainstream media, thus, comes under pressure".[59]

Conclusion: Where Do We Go From Here?

To say India's relationship with its neighbourhood is complicated—would be as un-nuanced as it is over-simplistic. However imprisoned as we are in our predisposed attitudes and burdened histories, the yearning for peace has always been strong. Even Indo-Pak relations, where over time negative attitudes are gaining prominence, the choice of peace and rejection of war, among both nations, has remained unchanged.[60] The foundation for improving perceptions and breaking stereotypes even in extreme scenarios do exist, we need to build on this.

The media is not a monolith, and as in India, there are many different actors participating in debates across South Asia. This needs to be acknowledged. There is a need for more overseas correspondents and less reflection of opinion which form the basis of many news reports today. This might be easier said than done. For media houses this means re-evaluating their business models and decreasing dependence on advertising revenues and consequently re-prioritising news and rejecting 'infotainment'. For the government, it means making strategic communication on matters of foreign policy unambiguous and granting more visas, access and transparency to encourage comprehensive reportage in the media and nip hyper nationalism in the bud. While it is the media's job to report accurately, it is unrealistic to expect private media houses surviving under competitive pressures to shoulder responsibility of bilateral/regional relationships. Blaming the messenger entirely in times of crises, is often reflective of the government's inability to get its act together and being in denial of strategic realities.

Media dialogues are a great opportunity to explore new ideas and gain fresh perspective, but in the case of South Asia they have had limited impact. *Aman ki Asha* (Hope for Peace) a joint campaign between the Jang Group in Pakistan and the *Times of India* group in 2010 aimed at creating a new conversation between the people. Cultural and business exchange, journalist workshops, track II level dialogues were all held within this framework. While they helped calm the nerves on both sides of the border, the scope was often limited, held hostage to the ups and downs of Indo-Pak relations. Organisations like SAFMA (South Asian Free Media Association) have done their bit to bring journalists together in the neighbourhood and "enable exchange of ideas and developing contacts" but many reporters feel "these were reduced to media junkets, with core issues of restricted access, visas, etc. never being dealt with".[61]

Reportage within the Indian media, needs to find points of convergence moving beyond the threat-security paradigm. Themes focussing on "societies in transition", health and education have takers and need more coverage. There is a need to 'humanise' coverage in the neighbourhood. Remember the idea of the Lahore bus service was mooted in a media interview. Also, the phenomenon of terrorism ails the whole of South Asia and the media can collaborate on narratives that counter extreme propaganda.

Censorship of the airwaves has meant that many South Asian neighbours have very little clue as to what their neighbourhood looks like, but are at ease with culture and people of western societies who they are separated from by hundreds of miles. The popularity of Zee Network's *Zindagi* channel, which airs Pakistani shows for the Indian audience is an indicator of how perceptions can change when societies have a window to each other's communities.

Having said that, there are critical challenges confronting South Asian media with media freedom coming under severe attack from several quarters. While some pressures still emanate from the state in the form of censorship and control, there is also rising intolerance from non-state actors, such as terrorists, violent extremist groups, and religious fundamentalists.[62] Many journalists in South Asia have found themselves threatened with repercussions for certain types of reporting—from physical attacks and legal action; and self-censorship in such an environment is only natural.[63] These pressures also have curbed the media's ability to represent diverse views.

Finally, electronic media, especially in India has been held responsible for always being a rabble rouser, fixated on black and white discussions and reducing debates to binaries—even on complex issues like foreign policy. However, it is important to point out that such generalisations may perhaps be unfair to the entire media landscape and need to be seen with the churning underway in the business of Indian media as discussed in previous sections. There has been introspection among many senior journalists in India on what is being called the "dumbing down of the medium". Prime time anchors/ editors criticised on the role of the media post the 26/11 attacks noted: "There is a trend to scream, to be loud, to be extreme because you realise that the viewer's or reader's attention span is becoming more and more fleeting. This is forcing you to have bolder headlines and bigger pictures in newspapers. In television it is forcing you to push for more polarised, extreme opinions—something I don't agree with (…) There is a lot of bad journalism in TV, terrible journalism. But that's not a reason to tar the entire medium in the manner that is happening".[64]

Karan Thapar, one of India's leading current affairs broadcasters wrote on the plight of Indian television debates "…this will only change when anchors and channel heads accept that current affairs discussions are not mass audience programmes and must not be thought of as entertainment. They are for those who care and want to know. And this group will always be a minority. Now, if this comes up against the imperatives of commercial survival that is a conundrum our television producers must address and solve. I accept it won't be easy. In fact, it could be expensive, both in terms of money and audience. But if it does not happen television discussions will soon cease to matter—except in a negative sense".[65] The absence of a robust public service broadcaster in India, which is not seen as propaganda tool for the government, is at such times, felt the most. There is growing viewership of serious new programming on state-owned Doordarshan, but mass public interest remains elusive.

It would be naive to believe that strategic imperatives will not overshadow reportage on the India-South Asia relationship. Yet, there is evidence of introspection and realisation among stakeholders that there is a need to inform opinion and discard stereotypes to overcome the crisis of credibility. There are no instant solutions. Increased interface and interaction among the media and transparency and clear communication from the government are essential to course correction. Perhaps Johan Galtung's idea of *peace journalism* needs to be revisited in the South Asian context. One of its basic tenets was to base reportage beyond narrow national constructs, giving voice to all sides of the conflict and to non-demonise the 'other'.[66]

NOTES

1. "Live coverage: Modi Swearing In: Can Modi Change India-Pak zero-sum game relationship?", NewsX, May 26, 2014, at https://www.youtube.com/watch?v=WQho1bstRfI (Accessed October 10, 2014).
2. For more see: "The Newshour Debate: Pakistan shown the door—Full Debate", August 18, 2014, at https://www.youtube.com/watch?v=3xiNBZX2lqo (Accessed October 10, 2014).
3. Ibid.
4. "Coward Modi Trends in Pakistan as Twitter Erupts with Anti-India messages", October 8, 2014, *First Post*, at http://www.firstpost.com/world/cowardmodi-trends-in-pakistan-as-twitter-erupts-with-anti-india-messages-1747247.html (Accessed October 10, 2014).
5. For more see Shruti Pandalai, "Who Sets the Agenda? Does Prime Time Really Pace Policy? The Indian Experience", IDSA Monograph Series No. 13, January 2013, at http://www.idsa.in/monograph/WhoSetstheAgendaDoesPrimeTimeReallyPacePolicy_spandalai.
6. B. Cohen, (1963), p. 13, quoted in Ibid, p.12.
7. The three stages of media agenda setting and influence are discussed by M.E. McCombs and D.L. Shaw, (1972), Media framing and priming by S. Iyengar and D. Kinder, (1987); For more elaborate literature on agenda setting theory see Shruti Pandalai, no. 5.
8. C. Naveh, 2002, quoted in Ibid, p. 10.
9. P.P. Basu, 2003, pp. 18-21, P. Seib, 1997, D.B. Miller, 2007, E. Gilboa, 2003, C. Naveh, 2002. For a more detailed literature review see Shruti Pandalai, no. 5.
10. Walgrave et al., 2006, p.104. For more see Ibid.
11. See detailed literature review on conditions for media influence in foreign policy in pp. 21-23, in Shruti Pandalai, no. 5.
12. Ibid.
13. E. Gilboa, 2003, p. 97.
14. D.B. Miller, 2007, pp. 192-197, quoted in Shruti Pandalai, no. 5, pp. 21-23.

15. Discussion based on interview with Syed Akbaruddin, former Foreign Office Spokesman, Ministry of External Affairs, GOI, on October 15, 2013 in New Delhi. He is quoting figures based on information given by the Ministry of Information and Broadcasting.
16. E. Kumar Sharma, "Indian media's poor coverage of world news, foreign policy", *India Today*, August 20, 2013, at http://blogs.intoday.in/businesstoday/indian-media-coverage-of-foreign-affairs- world-dismal-63061.html (Accessed October 10, 2013).
17. Conversation with journalists covering the Foreign Affairs beat for English News Media in India, many of whom requested to be quoted anonymously.
18. Interview with Suhasini Haidar, Diplomatic Editor, *The Hindu*, Former Senior Editor and Host of World 360 on CNN-IBN, English News Network of The Network 18 group in India; on October 10, 2014 in New Delhi.
19. Ibid.
20. "Indian Foreign Policy: A Big Draw on Social Media", *New Indian Express*, October 13, 2014, at http://www.newindianexpress.com/nation/Indias-Foreign-Policy-a-Big-Draw-on-New-and-Social-Media/2014/10/13/article2475901.ece1 (Accessed October 13, 2014).
21. Conversation with journalists covering the Foreign Affairs beat for English News Media in India, many of whom requested to be quoted anonymously.
22. "Controlling the message: Modi chooses State Media over Private News Media", *Times of India*, October 20, 2014, at http://timesofindia.indiatimes.com/india/Controlling-the-message-Modi-chooses-state-media-over-private-news-outlets/articleshow/44883704.cms (Accessed October 2014).
23. Ibid.
24. Interview with Suhasini Haidar, no. 18.
25. No. 22.
26. Interview with Suhasini Haidar, no. 18.
27. Ibid.
28. "Why mainstream media is feeling disempowered under Modi", *Rediff*, August 6, 2014, at http://www.rediff.com/news/column/why-mainstream-media-is-feeling-disempowered-under-modi/20140806.htm (Accessed October 10, 2014).
29. Interview with Suhasini Haidar, no. 18.
30. Ibid.
31. Interview with Indrani Bagchi, Senior Diplomatic Editor, *Times of India*, in New Delhi on October 21, 2014.
32. Ibid.
33. Rajdeep Sardesai, Consulting Editor, Headlines Today, India Today Group and Former Editor-in-chief CNN-IBN, for IBNLive.com, "Making Sense of Sensationalist TV Journalism", February 8, 2013, at http://ibnlive.in.com/blogs/rajdeepsardesai/1/64305/making-sense-of-sensationalist-tv-journalism.html; Karan Thapar, current affairs host of Last Word, Devil's Advocate on Network 18, currently host of To The Point, Headlines Today, India Today Group, for Hindustan Times, "Television: A Mea Culpa", *Hindustan Times*, February 9, 2013, at http://www.hindustantimes.com/news-feed/columnskaranthapar/tv-a-mea-culpa/article1-1009279.aspx (Accessed October 10, 2014).
34. Dwaipayan Bose, "Journalism Caught in Narrow Nationalism: The India-Pakistan Media War", Reuters Institute for the study of Journalism, Oxford University, 2011, at https://reutersinstitute.politics.ox.ac.uk/sites/default/files/Journalism%20Caught%20in%20Narrow %20 Nationalism%20The%20India-Pakistan%20Media%20War% E2%80%99.pdf (Accessed October 20, 2014).
35. Ibid.

36. Ibid. quoting Maroof Raza, Strategic Affairs Expert with Times Now, Indian English News Network.
37. Ibid.
38. For a more detailed exposition read Shruti Pandalai, no. 5.
39. Ibid for more details on sources and timelines.
40. Ibid.
41. Ibid.
42. "Abject Surrender at Sharm-el-Sheikh", Op-ed, *New Indian Express*, July 2009, at http://www.newindianexpress.com/columns/article146654.ece (Accessed October 10, 2014).
43. "Prime Minister's statement in Lok Sabha on the debate on the PM's recent visit's abroad" on July 29, 2009, transcript accessed on Speeches and Statements, at www.mea.gov.in on August 10, 2010.
44. Salman Haidar, "Sharm-el-Sheikh revisited", Op-ed column, *The Hindu*, September 29, 2009, at http://www.thehindu.com/opinion/op-ed/sharm-el-sheikh-rea%20visited/article23769.ece (Accessed October 20, 2014).
45. H.Y. Sharada Prasada, "Agra summit, in brief", *The Asian Age,* July 25, 2001, at http://www.mea.gov.in/articles-in-indian-media.htm?dtl/18606/Agra+summit+in+brief (Accessed October 20, 2014).
46. Ibid.
47. Bharat Wariavwalla, "Learning the limits of diplomacy", *The Tribune,* July 29, 2001, at http://www.tribuneindia.com/2001/20010729/edit.htm#2 (Accessed October 20, 2014).
48. Prabhu Chawla, Raj Chengappa and Shishir Gupta, "Cover Story: Hit and run : Indo-Pak Agra Summit: Positions of Delhi and Islamabad remains incompatible", *India Today,* July 30, 2001, at http://indiatoday.intoday.in/story/indo-pak-agra-summit-positions-of-delhi-and-islamabad-remains-incompatible/1/230813.html (Accessed October 20, 2014).
49. Author used Google Analytics to analyse search "China in India's backyard" having chosen 453 English media news reports between October 2005-October 2014. The peak in coverage and gradual rise in reports of China's interest in South Asia was seen in 2010, when most articles spoke of China's investments in South Asia.
50. Sudha Ramachandran, "China moves into India's back yard", *Asia Times Online,* March 13, 2007, at http://www.atimes.com/atimes/South_Asia/IC13Df01.html; Pravakar Sahoo, IEG and Nisha Taneja, "China's growing presence in India's neighbourhood", ICRIER, East Asia Forum, February 5, 2010, at http://www.eastasiaforum.org/2010/02/05/chinas-growing-presence-in-indias-neighbourhood/(Accessed October 20, 2014); Shweta Punj, "The Castaway: India is steadily losing ground to China as a trading partner of South Asian countries", *Business Today,* December 22, 2013, at http://businesstoday.intoday.in/story/india-losing-ground-as-trading-partner-south-asian-countries/1/201078.html (Accessed October 20, 2014); "In Sri Lanka, India has lost the plot to China", firstbiz.com, March 25, 2013, at http://firstbiz.firstpost.com/corporate/in-sri-lanka-india-has-lost-the-plot-to-china-39988.html (Accessed October 20, 2014).
51. Interview with Suhasini Haidar, no. 18.
52. Conversations with journalists covering the MEA beat, no. 21.
53. Interview with Indrani Bagchi, no. 31.
54. View of all Indian journalists interviewed for this chapter.
55. Figures at: https://www.gov.uk/government/uploads/system/uploads/attachment_data/file/342442/India_-_Monthly_Trade_Report_July_2014.pdf (Accessed October 21, 2014).
56. Rahul Mediratta, "Media underreporting as a barrier to Indo-Pak Trade Normalisation—

Quantitative analysis of newsprint dailies", ICRIER Working Paper, 288, October 2014, at http://icrier.org/pdf/Working_Paper_288.pdf (Accessed October 21, 2014).

57. Nitin Gokhale, "Case—A beheading along the Line of Control", Takshashila Policy Research, April 2013, at http://takshashila.org.in/wp-content/uploads/2013/04/TCPP-NitinGokhale-LoCBeheading-April2013.pdf (Accessed October 20, 2014).
58. Ibid.
59. Ibid.
60. Data gathered from the Pew Global Attitudes Project 2014, at http://www.pewglobal.org/2014/07/14/chapter-4-how-asians-view-each-other/; BBC World Service Country Poll, June 3, 2014, at http://downloads.bbc.co.uk/mediacentre/country-rating-poll.pdf; Low Institute India Poll 2013, May 20, 2013, at http://www.lowyinstitute.org/publications/india-poll-2013; all (Accessed October 20, 2014).
61. Conversation with journalists covering the MEA beat for English News Media in India, many of whom requested to be quoted anonymously.
62. Naureen Chowdhury Fink, Karin Deutsch Karlekar, and Rafia Barakat, "Mightier than the Sword? The Role of the Media in Addressing Violence and Terrorism in South Asia", Centre on Global Counter Terrorism Cooperation, October 2013, at http://globalcenter.org/wp-content/uploads/2013/11/2013Oct_CGCC_MightierThanTheSword_Report.pdf (Accessed October 10, 2014).
63. Ibid.
64. "Rajdeep Sardesai and Barkha Dutt respond to criticism of the 26/11 coverage at the Indian Express Ideas Exchange", December 29, 2008, at http://thehoot.org/web/storypage/3554-1-1-14-true.html (Accessed October 20, 2014).
65. Karan Thapar, no. 33.
66. Jake Lynch and Annabel McGoldrick, *Peace Journalism*, Hawthorn Press, Stroud, UK, 2005.

PART III
Influence of Media on Foreign and Security Policies of States

13

News Media Re-Presentation and Agenda-Setting in Public Discourse on Foreign Relations: The Case of Sri Lankan Popular Attitudes Towards India

Lakshman F.B. Gunasekara

Introduction

Apart from the South Asian Free Media Association (SAFMA), the region's only major grouping[1] of journalists, there is not any major initiative to facilitate a consultation among media professionals and experts on a theme long espoused by the media community of the South Asian region. South Asia is not only one of the world's largest demographic formations, but it is also home to a major, and yet blossoming, global locus of human creativity and industry. The challenges faced within the region, both inter-state as well as intra-state and, the challenges from the outer regions are well understood.

The role the mass communication media plays in all this, especially that of the news media, is understood and discussed in varying ways. An attempt has been in this paper to problematize the subject of the 'role of the media' and to offer an approach drawing on the author's experience as a media professional and rights activist and also as a student of the news media and its core ideological function.

For this purpose, it is useful to discuss the general role and societal function of the news media as both an industry and as the predominant—and increasingly widespread—social communication structure of South Asian society. This discussion will include a critique of currently popular approaches to the news media by key relevant societal actors, and will offer what is considered to be the most effective way of examining this increasingly wondrous but, baffling, phenomenon that we so simply term 'the media'. This paper looks at the news media's role in the complex of Sri Lankan social conflict and draws a picture of the attitudes and perceptions that form ideological 'base content' of the social communication, dynamic, and structure within which the news media operates. In doing so, the paper does not use the traditional 'mass communication' theoretical model that is yet (surprisingly) predominant in media analysis discourses in South Asia, but what is called the 'Cultural Studies' theoretical model. Finally, the paper sketches the contours of Sri Lankan social attitudes towards the country's immediate regional neighbour, India, and offers an understanding of the way in which the news media thrives on these attitudes while, at the same time, nurturing and reproducing them.

The News Media as Industry and Ideological Structure

Media Misunderstood as an 'Instrument': A range of non-journalist actors—including even some media owners—had a misunderstanding of the news media's role. It is being used to refer to what is called the 'instrumentalist model' that is applied in South Asia in attempting to understand the news media, almost across the board, by the mass of citizenry, politicians and political activists, much of the intelligentsia including the social action and social service sectors and, culture sector, and, government and bureaucracy. By 'instrument' is meant that the media is primarily seen as a tool, supposedly, for a set of purposes: of, apparently,

- informing, and therefore, instructing and educating people;
- guiding and motivating people;
- animating and provoking people.

Thus, the news media is seen as useful, and a key instrument, for political management, for 'development' and 'modernisation', for responding to social crises and problems, ranging from health issues to natural disasters. The news media is also, therefore, apparently blamed for actively provoking and arousing people and motivating them—both individually and as groups—into socially harmful and negative behaviour ranging from violence to minor 'anti-social' behaviour. Different social interest groups accuse the news media of being deliberately sensational, promoting misperceptions between communities, sexism, and all kinds of other 'sins'. Bureaucrats as well as NGOs (non-governmental organisations) workers and even religious leaders frequently complain that the news media does not fulfil its function of 'educating the masses' whether it is for modernisation or for social survival.

News Media as Industry First, Second and Third: In the West, where the mass media originated as a modern industry in the 17th and 18th centuries and quickly evolved as a predominantly market-based social communication structure in the 19th century, the news media has long been well understood as to what it is—a commercial industry and little more.

The news media encompasses commercial, profit-driven, companies (including massive conglomerates) that function as market-driven entities. They must make profit if they are to survive and deliver income to their owners (including all share-holders) who have invested capital in them. The employees of these companies produce goods and services that fulfil this purpose and these products must be successfully marketed. The better the 'business model' of the media company, the better its prospects of surviving and thriving as a business entity.

Even if starry-eyed cub reporters begin their work as journalists and see it as adventure and mission, they quickly learn the contours of their profession as a livelihood first and mission later—if at all. Indeed, most journalists see their profession as a livelihood and little else, although, once imbued with the company's work culture, the market savvy ones are happy to expound their 'service mission' as professionals. And what is wrong with paid workers seeing their livelihoods as what it really is?

Even the chief editor of a newspaper has the primary duty of delivering a successfully marketable newspaper to his management. Otherwise, he expects to be fired or demoted just like any employee in any other commercial institution.

How does the news media make income on the market? It is certainly not by sales of copies of newspapers or sale of radio/TV subscriptions. Such direct media consumer revenue is a very small component of the media industry. This is why, even some newspapers are circulated free.

The news media's direct income is from advertising. In reality, as all media industry analysts recognised long ago, the news media industry's 'product' that is sold in the market is not 'news' at all. The essential, revenue earning 'product' is its audience (or, audiences) which are provided (sold) to advertisers. The larger and richer the audiences, the more lucrative the advertising, hence, resulting in worthwhile advertising revenue for the news media industry. Hence, the eternal battle is between Editorial/News Room and Advertising for newspaper space or TV/radio time. The 'business model' is that fine, mathematically calculated (easy today, thanks to computers) balance between rich advertising, cunning lay-out or programming and audience-attracting 'news'.

Following are some of the core characteristic of the news industry:

News Media Audiences and 'Constituency': Hence, 'news' establishes what is most attractive and useful to a particular target audience of a news media venture. The way that news is presented is also a means of pursuing that audience. That audience is the 'constituency' in more ways than simply being the target of news production. The very news producers themselves—the journalists, editors/directors, news processors—if to successfully 'treat' (package) their news for their intended audience, must be in close touch with those audiences. Indeed, the media labour market successfully recruits workers from the very broad social layers (or proximate layers) that constitute the audience.

That is, the news producers are broadly part of their audience or, in reverse, the audience constitutes the producers as well. The more one is part of one's audience, the better one can successfully communicate. Thus, the content of 'news' is a shared ideology between the journalist and her/his audience—her/his constituency. This is where the 're-presentation' function takes place—so well explained in the Cultural Studies model of the news media.

Thus, the political, ideological and social functioning of the news media industry is better understood through this perspective.

News Media Industry's Ideological and Political Function: When politicians or social actors of the advanced industrialised societies talk about the news media, they do not have any illusions of structurally using the news media as a mechanism of informing and educating. They do not see the media being 'meant to' perform these functions; not in any direct manner.

The exception to this was in the communist states where the media as a whole was not a market-based industry at all. In those societies, the news media were state-run institutions and functioned as little more than content producing and circulating bureaucracies. Even in China, which is a one-party state, the news media today is still only somewhat market-based, and must be rather considered as exception. Whether capitalism is allowed to evolve in China (and Vietnam, Cuba and Burma) in the way it has in the rest of world, will decide whether the news media there becomes a fully market-driven industry.

As the 'constituency' nature of the news media is vibrant, the 'instructional' dynamic operates in a hidden manner through catering to specific target audiences by specific news media ventures, installing content that is shaped by audience interests. This is why, for example, the mainstream media in the US almost never raises the issue of Israel's nuclear weapons industry whereas Iran is rarely far away from their news pages or bulletins. It is the industry-audience ideological nexus that is crucial for successful media market survival. Of course, on top of the almost 'natural' market dynamic, the various agendas of the ownerships also influence news conduct. So, while the *Washington Times* will be shrill on Iran, the *Washington Post* may occasionally have 'soft' a piece—that has sensational market value—on Israel's nuclear power.

Certainly, in the affluent, industrialised societies (including Japan, Australia, South Korea, etc.), the news media's 'instrumental' role is, at most, seen as a kind of 'courtesy' provided by the media industry and not as a core function. This understanding of the media industry is the pragmatic and realistic approach which, then, does not result in a mismatch between social expectations and industry function. It enables better political and social management because there are no unrealistic presumptions and no one—certainly not the bureaucracies and political classes –sits back and waits for the media to 'do its duty', not even in nationalist terms. By 'realistic', it is meant there is an understanding of the contours of control and deployment that could be applied successfully on the news media by social and political managers. If this was not the case, it would be impossible to explain the way *The New York Times*, at the height of the Cold War, could expose the rule-breaking and unethical actions by state security and espionage agencies in the 1960s, nor, for example, the publication of '*Inside the Company: a CIA Diary*' by commercial publishers—a book that not only described the way the CIA operates but also went on to list hundreds of commonly known institutions and organisations that had been infiltrated by the CIA!

It is the very industrial nature of the news media, and its recognition as such (in the advanced, industrialised countries), that enables it to exploit such spaces for its own industrial gain but, at the same time, provides information to society that enables interest groups to use such information for the social good (and, social 'bad', where loopholes are not closed). Most of them are the well-meaning journalists who also exploit this space to do social good. And some of them have sacrificed their careers if not their lives in this mission.

It must be noted, however, that this paper focuses primarily on the current news media industrial structure which is the press, radio and television. The new internet media must be seen as an emerging, entirely new phenomenon that surpasses traditional forms of social communication. In any case, the internet media offers an even less facility of being used as an 'instrument' compared with the traditional news media industry.

It is vital and urgent that society in South Asia reconciles itself to shed the instrumentalist approach to the news media. It is time to recognise the news media as a market-based business first, second and third with only some default (and not active and institutional) services and courtesies that it can provide to various socially important needs—ranging from supporting democracy by informing citizens. Ironically, this is exactly how the news media industry is treated in the affluent, industrialised capitalist democracies (now almost a global phenomenon)—the very news industry that is often touted as the model of "democratic media"! Ask any western media industry journalist about the 'social service' they provide, and they laugh sarcastically before going on to argue that theirs is not a 'communist system' but "a democracy" (i.e. a capitalist democracy).

The argument is: having recognised the news media as to what it is, one is able to use 'the beast' usefully although not necessarily in the simplistic ways we thought we could. This approach has best served when one acts as an 'intermediary'—where, as an industry journalist, one has to also fulfil the role of a social activist. This role helps social action groups engage with the news media and use its 'default' services for the purposes of their goals and the benefit of their social constituencies.

News Media Industry as a Social Communicator in Sri Lanka

The ideological function of 'constituency' operates very starkly in Sri Lanka and has been noted by the few analysts who have studied the problem. It is, indeed, a big problem.

In Sri Lanka, the news media functions—in terms of industrial size and impact—mainly in the Sinhala and Tamil languages and, hence, the news media 'constituency' architecture comprises discrete audiences as per ethnicity. Thus, we have Tamil news media that caters virtually exclusively to the Tamil-speaking communities and Sinhala news media catering exclusively to the Sinhala communities. When one community is the demographic majority, and the other is the minority, in a competitive capitalist democracy (socialist democracies are not 'competitive' in the same way) there is the continuous competition among political actors for electoral success drawing on base vote banks that comprise ethno-linguistic communities. And, in a developing country like Sri Lanka, there is intense competition for shares in the 'development pie', especially for control of the State that leads 'development'. And the moment the vote bank comprises the numerical ethnic majority, there is an inevitable imbalance between majority and minority (and other socially marginalised sectors like women and lower castes) in that share of the pie.

Hence, there is a critical need for structured multi-culturalism, social pluralism and political devolution in societies like Sri Lanka.

With an understanding of the 'constituency' dynamic in the news media industry, it is easy to see how, parallel to the competitive political mobilisations between ethnic communities for the purposes of elected government, the media adds to the community rivalry by its own industry dynamic of catering to ethno-linguistic audience-markets. The combination is explosive and, in Sri Lanka's case, it has been so due to a long history of the ethnic conflict.

News Media, Ethnic Ideology and Community Perceptions

Ethnic Conflict: Today, such ethnic based 'news communication' is in full maturity and simply the providing of news of events and trends constantly serves to fuel inter-ethnic suspicions and fears. When the Sinhalese are taught in their schools, a majority understanding social history and 'national' political evolution, it is not surprising if, as adults, their social interest in terms of 'news' is framed accordingly. And, it is but logical—in terms of our market-driven industry—to employ Sinhala speaking journalists to cater to Sinhala news audiences and Tamil speaking journalists for Tamil audience. Thus, we have what media studies doyen Arjuna Parakrama calls the 'closed circuit' of linguistic media audiences—the Sinhalese and Tamils live in their own worlds of 'news'.

Perceptions of India: The understanding of 'Sri Lankan' history is replete with spectres of 'Tamil invaders' from across the Palk Straits in South India. The fact that the Sinhalese themselves were 'invaders' from the same origin is ignored by the majority community-precisely because, as the majority, they have dictated what is understood by 'history'.

Hence, India is seen as the source of invasion and intrusion and the source of undermining of 'Sinhala civilisation'. Today, while the European colonial invasion (which is considered to be the really devastating invasions over nearly 500 hundred years) is now a distant memory, the modern ethnic rivalry and conflict and the cultural link of the Tamils with Tamil Nadu and consequent South Indian political dynamics has resulted in the worsening of the 'invader' perception of India.

New Delhi did not help when it, rather simplistically, offered not just sanctuary to Tamils fleeing massive and successive ethnic pogroms but also a hinterland or 'fall-back area' to the Tamil secessionist insurgency. One is aware of the geo-political provocation of J.R. Jayavardhana's equally simplistic pro-West policy in the 1970s and 1980s that prompted Delhi's policy option. However, it is still felt that a more nuanced policy perhaps would not have brought the bitter animosity being witnessed today among the Sinhalese. All that the news media has done is to sell its news to its logical audience and, in terms of capitalist market dynamics, it is news that was produced and multiplied on large scale by rival media outlets all competing for the same linguistic audience. Thus, we cannot be surprised with the kind of media behaviour that we see in relation to India in Sri Lanka today among the Sinhala language news media, and also, to a lesser extent, in the English language news media as well, since the bulk of its audience is also Sinhalese.

NOTES

1. Founded in 2000 in Islamabad, SAFMA has national chapters in all 8 SAARC member states and is affiliated with the SAARC Secretariat. It is an organisation of socially concerned journalists and facilitates joint actions by, and knowledge-building among, the region's journalists about a range of issues from inter-state conflict, ethnic & gender discrimination, and, poverty & development, to nuclear weapons controls, regional trade and, media rights.

14

The Role of Media in Shaping Foreign Policy Discourse in Myanmar

Khin Maung Soe

Myanmar's History: A Brief Introduction

Myanmar (Burma) remained under military rule, although the government held its first elections in 20 years on November 7, 2010. It has been under military rule since 1962, when General Ne Win staged a coup against the democratically elected government led by Prime Minister U Nu, claiming that the military had to step in to save the country from disintegration. After Myanmar's independence from Britain in 1948, the Communist Party of Burma and various ethnic groups took up arms against the central government, despite the introduction of parliamentary democracy. The military sought to achieve national unity, but could only do so by coercion without achieving a viable political solution to deep rooted ethnic conflicts especially in Kachin and Shan states.

When the military assumed power, it abolished democratic institutions and replaced them with the Revolutionary Council, chaired by General Ne Win. The army led the country into isolation, cutting off all contacts with the outside world, driving foreign companies out of the country and nationalising all private enterprises. Many successful entrepreneurs including those of Indian origins were forced to leave the country. In 1974, the junta (military group controlling a government) pushed through a constitutional referendum to transition from direct military rule to indirect military rule. Thereafter, a socialist planned economy and one-party rule by Ne Win's Burma Socialist Program Party (BSPP) resulted in resource-rich Myanmar becoming one of the least-developed countries in the world.

When the country began experiencing serious economic problems, Ne Win stepped down as President and was succeeded in office by his confidante, retired General San Yu. Yet, Ne Win remained chairman of the country's only political party, and continued to play a decisive behind-the-scenes role in formulating governmental policies. In 1988, continued economic problems led to country-wide demonstrations and the collapse of the ruling party. However, the military staged a coup on September 18, 1988, killing thousands of people. General Saw Maung, then commander-in-chief of the defence forces, led the military junta while Ne Win remained influential behind the scenes.

The new military junta promised to hold free elections, which took place in May 1990. The opposition leader, Aung San Suu Kyi, was placed under house arrest while the electoral campaign was underway. However, the elections resulted in her party, the National League for Democracy (NLD), winning more than 80 per cent of the parliamentary seats. Despite this clear victory for the opposition, the army refused to accept the election results and continued to rule the country.

On the economic front, the new junta formally incorporated market economic principles, but in practice continued to control the economy with poorly managed policies. Foreign investors hesitated to invest in the country because of the unstable political situation there (e.g., violent minority conflicts and legal uncertainty) and because of concerns about their public image (e.g., fear of boycotts associated with the regime's human rights violations and repression of the democratic opposition). Investments are primarily concentrated in the natural-resource extraction sectors, especially oil, gas, timber and gems, while other industries have received little attention. While western countries have imposed sanctions on Myanmar for the regime's refusal to democratise; and for its systematic human rights abuses, neighbouring Asian countries (including Thailand, China and Hong Kong) have invested heavily. According to information as of December 31, 2013 by the Directorate of Investment and Company Administration, Ministry of National Planning and Economic Development, there are 10 major countries making foreign investments : (1) China (US$14.2 billion), (2) Thailand (US$10 billion), (3) Hong Kong (US$6.5 billion), (4) UK (US$3.1 billion), (5) Republic of Korea (US$3 billion), (6) Singapore (US$2.8 billion), (7) Malaysia (US$1.6 billion), (8) Vietnam (US$0.5 billion), (9) France (US$0.5 billion), and (10) Japan (US$0.3 billion).

In 1995, Aung San Suu Kyi was released for the first time, but the authorities repeatedly prevented her from leaving the then capital, Yangon (formerly Rangoon), to undertake political activities elsewhere in the country. The opposition leader was placed under house arrest again at the end of 2000 during her attempt to travel outside of Yangon, and was only released again 19 months later. Suu Kyi did not try to travel outside of Yangon for a year after her second release, waiting instead for the junta to accept her proposal for dialogue. When the regime did not respond to her requests, she began travelling to various parts of the country to revitalise her party, and large crowds of people, sometimes numbering in thousands, gathered to see her wherever she went. The military attacked her motorcade on May 30, 2003, killing number of NLD supporters and injuring dozens more. She was imprisoned for three months and then placed back under house arrest. The violent crackdown triggered another outcry of criticism from the international community. The United States imposed an embargo against imported goods from Myanmar, and the European Union imposed the ban on large number of people on the travel list and demanded that all political prisoners be released.

In response to international criticism, the military announced a roadmap to democracy in September 2003, which envisioned a "disciplined democracy" for the future. The government resurrected a constitution-drafting process that had begun in 1993 and come to a halt in 1996. The National Convention, which was convened from 2004 to 2007 in order to draft a new constitution, was given detailed guidelines so as to safeguard the military's dominant position. In response to strong international criticism of the 2007 crackdown against monk-led demonstrations, in which more than 30 people were killed and several hundred arrested, the regime expedited the constitution-drafting process, announcing that the constitutional referendum would be held in 2008 and elections in 2010. In May 2008, the new constitution was ratified with 92.4 per cent of votes polled in a rigged referendum. The new constitution asserts that the head of state must have military experience, allows the military to select three key security ministers, and reserves 25 per cent of all seats in the upper and lower houses of parliament and in the regional and state-level assemblies for the military. In addition, the military leadership is accorded the right to declare a state of emergency and to seize power at any time it deems necessary with the approval of the National Defence and Security Council.

The Government and Media

Myanmar government has abandoned its pre-publication censorship in August 2012 on a number of magazines and newspapers, and issues concerning freedom of the press and freedom of speech are of great interest. News and information from the opposition, led by Aung San Suu Kyi, is now also covered in state-owned media. Her own party, NLD, is running a weekly journal namely *The Wave*. Websites which were previously blocked, such as YouTube, Facebook, and Google, as well as radio stations like RFA (Radio Free Asia), BBC and Voice of America, can now be accessed from within the country. Burma's sudden embrace of democratic reforms has allowed media to operate with relative freedom.

There are estimated to be approximately 1,200-1,500 journalists in Myanmar. The number of media outlets are increasing, with at least 248 weeklies being published (of which 138 are news and current affairs publications). While at present all 6 daily newspapers are owned and controlled by the state, 7 journals run daily newspapers including *The Voice*, *Popular*, *Eleven*, *Yangon Times*, *7 Day*, *Venus News*, and *Myanmar Times*. Radio is the most preferred source of information for the rural population and caters to large number of regular listeners in many cities, although it lacks capacity—both technically and the content side. The 6 semi-state owned FM/AM stations focus on "non-controversial" content such as music and entertainment from private producers. Almost every citizen in Myanmar listens to Voice of America, RFA or BBC for daily news and current affairs. The ban on these radio channels is gradually being lifted and foreign journalists are now allowed to report from Myanmar.

Although internet penetration in Myanmar is less than one per cent, social media such as Facebook and mobile phones are increasingly becoming tools for urban youth to communicate and interact socially. The Information and Communication Technology (ICT) and telecommunications sectors are also expected to experience a major boom within the next two years with the arrival of foreign Information Technology (IT) companies in the country along with new mobile operators like Ooredoo and Telenor from Qatar and Norway.

Because of the new openness: "The voice of the political opposition is being granted more space in the media, and publications are increasingly able to openly discuss government policies. Even the publications allied with or owned by the government are following this trend. The government has begun holding press conferences where media representatives can raise questions. This newfound situation of more openness and a relaxation of censorship pose a challenge for media in Myanmar and the question is whether the media is able to fulfil its role as society's watchdog with no experience to draw on or knowledge of professional ethical standards".[1]

A study shows that the country's young journalists, with an average age of 25, dominate the media and yet are facing considerable challenges. After more than 50 years of government content censorship, the responsibility of monitoring content now lies with the editors rather than the censors. This poses a challenge as many of the young, untrained journalists have little or no formal journalistic experience, and many have little knowledge of professional ethics or to conduct objective journalism. The report urges that it is important to not only support freedom of the press through media law reforms but also to strengthen the media sector and train journalists.

International journalistic professionals recommend that support to the Myanmar media environment is approached through three broad focus areas: (i) Strengthening national capacity to reform media-related policies and legal frameworks and to engage in democratic transition; (ii) Building the foundation for media and journalism to professionalise ("The process could start by identifying individuals, developing their capacity, assisting them in institution building, expanding their networks and building strategic partnerships")[2]; and (iii) Expanding access and outreach of media content to rural areas.

Media's Influence on the Foreign Policy Discourse in Myanmar

Thein Sein was sworn in as the President of the Republic of the Union of Myanmar on March 30, 2011. This reduced the unethical influence and economic, social and cultural invasion of China on its once-pariah state-which has reportedly been one of the priorities of the new government's foreign policy discourse. The assumption was proved to be more than the usual political propaganda.

The golden rule in foreign policy is—do not do to other nations what we do not want others to do to you. There is a growing importance of media in shaping foreign policy discourse in Myanmar. Media includes mass media like TV, news channels, newspapers, Radio, journals, magazines and most importantly, internet and email. The sphere of influence of media is increasing day by day as the coverage of even a small news article is very wide these days.

Media's Role in Shaping Public Opinion in Other Countries

Each country has its own "national media" which could also be thought of as specific "propaganda" aimed at their own domestic audience. It is obvious that each media specifically targets its own audience and caters to the sensibilities and desires of what they think may be of interest to that audience. This is how media survives in a competitive market. Not all audiences are the same. It depends on the credibility of a particular media such as newspapers or TV channels (print, visual and social). If readers (the public, the population) think a particular media is biased or not impartial in presenting the news, its influence on public opinion will only be minimal. In autocratic countries, media can provide a platform for the government for its propaganda. In democracies, majority of the media is usually independent. But even such media have their leaning towards one political or social belief or another. For example, *The New York Times* is in favour of liberal democratic order while the *Fox News* is with conservatives. In most countries, people read all media to have a balanced view on a particular issue. Sometimes, it is downright impossible to make a correct judgment on the media as there are many unseen factors. Now, we have a new media which is social media.

People themselves become citizen journalists and it is harder now for traditional media like newspaper and TV to lie to the public blatantly. If one looks at the history of modern media and its relation to "democracies" it is evident that leaders realised that they could no longer control population by breaking legs, so they became highly refined in shaping the public mind through "propaganda"—a term which has lost its original meaning. One of the pioneers of this, the modern public relations industry, was Edward Bernays, who was active in New York in the 1920s especially—and became an adviser to President Calvin Coolidge. Even Joseph Goebbels of the Nazis used Bernays' ideas to shape the public mind in Germany. It is well understood by the leadership agenda in modern "democracies" that concordant with the inability to break legs, population control is the province of modern media.

Undisciplined "social media" like Facebook opens a whole range of possibilities for spreading wrong stories as we saw in July 2014 in Mandalay when an innocent Muslim man was killed by a thug with a machete-based on a false report of rape by two Muslim brothers (the lady who filed the case admitted she had been paid to do it). The story was posted on a militant monk's website and then propagated furiously by a Burmese man in the US with a large Facebook following.

We live in what is called "The Nation-State System" which dates back to the Treaty of Westphalia of October, 1648. Since then, the old system of a variety of city-states consisting Muslims, Buddhists, Christians, some worshipping other things, approachable by camel or horse back, came to an end as lines were drawn around the world by the great colonial powers of Europe. This later culminated with the horror and conclusions of the two World Wars. Today, nationalism remains a powerful element of control all around the nation-state system—with the US, China, Russia, Japan, Thailand, Vietnam, even places like Bolivia, and New Zealand, India, Pakistan, Afghanistan, Italy—have their distinct "nationalisms". The state-owned media, often, develops a nationalistic agenda—and even privately owned media would necessarily have to keep nationalism in their agenda to boost their business.

Media's Influence on Foreign and Security Policies of States

Governments in every state take note of the opinion of independent and influential journalists in their own countries on security issues. Similarly, media representing the voice of the government is avidly watched by foreign countries to guess the government's stance on certain issue (for instance *The Global Times* of China). Vernacular media catering to the domestic readers often has a profound influence on popular opinion. All policy makers read the newspapers and their policies are influenced by what they read.

Thus, media will continue to influence both foreign policy and security policies of states, more in democracies, and less so in totalitarian regimes. Even in non-democracies, they are able to shape public opinion against the wishes of the government. A case in point is the Myitsone Dam in Myanmar—a 50-storey-tall project planned to be built on the Ayeyarwaddy (Irrawaddy) River by China Power Investment Corporation (CPI). It was expected to produce 6,000 MW of power for export to China, and was the first in a series of seven Chinese dams planned on the Ayeyarwaddy and its tributaries. Since early 2010, affected villagers have highlighted human rights and environmental concerns, including the displacement of 15,000 people and the likelihood of a disastrous break in an earthquake-prone area. The dam project was stalled by the government in the wake of heavy criticism of the policies of the government by the media.

Forces Influencing Media and its Approach to Regional Issues

The people managing media have to carefully look at the audience and its taste. It is well known how Rupert Murdoch created *The Sun* in Britain and nurtured readers with his sensational stories and raised the scale of readership appreciably to attract advertising from business houses.

The Impact of Media Ownership

The ownership of the media does play a role in the way media sets its agenda and conducts itself. People who work for media companies are smart enough to know who their owners are and what their interests are. In the US, for example, General Electric owns the National Broadcasting Corporation (NBC). That is why, there is hardly anything bad about General Electric on NBC. Apart from narrow business interests, it also depends on the owner's political and social belief. For example, the Eleven Media Group in Myanmar is nationalist while *The Voice* is pro-third wave. With the spread of popular awareness in every state, the mainstream media nowadays cannot afford to be too biased and partial. People hate extreme ideas or doctrines.

Role in Promoting Jingoistic Nationalism

One can cite the case of Thailand and Cambodia in this regard. When Thailand was facing internal strife with the red shirts, they cooked up a border conflict with Cambodia in order to divert public attention away from the internal problems. It is somewhat similar to the 9/11 in the US. One can arouse popular sentiments through "manufacturing" tension and insecurity whereby the people of a country inevitably turn towards their government for safety, however horrible the government may be. A case in example are the developments in the wake of the displacement of *Rohingya* communities in Rakhine State of Myanmar. Generally speaking, the media does not oppose regional unity as long as the national interest is not affected.

Role in Promoting Regional Understanding

It needs to be kept in mind that media in most countries in the region cannot transcend the national interest as most newspapers and TV channels are principally for domestic audience. There are exceptions of course, like the 'Channel News Asia' in Singapore, which features stories about countries in the region in English and which can be watched across many countries in the region.

Through good coverage of issues and interviews with experts, one can make a big difference in enhancing public understanding and create popular awareness about important issues being debated at local, regional and international level. The media can follow the trends in regional economic interaction and show how cooperation can benefit one another. It can highlight complementarities among national economies. The AEC (ASEAN Economic Community) in 2015 will reinforce this ideology and dreams envisaged by farsighted leaders in the region.

Media can and should play a vital role in promoting regional understanding by doing, for example, special reports on different countries as they do at the *The Myanmar Times* (the leading English weekly of Myanmar). This gives a chance for foreign ambassadors and their associated business houses to explain to the public the efforts they are making to contribute towards economic development of the host country and the region. Media should resort to innovative ways of showcasing examples of regional cooperation and integration and facilitate interstate understanding and reconciliation.

NOTES

1. An Assessment of Media Development Challenges and Opportunities in Myanmar: Change is in the Air, January 11, 2012, at http://www.comminit.com/node/9287948.
2. Ibid.

15

The Role of Bhutanese Media in Amalgamating South Asia: Quest for a Happy South Asian Society

Dawa Penjor

Introduction

South Asia with a population of more than 1.67 billion people is well endowed with natural resources and human capital to become a leading economic hub in the world. However, there are millions of people still living in extreme poverty. It is a region not just interconnected by land and ocean, but also linked socially, historically, culturally and economically. Yet we do not trust each other or cannot seemingly find a common ground for mutual progress despite creating bodies such as the South Asian Association for Regional Cooperation (SAARC) and having pledged "to work together in a spirit of friendship, trust and understanding" with the aim "to accelerate the process of economic and social development in Member States."

South Asia is known more in the international circle for its ethnic tensions, religious intolerance, and border disputes, terrorism and not to mention the intense rivalry between the two largest nations-India and Pakistan. Over the years, there has been growth in transnational terrorists groups, at times with state patronage. Given the porous borders and linkages amongst the people, political instability or terrorism related violence in one country inevitably has direct adverse effect on the security and wellbeing of the neighbouring states.

The efforts made by the only regional organisation—SAARC—to promote cooperative spirit and bilateral relationships among the member countries for the last two decades are hardly recognised and moreover, many within South Asia believe that the SAARC has functioned more as a talking shop and does not get much done. At the 16th SAARC summit held in Thimphu in 2010, leaders pointed out that, despite having close to 200 meetings a year, the association failed to bear fruits in equal proportion. The Maldivian President, Mohamed Nasheed, in his address at the 16th SAARC summit in Thimphu held India and Pakistan responsible for the slow progress in regional cooperation.

Consequently, due to the lukewarm relations within the region and also owing to the political tension between India and Pakistan, the performance of not just SAARC, but other regional initiatives like Bay of Bengal Initiative for Multi-sectorial Technical and Economic Cooperation (BIMSTEC) and Mekong-Ganga Cooperation (MGC) are also affected.

At the same time, a close examination of the political dynamics of various states in South Asia reveals that the internal problems and issues are more critical than the regional ones. And most of these problems and issues originate either from state's inability to resolve issues of political grievances or economic aspirations.

However, one of the positive aspects for the region is its democratic evolution. The entire region now lives within civilian-led democracies. In between January 2013 to August 2014, six out of seven South Asian countries have voted for new leaders and political parties responsive to the will of their people. Fundamental human rights, accountability and transparency in governance are no longer mere concepts of political parlance and a text used to eyewash human rights watchdogs; these are today enshrined in the constitutions of the entire South Asian countries. With democracy taking stronger roots than before, it is hoped that the elected governments would take the right steps for good governance and economic development to cater to the demands of the constituents they represent.

Traditionally, media in South Asia is viewed as polarised and as an institution that is either marshalled in to serve the state or the leaders, and in recent decades, the market-state. Media has been at the forefront in transforming South Asia and showcasing to the world its triumphs and challenges. Democracy and media go hand in hand. With democracy, the number of media has exponentially grown and today, the citizens of South Asian states enjoy better access to information and their capacity to communicate and express themselves has leap frogged than a decade ago. The access to information has been fuelled by the booming of the traditional media, and further accelerated by satellite TV since the 1990s and now, with social media, it has grown by leaps and bounds.

Further, with the onset of democracy, it is not just the journalists and politicians but the common mass that has been harnessing the power of media to voice their concerns and keep the government accountable. At the same time, there has been a rapid change in the way media is regulated. Newsprints once controlled by national governments are witnessing greater deregulation and the private papers are hailed better in content than the state-owned. Even the rights to broadcast over the radio have been deregulated in Nepal; but in most other South Asian countries, governments still retain the final broadcasting rights.

The media landscape of South Asia presents diversity in ownerships, ranging from private, political and governmental, to that of religion and faith-based. The structure of the media domain and its institutional characteristics in South Asia has been heavily influenced by state and public policy.

As per the 2014 freedom of the press index compiled by Reporters without Borders, the levels of freedom experienced by print and broadcast media amongst the South Asian nations vary from 'noticeable problem' to 'difficult situation'. Bhutan enjoys the top most freedom index at 92 and Sri Lanka the least at 165 out of 180 nations worldwide.

Although the number of media outlets continues to grow, South Asia is rated as one of the most dangerous work region for journalists. Violence against media personnel and impunity against perpetrators continue to remain a major threat to media freedom. The recently published South Asia Media Monitor Report states that in 2012, at least 22 journalists lost their lives in the line of duty. The highest number of journalists killed were in Pakistan at 10, followed by 8 in India, 3 in Afghanistan and 1 in Bangladesh. "Courtesy of these killings, Pakistan and India have made it to the shameful club of the world's five deadliest countries for the media," the report noted.

Even though the media and number of journalists have expanded, it has not contributed to wider coverage of South Asia news; paradoxically, it has contributed to higher localisation. The few regional news are either unbalanced, biased or sensational. At the same time, one of the greatest challenges media faces in South Asia is the professional capacity of the journalists to provide quality reporting and independent news. Only a minority of the several thousand working journalists throughout the region is considered competent and professionally qualified. The regional media houses' investment in learning journalism and awareness on what it means to be journalists, is feeble.

Why Media Matters in South Asia?

South Asia has far more reason to work together towards a common future, since people and states are intertwined and destined by geography, culture and history. In many ways, our countries stand at a critical threshold, and an assessment of the numerous past and ongoing conflicts suggests that war and violence has never resolved issues in South Asia. It has only made the states adopt cautious policies towards the problem of regional integration. South Asian countries should learn from their past mistakes and move towards dialogue and discussion and have patience while striving for peaceful settlement of various disputes.

Our region ranks low on every human development indicator in comparison to other regions like East Asia or even Southeast Asia. Unless South Asian nations reset their policies and priorities, reconcile with their past and settle their disputes, our hope to see an economically prosperous region with improved human development index rankings would remain a mere dream.

Therefore, the role of media in the South Asian countries becomes crucial to envision a common regional future of greater economic cooperation and political stability. It is in this context that media can play an instrumental role in promoting cooperation and transforming mind-sets and hearts to bring in regional harmony and progress.

The media should strive to build a peaceful and stable neighbourhood, and groups like South Asian Free Media Association (SAFMA) should be more active and vibrant in building peaceful and mutually beneficial relations between neighbours. This is an issue of critical importance since in the absence of peace and harmony, our efforts to strengthen economic cooperation would be futile. Therefore, a peaceful and stable neighbourhood should be our topmost foreign policy goal and also, that of the media.

Till date, the efforts of SAFMA have been limited to carrying out exchanges within the region-editors, journalists, parliamentarians and academics. Being a well-established institution, SAFMA's objectives could go beyond media and journalistic exchange. The focus of SAFMA could shift to include exchange and interaction for students, scholars, researchers, artists from the region so they can understand and learn from each other and use the media as a channel to bridge differences among populations and states.

Recognising the crucial role that the media plays in conflict situations, South Asian media should adopt "peace journalism" as proposed by Johan Galtung, a Norwegian sociologist and the principal founder of the peace and conflict studies discipline. Peace journalism avoids giving undue attention to violence, instead focuses on the impact of war on communities on both sides of the divide and their efforts to bridge their differences.

It is important for media to conceptualise South Asia as a 'region' and emphasise the common challenges that confront its people and states. Instead of presenting only the negativities, the media must bring out the best practices from within the South Asian states to be recognised and build upon to further the region's common vision and address these challenges. There are several doable ideas to boost inter-state cooperation and people-to-people relations. The governments should relax visa regimes, facilitate media-to-media, journalist-to-journalist and journalist-to-people contacts and encourage exchanges in areas like culture, arts and cinema.

Recently, some commendable efforts in building bilateral relations have been made by Indian and Pakistani media and individuals. *Aman ki Asha* (A Hope for Peace) is a joint initiative made by *Jang* and *Times of India*, two of the largest media groups on either side of the border in the year 2010. They created a platform to foster people-to-people movement and rebuilt the ancient bonds among the people of these two nations to look beyond the 60-year-old political boundary and rivalry. Another initiative worth mentioning is Romancing the Borders (RTB), a platform on the social media site Facebook for people-to-people movement in 2012 created by Shirin and Rehman, an Indian and a Pakistani University student.

The Bhutanese Media Landscape

Compared to the media in other countries in South Asia, the media in Bhutan is a fairly young development. The concept of the media, as a player in the growth of a modern society began in the mid-1960s, with the establishment of the first Bhutanese newspaper, *Kuensel* in 1965 and the Bhutan Broadcasting Radio Station (then known as Radio NYAB—National Youth Association of Bhutan) in 1973.

Ever since Bhutan joined the global village through TV and internet in 1999, there has been a rapid growth in the number of print, audio and visual media, and entertainment industry. For a population of 6, 34,982 (Population and Housing Census, 2005), Bhutan's media environment is relatively vibrant.

With the liberalisation of media licensing after the enactment of the Bhutan Information, Communication and Media Act in 2006 and establishment of the Bhutan InfoComm and Media Authority (BICMA), there has been growth of several private media houses. Today, besides free access to numerous international media via internet and Cable TV, the people of Bhutan have the choice of 11 newspapers and 5 radio stations. While the BBS (Bhutan Broadcasting Service) and Kuzoo FM radio services have a nationwide reach, the remaining radios are available only in Thimphu. Magazines range from news to entertainment and travel.

Currently, BBS TV is the only Bhutanese television channel that provides news and programmes in Bhutan. The BBS launched its satellite television service in February 2006 and is now available in more than 40 Asian countries.

The Bhutanese film industry is still in its infancy and emulates Bollywood or Hollywood style. The number of Bhutanese films has been increasing over the years ever since the first Bhutanese commercial movie was produced in 1989.

Further, with the introduction of cellular mobile phone in 2005, communication and access to media has been revolutionised. In recent years, social media has gained popularity with an increasing number of Bhutanese on social networking sites like Facebook, Twitter, YouTube and Google+, accessing them either for news and information or interaction and discussion among others. Facebook has more than 80,000 Bhutanese and is the most accessed social media site in Bhutan.

With the change in media landscape, Bhutan is witnessing immense changes in the ways citizens are informed, government and corporations are made accountable, and societies fulfil their potential in politics, economy, social fabric and every other aspect of life.

Since 2006, media has had a major impact on the evolution of Bhutan's democracy, formulation and implementation of government laws and policies, disclosure of corruption, changing individual mind-set and system of governance. For example, due to media's reports, the government repelled tax proposals, amended the draconian Tobacco Act that criminalised an unhealthy habit, and helped introduce Right to Information Bill (2015) and retracted its policy to lower tourism tariff to generate higher tourism numbers.

The biggest and far reaching impact of the media has been in providing voices to the ordinary and fostering democratic mind-set among the Bhutanese. As per the Media Impact Study, 2013, the top three media that influenced people's decision on choosing elected representatives were the state financed BBS TV (48 per cent) followed by Bhutanese Radio (35 per cent) and Bhutanese Newspapers (11 per cent). Thus, statistics show that Television is the most preferred media that influenced people's electoral decisions.

However, one of the biggest flaws in the development of the Bhutanese media is its rural representation and reach. The Bhutan Information and Media Impact Study, 2013, finding notes that the difference in access to media between urban and rural settings is a significant issue. Only two radio stations, one TV station and one newspaper have nationwide coverage. Although the number of TV sets in the country has increased from 47,125 in 2008 to 74,836, the same study found that while 86.8 per cent of urban households have access to TV, only 43.9 per cent of rural households do. Only 23 per cent of survey respondents had access to the internet.

The rapid growth in the number of media outlets has been good for the evolution of democracy, and in projecting Bhutan as a free, plural and vibrant society. However, a serious scrutiny reveals a society bombarded with a large number of media outlets with questionable quality. Some sections of the society already feel that there is a serious disconnect between the liberal issue of newspaper licenses and the actual need. While a plural media guarantees multiple perspectives to issues in the public domain and stimulates exchange of ideas amongst diverse constituencies, in turn irresponsible and unprofessional media can ruin societies and crumble nations.

Independent and non-profit organisations, such as the Journalists' Association of Bhutan (2006) and Bhutan Media Foundation (2010) were established to develop professionalism and uphold the interests of media and journalists across the country and protect freedom and rights of the media.

However, owing to the weak Bhutanese economic climate, the financial sustainability of media companies remains a major challenge. To make matters worse, the media is overly dependent on government advertisements and public service announcements. An estimated 80 per cent of the revenue of the Bhutanese media is derived from advertising distributed by the government agencies. Currently, with the government adopting austerity measures, almost all the private media houses had to downsize by 50-60 per cent and some publish only when they receive advertisements. Such unhealthy trends could be detrimental to Bhutan's young democracy. Therefore, the government should be careful in implementing its media policies as media is the only thread connecting the people and the government.

Bhutan in South Asian Media and South Asia in Bhutanese Media

Bhutan seldom features in the South Asian region news streams. The stories from Bhutan that emerge in the South Asian media are either event based or about our pursuit of the Gross National Happiness. At the same time, South Asia features erratically in the Bhutanese media. Overall, the media content is more local than global.

Bhutan receives little coverage in the South Asian media. Unfortunately, even this limited coverage is full of biased opinions and does not speak too well of Bhutan and its governance. As far as the Bhutanese media is concerned, it has been reporting stories on South Asia with much sensitivity towards promoting peace, stability, amity and progress. Similarly, South Asian media should also adopt unbiased attitude in depicting Bhutan as a flourishing nation.

Media influence on foreign or domestic policies are more indirect in nature. Media do not necessarily influence policymakers directly, but may shape public opinion—what people know and want from foreign politics.

Large number of media reports in the past on 'People in the Camps' from the Nepalese media, especially those with vested interest have tried their best to paint Bhutan in a poor light despite Bhutan government's invitation to foreign media to visit and get first-hand information on the issue. There is a lot of misinformation. All reports need not be positive, but they should be factually accurate, objective, well-researched and well-written. Media reports overseas are picking up what they see in the regional media, including misreporting and misinformation. Most stories in this regard are far-fetched, the latest being that they are freedom fighters trying to establish democracy in Bhutan. The problem is that people around the world, who cannot find South Asia on the map, leave alone Bhutan, are beginning to believe such reports. These reports only fanned the flames of discord by taking sides, reinforcing prejudices, muddling the facts and peddling half-truths. Instead, the Bhutan and Nepal media must look beyond the 'People in the Camps' problem and strengthen bilateral relations and foster economic, tourism and cultural relations. The issue of illegal immigration and illegal incursion is not just confined to Bhutan. Most of the nations in South Asia have or are experiencing similar challenges and it is essential that the media does its best to produce balanced reports.

During Bhutan's 2013 general elections, we had an influx of reports from Indian media on different issues concerning Bhutan. The headlines ranged from Chinese incursion into the Bhutanese border and setting up camps, to removal of Kerosene and LPG (Liquefied Petroleum Gas) subsidy by the Indian government and non-payment of excise duty refund and scrapping subsidy on power generated from Chukha Hydro Power by the Indian Government, to our former Prime Minister Jigme Yoezer Thinley warming up to Chinese leaders during the Rio Summit of 2012 which apparently irked New Delhi. We do not know if these reports were deliberate or ill-timed, but it was looked upon by the Bhutanese intelligentsia as unwelcome.

The recent Indian media's reports have given many Bhutanese, from farmers to the bureaucrats, the impetus to view the Indo-Bhutan dependency relationship in the geopolitical context of India-Bhutan-China and the need to balance the nature of Bhutan's relations with India vis-à-vis China. This is evident from the opinions from numerous Bhutanese in the newspapers and online blogs. Such things were uncommon in the past. Besides India, Bhutan is the only country that has unresolved border with China. The Bhutanese are in favour of resolving the issue with China amicably without further delay so that Bhutan has a peaceful boundary with its northern neighbour as it does with India. Therefore, Indian media and politicians should uphold the revised Indo-Bhutan Friendship Treaty of 1949 in 2007 where the preamble of the Treaty clearly states the mutual reaffirmation of sovereignty and territorial integrity.

Bhutan and India have greater mutual interest that far exceeds the 'good neighbour policy' as we are strategic partners in development of economy and security. In the words of Bhutan's Prime Minister, Tshering Tobgay "good relations with India are the cornerstone of our foreign policy". So, it is certain that Bhutan would not at any cost jeopardise the Indo-Bhutan relationship that we have built over the past 45 years, as it would be a costly affair for both nations.

On the security level, we often have the Indian media reporting on re-entrenchment of Assamese and other north-eastern rebel groups within Bhutan despite Bhutan government's repeated reassurance that the existence of militants in the region not only undermines "the peace, stability and socio-economic development enjoyed by the Bhutanese people", but also "threatens the very sovereignty of the country". It is a matter of great concern to both governments and the Royal Bhutan government will not hesitate to act on the Indian insurgent groups in its southern borders similar to the action undertaken in 2003.

The media on both sides of the nation should provide a discourse to take our relationship further and look at 'win-win framework' or mutually beneficial schemes, and persuade establishment of a balanced and healthy economic interdependency between the two nations. If policymakers want to take advantage of the media's power to create communities, cooperation is a better approach than competition, and the media becomes relevant tool of foreign politics.

Media from Assam and Bangladesh often blames Bhutan for releasing the water from our hydro-power dams in the plains without advance warning and for the resulting floods. Such biased and factually incorrect reports create negativity in the minds of the people who are affected by such disasters and would develop ill-will for Bhutan. Instead, India, Bhutan, and Bangladesh media should work together to make our governments streamline policies and adopt joint media strategy to mitigate the impact of climate change in the sub-continent. This is important as Assam in India and Bangladesh, as lower riparian, would be severely affected by flash floods emanating from the glaciers of Bhutan.

In the last two years, there has been surge of border kidnapping of Bhutanese citizens by people from Assam. This is becoming a serious concern for people living on the border with India and causing uneasiness. However, it is only the Bhutanese media that reports these kidnappings and none of the Indian media carries such stories. The issue is not just confined to kidnapping, even human trafficking, drug trafficking, smuggling and flesh trade are rampant on the borders. The media on both sides of the border should consider joint investigative stories on these issues and pursue both governments to take actions to prevent such incidents.

Gross National Happiness

Since the late 1970s, Bhutan, a small country, dared to be different, offering the international community the concept of 'Gross National Happiness (GNH)'—a higher goal for human development and well-being at a time when the whole world is after the pursuit of material development that has had a tragic impact on the environment and climate.

It was in 1979, when the Fourth King of Bhutan, Jigme Singye Wangchuck landed in present day Mumbai, after attending the Non Aligned Summit in Havana. Indian journalists interviewed him at the airport and one of them asked: "We are your closest neighbour and yet we know nothing about Bhutan. For example, what is your GNP?" Then came the historic words: "We are not concerned about Gross National Product, we care about Gross National Happiness". Thereafter, the concept of GNH became an overnight headline, and academics and policy makers started to work on the concept.

Therefore, it is important to peel the profundity of the King's statement to understand GNH in its true sense. His Majesty firmly believed that happiness is an indicator, a signifier, and a sign of good development and good society. GNH was provided as a guiding philosophy for societal transformation and an alternative to the singular pursuit of economic development. It is development with values. Enhancing happiness forever is the Bhutanese constitutional pledge and it is the responsibility of the state or the government to create a conducive environment for citizens to pursue collective happiness.

GNH does not seek to devalue, demean or ridicule the natural materialist impulse in human aspirations, rather the goal is to find the right balance between the material and the spiritual; between economic growth and natural resource sustainability; between modernisation and preservation; and promotion of culture and traditional values.

Based on these considerations, the Royal Government of Bhutan has established a four-pronged strategy known as the four pillars of GNH that facilitate the pursuit and attainment of positive transformation. The four pillars are: (i) sustainable and equitable socio-economic development; (ii) conservation of environment; (iii) preservation and promotion of culture; and (iv) good governance.

Further, in July 2011, Bhutan proposed to the United Nations a resolution on Happiness as a more holistic development goal, and this was supported by every member of the United Nations. In October 2012, the United Nations declared March 20 as the International Day of Happiness. It is a big accolade for GNH and Bhutan. GNH is a well-researched and well received concept for growth and development and the South Asian nations could collectively pursue GNH.

South Asian Media Inspired by GNH

GNH is proposed for the South Asian media and journalists as a higher goal that makes them achieve their true purpose of existence. It is not a proposal for the media to carry happy or pleasant stories all the time but rather the necessity of making the media more conscious and reflective of the principles and values in their everyday work. Therefore, one can ask whether a model for media embedded in GNH values and principles can be developed. Can the South Asian media set a better example when the global media is busy disseminating unhappiness, characterised by consumerism, commercialism, sensationalism, corruption and lack of professionalism? Can South Asian media learn to treat their audience as people first and not consumers? So, how do we go about building a South Asian community where people and state can pursue GNH?

Currently, most of the media in South Asia focusses on the lucrative urban audience and neglect rural population where the majority of the people reside. Similar to media outlets in other parts of the world, media organisations in South Asia are also consumed by commercialism, concerned about generating profits as an end goal. Just as GNH is a response to globalisation and global interpretations of development, the media has the responsibility to resist and provide alternatives to global trends in the media. South Asian media needs to seriously commit to public service obligations and help citizens understand the aspirations of a society and pursue contentment of the people as the end goal of economic, political and social development.

A critical element of GNH media is the empowerment of the citizen, which is also the basis of democracy. It is not just providing access to information, but enabling the citizen to make reasoned decisions at the individual, community and national level. Citizens on their part must understand, analyse, evaluate and be able to control media products as well as contribute to the development of media industry in a way the society aspires.

Conclusion

To deliver a media based on GNH is not as simple as one might wish it to be. At the same time, it is not something that can never be achieved. It is the government's responsibility to identify policies that strengthen the public interest, maximise civic engagement, and make the most of the potential of innovation in media for the public good. And it is the duty of media owners and professionals to ensure that the media houses are run professionally so that they promote, respect and adhere to the fundamental principles and global standards of journalistic practice. It is necessary that media be run by trained professionals and be held accountable by common standards of journalistic practice and codes of conduct. Journalist associations, associations of editors, press clubs can help ensure the standard of professionalism in media and prevent media from indulging in undesired practices.

Therefore, our governments should invest in building a pool of trained media professionals to be able to deliver our aspirations. The governments should be able to commit certain portion of the public taxes for promoting the media and at the same time, adopt a policy of non-interference in the management and operation of the media house. Further, the South Asian nations should come together to establish a South Asian media and journalism award to recognise and honour media and media professionals that have been instrumental in promoting regional peace, stability and progress and endeavour towards building better South Asian relations. The South Asian nations should commit to provide the media and journalist the safe environment to practice their profession. The states should institute laws that guarantee the rights of the media and journalists and take quick and judicious action against those who try to silence or muzzle the media.

With internet and technology, the media landscape is changing at a greater speed than one could imagine. Internet has proven to be a much more democratic medium than newspapers or television, allowing a freer information dissemination and exchange of views for a larger number of audience. Therefore, our nations should come together to harness the power of the internet and develop prototypes to build ONE South Asia media that would minimise our differences and create harmony and peace and promote human progress within our nations.

REFERENCES

1. C. Arpi, "Chinese incursions: Bhutan suffers alongside India", October 14, 2013, at http://www.niticentral.com/2013/10/14/chinese-incursions-bhutan-suffersalongside-india-145505.html.
2. S.K. Datta-Ray, "A Distance Bugle-India's Bhutan policy must be far more nuanced from now on", *The Telegraph*, Kolkata, July 20, 2013, at http:// www.telegraphindia.com/1130720/jsp/opinion/story_17134356.jsp#.VEoTIYep38s.
3. K. Dorji, "India-Bhutan: A Model of Friendship", Institute of Peace and Conflict Studies, at http://www.ipcs.org/article/india/india-bhutan-a-model-of-friendship-3994.htm.
4. K. Dorji and S.S. Pek-Dorji, "The Media in Bhutan in the service of the public", 2nd Conference on Gross National Happiness, Centre for Bhutan Studies, Thimphu, Bhutan, 2005.
5. Y. Dorji, "Indo-Bhutan Relations: A Reality Check-I, II, III & IV", August 27, 2013, at http://yesheydorji.blogspot.in/search/label/International%20Relations.
6. S. Dikshit, "Fuel subsidy cut a 'goof-up' but Bhutan result 'unaffected'", *The Hindu*, Chennai, July 16, 2013, at http://www.thehindu.com/news/national/fuelsubsidy-cut-a-goofup-but-bhutan-result-unaffected/article4918291.ece.
7. "How India is losing Bhutan, its last 'friend' in South Asia", *Firstpost World*, July 9, 2013, at http://www.firstpost.com/world/how-india-is-losing-bhutan-its-lastfriendin-south-asia-942269.html.
8. S. Gosh, "Understanding India-Bhutan relations", *One India News*, June 18, 2014, at http://news.oneindia.in/feature/understanding-india-bhutanrelations-1467521.html.
9. "India Bhutan China Strategic Triangle", *Gurkha International*, at http:// www.gurkha.com.hk/index.php/seatank-limited/shipping-information/53-indiabhutan-china-strategic-triangle.
10. W. Sangye, "The after effects of Indian intervention in Bhutan Election", at http://wangchasangey.blogspot.in/2013/08/the-after-effects-of-indian_8.html.
11. *South Asia Media Monitor 2012*, at http://www.southasianmedia.net.
12. K. Tshering, "Curse of the middle kingdom on Indo-Bhutan friendship", at https://www.bhutantimes.com/2013/06/curse-of-the-middle-kingdom-on-indo-bhutanfriendship.
13. "India, Bhutan sign friendship treaty", *IANS*, February 9, 2007, at http:// www.hindustantimes.com/world-news/india-bhutan-sign-friendship-treaty/ article1-193104.aspx.
14. "Conflict, Media and Human Rights in South Asia"—Report from a Roundtable, International Council on Human Rights Policy, 2011, at http://www.ichrp.org/files/ assets/260/south_asia_roundtable_report.pdf.
15. Anand Kumar, "The Terror Challenge in South Asia and Prospect of Regional Cooperation", Institute for Defence Studies and Analyses, New Delhi, at http:// www.idsa.in/system/files/Book_TerrorChallengesSouthAsia.pdf.
16. Proceedings of the Second International Seminar on "Bhutan Studies, Media and Public Culture", June 2006, at http://www.bhutanstudies.org.bt/media-and-public-culture/?print=pdf.
17. D. Mitra, "'Yam' Between Two Boulders: Re-Assessing India-Bhutan Relationship",

Jadavpur Journal of International Relations, 2013, at http://jnr.sagepub.com/ content/17/2/185.

18. K.T. Ngyamtso, "India-Bhutan Relations-Sailing in Trouble Waters", *Kuensel,* July 10, 2013, at http://www.kuenselonline.com/bhutan-india-relations-sailing-introubled-waters/#.VEoLs4ep38s.
19. S. S. Pek-Dorji, "Engaging in the realm of ideas", 2010, at http://www.indiaseminar.com/2010/614/614_siok_sian_pek_dorji.htm.
20. S. S. Pek-Dorji, "Opening the Gates in Bhutan: Media Gatekeepers and the Agenda of Change", November 2007, at http://www.bhutanstudies.org.bt/publicationFiles/ConferenceProceedings/3rdGNH/7.3rdGNH.pdf.
21. K. Pradhan, "Bhutan Happy? Not when India is leaning so hard", *Times of India,* July 11, 2013, at http://timesofindia.indiatimes.com/world/south-asia/Bhutan-Happy-Not-whenIndia-is-leaning-so-hard/articleshow/21010529.cms.
22. P. Stobdan, *India and Bhutan: The Strategic Imperative*, Institute for Defence Studies and Analyses, New Delhi, India, 2014, at http://www.idsa.in/occasionalpapers/OP_Indiaand Bhutan_pstobdan_260914.html.
23. S. Tamang, "LPG/Kerosene subsidy: What is it about?", July 10, 2013, at http://sangpatamang.blogspot.com.
24. N. S. Tere, "Bridging Barriers: Media and Citizen Diplomacy in India-Pakistan Relations", at http://www.academia.edu/3692462/ Bridging_Barriers_Media_and_Citizen_Diplomacy_in_India-Pakistan_Relations.
25. *The Media Impact Study*, Department of Information and Media, Ministry of Information and Communications, Royal Government of Bhutan, 2013.
26. J. Y. Thinley, "A vision of common purpose", 2010, at http://www.indiaseminar.com/2010/614/614_jigmi_y_thinley.htm.
27. "Treaty of Friendship between India and Bhutan", UNHCR, at http:// www.refworld.org/docid/3ae6b4d620.html.
28. K. Ura, "Measuring happiness", 2010, at http://www.india-seminar.com/ 2010/614/614_karma_ura.html.
29. S. Verma, "Bhutan Elections: A case of India's diplomatic bankruptcy", *South Asia Citizen Web*, July 21, 2013, at http://www.sacw.net/article5100.html.
30. L. Zongyi, "New Delhi sees Bhutan as little more than potential protectorate", *Global Times*, Beijing, August 14, 2013, at http://www.globaltimes.cn/content/ 801348.shtml.
31. "Reporters Without Borders", World Press Freedom Index 2015, at https://index.rsf.org/#!/.
32. "Bhutan Chapter launched South Asia Media Monitor 2012 reports", *Bhutan Observer,* December 31, 2012, at http://bhutanobserver.bt/1276-bo-news-about-bhutan_chapter_launched_south_asia_media_monitor_2012_reports.aspx.

16

The Role of Media in Shaping Foreign Policy Discourse in Nepal

Deepak Adhikari

Introduction

Nepal today stands at a very critical juncture of its history. It is in a prolonged process of charting a political future. Since the end of the Maoist insurgency in 2006, Nepal has been struggling to draft a constitution through a Constituent Assembly and complete the peace process. After a long gap, the constitution was finally promulgated in September 2015. Surrounded by two giant neighbours, India and China, Nepal is also on the cusp of redefining its foreign policy aimed at strengthening its ties in the immediate neighbourhood and expanding its reach in the larger world community.

Over the years, Nepal's news media, whose professional journey began only in the early 1990s following the restoration of democracy, have been at the vanguard of the country's quest for democracy and stability. This paper attempts to explore the role of news media in shaping foreign policy discourse in Nepal. While an attempt to trace out the history of Nepal's foreign policy and the influences of the media in formulating it is well within the scope of the paper, it primarily focuses on more recent developments.

In this context, the essence of this paper is that Nepal's news media has played a significant role in shaping and influencing foreign policy discourse and debate in the country. But the fact remains, it is still a young industry and its members who are learning on the job have a long way to go in delivering its full impact. The Nepali news media has failed to engage readers through reportages on foreign policy issues. It has also shied away from publishing more rigorous, well-researched opinion pieces that help policymakers see things from new, fresh perspectives.

Though the two neighbours get lion's share of coverage in Nepal's news media, it has hardly gone beyond covering bilateral visits, parliamentary hearings of the ambassadors—designate and activities of the foreign missions. But as was apparent during the recent visit of Indian Prime Minister, Narendra Modi, Nepali news media can play a positive role in dispelling distrust and building cordial relations. In this regard, the paper also examines how the Nepali news media shaped opinions and helped allay fears about the deals between India and Nepal after Modi's maiden trip to the country.

Given the absence of similar studies in Nepal, this paper draws from the authors' experience of working at Nepal's leading news publications for more than a decade and writing for international outlets on the geopolitics for past 4-5 years. The paper also purports to incorporate studies based on the coverage of the Mahakali Treaty and the Power Trade Agreement between Nepal and India. This sheds light on how the news of the two deals were played out in the Nepali news media and the role it played in shaping the foreign policy discourse. Nepali news media's impact on Nepal's foreign policy mandarins and the public is huge, but it is yet to exploit the full potential when it comes to influencing foreign policy in the country.

Covering Shital Niwas[1]

The restoration of democracy in 1990, after three-decades of the king-led Panchayat autocracy, heralded a new era of professional news media in Nepal. During the Panchayat years, most of the media was controlled by the state: *Gorkhapatra*, *The Rising Nepal*, Nepal Television and Radio Nepal (Indeed, it is very rare for the government now to run all three news media). In contrast, there were popular weeklies supported by then underground political parties. These tabloids in Nepali language had a cult following and played crucial role in garnering support and mobilising masses against the regime. Their journalism essentially that of dissent had a name: mission journalism.

In early 1990s, after promulgation of constitution that guaranteed press freedom and freedom of expression, among others, a number of media groups were set up, allowing for the first time in Nepal's history, independent and professional voices. The Kantipur Publications, one of the major ventures set up in 1993 by an Indian-origin businessman (later two Nepali businessmen bought it from the Indian owners) took the lead by publishing Nepali and English broadsheet dailies: *Kantipur* and *The Kathmandu Post.* Soon, other media houses followed. But some of them folded after a few years.[2] They could not survive because the market was not ready for a proliferation yet. It was a new world and there was excitement and elan. However, mere enthusiasm could not sustain a business that required huge financial investment, trained and skilled professionals and a substantial readership.

The rest of the news media that survived rarely prioritised the foreign affairs beat amid the plethora of issues—burgeoning identity politics, corruption, water resources, parliament and political protests that consumed the journalists. During the mid-1990s, these papers covered Nepal's foreign policies but there was not a single reporter assigned to report on it. He or she had to juggle several areas including politics.

The foreign affairs reporting evolved in the late 1990s following the extensive coverage of Bhutanese refugees, who were expelled from Bhutan in late 1980s and early 1990s.[3] This was the first time Nepal had received such huge influx of refugees. Naturally, the news media focused on the issue. By late 1990s, with the refugees protesting in Kathmandu and in eastern Nepal (over 1,00,000 refugees lived in the UN-managed camps in Jhapa and Morang districts), this received widespread coverage in the mainstream Nepali news media. Journalists from Kathmandu descended upon the camps and filed dispatches on the plights of refugees. The bilateral meetings were going on between Bhutan and Nepal to resolve the issue and this naturally remained a crucial topic. India, by virtue of being the country whose land was used to transport the Nepali-speaking refugees from the Indo-Bhutan border to Kakarbhitta, on the Nepal-India border, held centre stage in the coverage.

Most media houses entrusted the reporters who covered the refugee issues (while the Tibetan refugees had begun to arrive in Nepal since 1950s, the focus remains on the Bhutanese, partly due to their Nepali-origin) with more ambitious topics such as SAARC (South Asian Association for Regional Cooperation) and bilateral relations, which particularly focused on India-Nepal relations.[4]

While this was institutional attempt at diversifying coverage and accord significance to an important aspect of Nepal's diplomatic overtures, there were also individuals who began to write on the foreign policy issues. A veteran foreign correspondent credited Manoranjan Joshi (known as M.R. Josse) for a pioneering work on Nepal's foreign affairs. Josse wrote a column on foreign affairs first in *The Rising Nepal*, where he worked in late 1980s and later in *The Independent* (now defunct English weekly) which he founded in early 1990s.[5]

By early 2000s, *Kantipur* and *The Kathmandu Post* had assigned one reporter each to cover foreign affairs. Nepali news media has not gone beyond covering bilateral visits, parliamentary hearing of the ambassadors—designate and activities of the foreign missions. The first generation of foreign affairs reporters usually came with a degree in English literature or from English medium boarding school background. They mostly reported on bilateral visits, foreign missions' activities and the appointments of ambassadors.

Foreign affairs in Nepalese media gained some momentum in January 2002 when Nepal hosted the 11th SAARC Summit in Kathmandu. Around this time, the Bhutanese refugee issue, now over a decade-old, reached a new stage. In the tenth round of ministerial talks between the two countries in December 2000, it was agreed that a Joint Verification Team (JVT), comprising representatives of both countries would verify and categorise the refugees.[6] While this was not the best of the solutions, it was something close to the Thimphu mandarins who had come to resolve the protracted crisis. In June 2003, the Bhutanese delegates came under attack by the refugees, leading them to abandon the process citing safety concerns. This issue was widely covered by Nepali media, which helped shape opinions about the problem.

In early 2005, Kantipur Publications decided to set up a bureau in New Delhi, becoming the first Nepali media house to open such office in a foreign country.[7] *The Kathmandu Post* reporter, Surendra Phuyal, became the first bureau chief (although it is a one-person bureau) and the media house has maintained it ever since. This showed how, despite severe limitations at home, the Nepali news media has been trying to reach out beyond borders to get on-the ground reports from its correspondents. Soon, a few media houses followed suit, but they have not been able to have a permanent presence.

A Tale of Two Deals

Today, the second generation of Nepali reporters has taken over the 'foreign affairs beat'. Almost every major daily newspaper and most television channels and Kathmandu-based FM radios have a diplomatic correspondent. The group even has a loose network called Diplomatic Correspondents of Nepal. The issues related to foreign affairs, if not foreign policy, get ample media coverage. How did this come about? What are the factors that pushed Nepali media in this direction? How did this evolve over the years? To answer these questions, it would require a retrospective view. Perhaps a comparative analysis between the coverage of Mahakali Treaty in the mid-1990s and the Power Trade Agreement (PTA) between Nepal and India in 2014 helps us understand the trajectories. The Mahakali Treaty, signed by the Foreign Ministers of India and Nepal on January 29, 1996 became an issue that provoked passions of nationalism coupled with the lingering doubts about the past water sharing treaties (the Gandak and Kosi Treaties with India in the 1950s and 1960s). The treaty was ratified by two third of the parliament to fulfil the requirement of the constitution's Article 126.

First, it is useful to provide some background on how the two countries struck the pact.[8] In 1991, Girija Prasad Koirala, the then Prime Minister, agreed to allow India to complete a left afflux bund on Tanakpur barrage in western Nepal, which lies within the Nepali territory. When faced by the media and opposition, Koirala stated that it was an 'understanding' and did not require two third approval by the joint sessions of parliament as stipulated in the constitution. But responding to a petition filed at the Supreme Court of Nepal, the apex court ruled it was a treaty and thus the Article 126 was attracted. So, the Tanakpur debacle led to the Mahakali Treaty, an integrated deal that included the Pancheshwar Multipurpose Project, with the water-storage capacity of 12.3 billion cubic metres and a 6,480 megawatt power plant.

After intense debate, the agreement was finally ratified on November 27, 1996, but deep disagreements led to the split of main opposition party—the UML (Unified Marxist–Leninist). The treaty stipulated that the Detailed Project Report (DPR) would be completed in six months, but more than 18 years after signing it, India and Nepal have failed to make significant progress in this direction. The debate generated by the treaty encompassed the whole spectrum of institutions including the court, parliament, political parties and the government. But nowhere was it played out more prominently than in the news media.

As explained earlier, the rise of professional media followed the restoration of democracy. The mass protests in the spring of 1990 itself had been organised in the wake of a sanction imposed by India in 1989. Apparently, New Delhi was unhappy with the King's overtures to Beijing. (This was seen as a punitive action against Nepal's purchase of some anti-aircraft guns from China). At that point of time, the regime had used the popular Radio Nepal to mobilise opinions against the Indian move.

The first generation of the reporters who covered this issue grew up during the Panchayat years. Moreover, the political landscape post-1990s was dominated by the Left parties who had inculcated the anti-India sentiment among its cadres and supporters. In addition to this, popular left periodicals including *Mulyankan* (now defunct) played key role in creating a discourse about the merits and demerits of the treaty and, thereby, helped build opinions. Left-leaning weeklies such as *Drishti*, *Jana Aastha*, *Budhabar* that were popular in those times extensively reported on the protests during the Supreme Court hearings.

Fast-forward to 2014: On September 5, Nepal and India signed Power Trade Agreement (PTA), which enables Nepal to export hydro-power to India. This deal was supposed to be signed during Indian Prime Minister Narendra Modi's visit to Nepal in August 2014. However, it got stuck because, according to local media, India's draft proposal included provisions that India could monopolise the hydro-power development in Nepal. Nepal does not want to give monopoly over its rivers to India as China is also interested in investing in hydro-power sector in Nepal.

A Power Trade Agreement that guarantees market for Nepal's hydro-power in India was long overdue. It would pave the way from realising Nepal's long-delayed hydro-power development. As Nepali officials were keen to sign the agreement, they might have gone ahead with the proposal which was not in Nepal's interest.

In late July 2014, Nepal's Energy Ministry sought suggestions from hydro-power experts and former energy ministers after India sent a proposal. A couple of ex-ministers shared the contents of the draft proposal with the Nepali media. The leak generated sharp criticism that some provisions were against Nepal's interests. This prompted the government to form a panel including lawmakers from the three major parties. Based on the panel's recommendations, Nepal forwarded another proposal to India.

On the PTA of Upper Karnali too, media played key role by publishing the stories about the benefits Nepal would make if the deal was struck. Similarly, the media also gave prominence to the voice that this was a great test if Nepal was to embark on harnessing its hydro-power resources. There were dissenting voices too, most prominently, of the hard-line Maoist faction, but in the face of growing support for the deal, which was backed by the media, the hardliners were forced to annul the protests.

Unlike in the mid-1990s, the Nepali newspapers covered the issue cautiously.[9] For example, *Kantipur Daily* invited experts and former government officials in its office complex and held a brainstorming session on the PTA. During Prime Minister Modi's visit to Nepal, the two countries agreed that the PTA would be signed within 45 days. This could have stirred up a hornets' nest in the polarised political landscape of Nepal. But the Investment Board Nepal, which provided technical expertise on the pact to the government, reached out to the news media and held discussions with editors and reporters on the proposal.[10] This helped them understand the issue better and counter the anti-deal narrative. As a result, the news on the PTA was published in the front pages. Editorials were written on why the deal was important for Nepal—should it develop and sell hydro-power.

Also, noteworthy was the fact that the news of the opposition to the deal was given less coverage. An alliance of 33 left and ethnic political parties (the CPN-Maoist (Communist Party of Nepal-Maoist), the splinter group is the biggest among these) had opposed the deal, threatening to launch protests against it. But they had to cancel the protests as the mood was overwhelmingly in support of the deal.

A Fulcrum of Debate

Over the years, particularly after King Gyanendra's takeover on February 1, 2005, New Delhi began to play an important role in resolving Nepal's then nine-year-old Maoist insurgency.[11] In November 2005, India mediated a deal between the Maoists and 7 political parties that were unsuccessfully agitating against the King's autocracy. The 12-point deal was a landmark pact that paved the way for the popular protests in the spring of 2006, helping end the insurgency and turning the country into a republic.

As India's role in Nepal's peace process grew, the news media began to devote attention on New Delhi's decisions that would have implications on Nepal. This was also when the Kantipur Publications set up its first bureau outside Nepal, having a permanent presence in New Delhi. So far, 4 senior reporters had their stints in New Delhi. Given the fraught relations between the two countries and the flow of people—from students to migrant workers, to patients seeking advanced medical treatment—to India from Nepal, the assignment is perhaps one of the toughest for Nepali journalists.[12] However, over the years, reporting from India has become more nuanced and in-depth, thanks to the experienced and well-trained journalists deployed south of the border. Not only New Delhi, but Beijing also is getting substantive media coverage in Nepal. Nepali media houses have yet to have a reporter based in China, but two leading dailies—*Kantipur* and *Nagarik* have their reporters in Hong Kong, who cover China as well. According to one of the reporters, an attempt to open a bureau in Beijing went unsuccessful.[13] In covering China, the two reporters not only focused on the bilateral ties, but also wrote about the Chinese Communist Party's national convention and other important issues. In recent years, China's engagement with Nepal has increased, which gets reflected in the news coverage.[14]

Research organisations and policy think tanks are vital to create a foreign policy discourse in any country. Both the non-governmental and government think tanks contribute a great deal to the discourse. These organisations carry out research on any particular topic related to the foreign policy and publish the findings. Such academic exercises are vital to the news media that is forever striving to get a new angle for a news story.

Nepal's Ministry of Foreign Affairs has its own Institute of Foreign Affairs (IFA). Founded in 1993 as a think tank to study Nepal's national interest and its relations with foreign countries, the IFA was reconstituted in 2012. It regularly holds seminars and meetings and publishes occasional reports.[15] The IFA is headed by an executive director, who is a political appointee. Over the years, the IFA has done little work and has been rather beset by political instability which prompted the change of guard at the IFA as well.

Academic think tanks, too, can contribute to the debate. In the past, Nepal had robust university-affiliated research organisations. Centre for Nepal and Asian Studies (CNAS) was once a premier think tank of Nepal. Hosted by the state-run Tribhuvan University, it published a journal, providing space for academic research. It did not cover foreign policy much, but it was an important initiative in the field of knowledge production. However, the Tribhuvan University itself was marred by politicisation, frequent transfers of the scholars and protests leading to the early demise of the think tank.

In such a situation, news media seems to be the only space for debates and discussions. The leading dailies publish op-ed from university professors and thinkers. These pages create important forum for debates, a fact reflected by its impact on the political leaders and policy makers. In most cases, politicos raise an issue in the parliament or in other forums once news media highlights it.[16]

Conclusion

Nepal has undergone a crucial phase of writing a constitution, a task that has prolonged, gnawing away at the vital post-war reconstruction and growth. As of now, Nepal's foreign policy has been based on United Nations Charter, Non-Aligned Movement and Panchsheel, the five-point principle. These were formulated during the 30-year Panchayat regime and the official policy has remained more or less the same.

In the first constituent assembly, the human rights and foreign affairs committee was most active, organising discussions on the contours of Nepal's foreign policy. The same committee of the second Constituent Assembly, however, has been lackadaisical.

Nepal's new media itself is hamstrung by lack of human resources, lack of training and exposure and lack of editorial priority vis-a-vis foreign affairs reporting. The reporters are not well-equipped to handle complex geopolitical matters that require understanding of cross-cutting issues. In recent years, the issue of trilateral cooperation between Nepal, India and China has gained traction. The notion is that the three countries should work together in areas including hydro-power, Buddha's birth place of Lumbini and vital infrastructure development such as roads, etc. Unfortunately, there has been no detailed in-depth report on the issue although it was the Nepali media that first raised the idea a few years ago. The extradition treaty, the border dispute, the collaboration between Nepali and Indian security officials, etc. hardly get the kind of significance and coverage it deserves.

Social media has become an important element of foreign policy today. But unlike in India, there is no foreign affairs spokesperson or minister disseminating information and important announcements through social media. While Nepali mandarins are slow to catch up with the social media, similar outreach by the former American ambassador had caught the limelight in Nepal a few years ago. Unlike in the United States, television and radio channels do not have in-house commentators in Nepal. Therefore, the popular channels fail to provide the larger picture. Everyone is reporting the same topic and there is lack of well-informed viewpoints or analysis.

To sum up, Nepali news media is well placed to play a prominent role in creating a vibrant discourse on its foreign policy. It has made some strides, but must make a leap from routine, event-based reporting to conducting in-depth reportage and publishing unconventional and forward-looking opinion pieces that help public understand the complex world of 21st century.

NOTES

1. Shital Niwas, now the office-cum-residence of the country's President, used to house the Ministry of Foreign Affairs (MFA) which moved to former Narayanhiti Palace in 2012.
2. Three dailies (two had English versions as well)—*Sagarmatha*, *Lokpatra* and *Space Time* folded in the late 1990s and early 2000s.
3. Author's interaction with a senior reporter of a leading Nepali-language daily.
4. Ibid.
5. Author's personal interaction.
6. For an excellent introduction to the Bhutanese refugee issue, see Michael Hutt's, "The Bhutanese Refugees: Between Verification, Repatriation and Royal Realpolitik", in *Peace and Democracy in South Asia*, 1 (1), January 2005.
7. Author's interaction with a former bureau chief.
8. For an excellent overview of the Mahakali Treaty, read Glen Hearns, "The Mahakali River Treaty: Applying a New Lens to Past Efforts for Future Success", *Natural Resources Security in South Asia: Nepal's Water*, February 12, 2006.
9. Akhilesh Upadhyay, "Price of Water", *The Kathmandu Post*, June 30, 2014, at http://kathmandupost.ekantipur.com/printedition/news/2014-06-29/price-of-water.html.
10. Author's interaction with the editor of a local daily.
11. Two recent books—Prashant Jha's, *Battles of the New Republic* and Sudheer Sharma's, *Prayogshala* (Laboratory) extensively document India's role in Nepal's political transition.
12. Author's interaction with a former New Delhi bureau chief of *Kantipur*.
13. Author's interaction. The reporter did not divulge the reason behind the failure.
14. Author's interaction with the editor of a daily newspaper.
15. For details see: Rishi Adhikari, Yam Prasad Chaulagain, Tika Prasad Dhakal and Shyam Bandhu Subedi, "From a Buffer Towards a Bridge: Nepal's New Foreign Policy Agenda", Institute of Foreign Affairs (IFA), Ministry of Foreign Affairs, Government of Nepal, December 2013, at http://ifa.org.np/wp-content/uploads/2014/01/From-a-Buffer-for-Mail.pdf.
16. Author's interaction with the editor of a daily newspaper.

ANNEXURE

Can Media Play a Role in Promoting Regional Understanding?

(Transcript of the Panel Discussion* held on October 29, 2014 at the 8th South Asia Dialogue)

The transcript of the Panel Discussion on the topic, "Can Media Play a Role in Promoting Regional Understanding?" is provided below. The panel discussion was held on October 29, 2014 as the final session of the Dialogue. The discussions in this session by experts from each of the countries in the region intended to reflect on key issues raised during the preceding sessions of the Dialogue. More importantly, the participants dwelt on the way the media can play an effective role in promoting regional understanding in South Asia. Several observations made during the course of panel discussion are being served here as recommendations from the dialogue participants which could provide the way forward for media in the region. Given the free flow of the discussions during this session and many useful points raised by both the speakers and participants, it was deemed necessary to carry a partially edited transcript of the session as an annexure to this volume. It may be read as a concluding part of this volume where all the contributors provide actionable inputs for the media and the governments of different states to act upon.

The session was chaired by Dr. Chandan Mitra, Hon'ble Member of the Parliament. The panel comprised some of the distinguished participants of the South Asia Dialogue 2014 and few eminent journalists. The country

*The transcript of the panel discussion has been edited and abridged to provide better clarity and understanding. However, best effort has been made not to tamper with the original remarks of the panellists in order to preserve the flow, fervour and essential arguments of their presentations.

perspectives on the subject were provided by Rasul Bakhsh Rais (Pakistan), Syed Badrul Ahsan (Bangladesh), Amrullah Saleh (Afghanistan), S.D. Muni (India), Ibrahim Waheed (Maldives), Myo Lwin (Myanmar), Kunda Dixit (Nepal), Dawa Penjor (Bhutan) and Dilrukshi Handunnetti (Sri Lanka). Perspectives from the media were shared by Suhasini Haidar, Diplomatic and Strategic Affairs Editor at *The Hindu* and Nitin Gokhale, Security and Strategic Affairs Editor, NDTV.

Brigadier Rumel Dahiya (Retd.): Ladies and gentlemen, I think we have had very useful discussions over the period of last two days and this last session is the crux of all that. Can the media really play a role in promoting regional understanding? I will be standing in for Dr. Chandan Mitra. We have a very distinguished panel. To start off the discussion, I shall request Nitin Gokhale to give his views on the subject.

Nitin Gokhale: The topic is "can media play a role in promoting understanding in South Asia region?" Certainly it can play a role. But whether it has played the role is the question, and unfortunately the answer is, to my mind, we have not played the role that we should. At least in India, I can say with honourable exceptions, we seem to know more about the US and perhaps the UK in the olden days than our neighbours. We do not know much about what is happening in Myanmar, what is Myanmar all about, what is Bangladesh, what is Bhutan, and rightly so, I think our friends from all these countries, I heard them sporadically yesterday and today, have that complaint or observation that India does not care about its neighbours until the prime minister goes there or until there is some trouble. For instance, on Bhutan you will only find headlines in Indian media when there is the kerosene subsidy being withdrawn or when the prime minister visits the country. We have not gone deeper into it. One reason, of course, in the current scenario, I think is the shrinking budgets and also the lack of understanding about the region itself in the newsrooms in general. We are overly obsessed with Pakistan and that is the reality. In the strategic community as well as in the newsrooms, even the smallest thing in Pakistan would be a headline in at least the English language media. China is just beginning to become a matter of interest to the Indian media. So we in South Asia know very little about each other really. We are trapped in stereotypes. When it comes to Bangladesh, it has to be either a fight between the two Begums or some influx stories from northeast when there is some trouble. About Bhutan, I think, friend Dawa Penjor has already mentioned what kind of stories come from Bhutan. So what should we do to overcome these shortcomings? I can go on and on about how illiterate we are about our neighbours and how we treat the countries around us without any information, without any insights. But all that has been said.

What I would suggest and as a matter of personal experience and personal visits that I have had to all these countries, be it Sri Lanka or to Bangladesh and reported from there, or from Bhutan or from Myanmar. Incidentally, I must tell my friends from Myanmar that I took a holiday in September (2014) to Myanmar and I really was besotted with that country. I had travelled from Tamu to Kalemyo earlier in 2004 by road. But I wanted to see the rest of the country. So I went to Bagan, I went to Inle, I went to Mandalay and to Yangon and I must say that this country is on the cusp of big changes and many congratulations for that. I am sure the media will also keep pace with what is happening around the country itself. Having said that, I think what we need to do to promote understanding about each other is to have more exchanges of media personnel amongst each other. I do not know whether the government will promote it or should the media organizations and media associations should do it—more exchanges, more visas freely available to media. I had trouble in getting, incidentally, a visa to Myanmar. They said I am sorry your passport says media and so we will have to refer it back to the headquarters. Fortunately, they did not find anything adverse and so they allowed me to go and we had a wonderful holiday there. But more visas are required, more freely and more frequently. Perhaps the other thing, apart from physical travel to each other's countries, is to have cross-posting of articles, a cross posting of views which Syed Badrul Ahsan used to do for *The Indian Express*. He writes or they take his articles or somebody else writes from here in other newspapers. Maybe just a free exchange, kind of reciprocal arrangement from various newspapers about each other. Maybe even share our stories on television, video stories or video footage. That we must do. Otherwise, what is happening is, we tend to be very episodic in our coverage about each other, be it Sri Lanka, be it Bangladesh, any of these countries.

Therefore, more exchanges, more dialogues like this, more information and maybe something that has an institutional backing, more organizations like IDSA and similar organizations and think-tanks in other countries may take the initiative to really have more exchanges and more visas and more cross-postings of articles. I remember, in the *Statesman*, in its heydays, used to have this pool of (it still has I think) articles coming from various newspapers in various countries. They all used to come and they used to print each other's article. So maybe that is one way of promoting understanding about each other and let us not get trapped into stereotypes. The jingoistic narrative that many speakers spoke about is a by-product of the closeness with which we work with foreign policy and defence establishments. I may be also guilty of that in some cases. But going beyond that, I think we need to promote our own understanding within the media circles to get neutral or maybe get the other side of the story rather than just sticking to one kind of a narrative from this side of the border criticising or trying to interfere, like somebody put it, into the foreign policy or into the national policy of a smaller country or a neighbour. To end, I will leave you with a thought that if we have more exchanges within ourselves, between ourselves and between newspapers and other media organizations, informally as well as through think-tanks and through governments, I think we would do ourselves a greater service to understand what the region is all about. We are in a very exciting region, volatile, of course, lots of problems, poverty stricken, all that we know, but we are also on the cusp of big changes in this Indian sub-continent and sometimes this term is also objected to, "Indian sub-continent", maybe South Asia is a better term. But certainly we need more exchanges and more views like this and more conferences like this.

Rasul Bakhsh Rais: I have been drafted to this role because of the absence of our compatriot Saleem Safi. On the subject, personally I am very pessimistic about media and I am looking at Pakistan in particular. Why I am pessimistic? I think we are putting too much hope on media that media alone can promote understanding among societies across the border, among citizens. Our emphasis should be somewhere on the state and those who hold powers. If they take right decisions in creating stable, peaceful, harmonious environment within the region, things will begin to change and I also think we are giving too much perceptual power to the media that media can do this, media can do that. There is only so much that the media can really, undermine peace or promote peace. It has limited capacity, a limited power because we are making an assumption that perhaps those who are anchors or the guests and the questions and what goes on in the media, the whole world is actually watching them in the first place and at the same time considers them very credible and believes in their story or the views that they express and also we are making a wrong assumption about the citizens, the audience, the viewers that they are perhaps not intelligent enough and they can be manipulated very easily by the false stories or by their views.

I think the important thing is if we have to consider the role of the media, the important thing is that the media, and particularly in the electronic media, the focus appears to be on the very young. It is just 10 or 15 years old and many very important positions are occupied by young journalists or by those who were never journalists in their last incarnation. So, they are there because of connections, they are there because they have been pushed into that. They are not there because they actually wanted it as a profession, in most of the cases. They have not come from the print media and I do not think many of them are really trained as media persons or journalists. Therefore, in a young media, where you are competing channels and they are dying for rating they will continue to say things and raise some of the issues. What many panellists across the South Asian countries have brought are very true in Pakistan that they want to say things which are sensational and where they demonize certain parties, certain individuals, certain countries and they will continue to do it. I think we have to bear with that and the immediate sense, I always advise people who are very unhappy, sad, and I detect the source of their unhappiness and I say that if you are reading newspapers, that if you are watching TV please stop doing it, read some book or take a hike, you will be a happy person. What we can actually do is, three things, I think are very important. One is that columnists in India who write about South Asian issues and even about India they should get published in Pakistani newspapers. They should get published in Sri Lankan newspapers and it is happening. There are two or three who write very frequently from India—Javed Naqvi and Praful Bidwai. There is another person who writes weekly column for the *Dawn* newspaper's economic section every week and that is about Indian economy. We are very much interested in what is happening in India. If there are more columnists writing in the print media and also if there are more Indians and Pakistanis who are not really shouted down, but that there is a very civilized exchange of ideas on talk shows in India where Pakistanis participate. I think we have to develop that culture of mutual respect. It does not happen on Pakistani television talk shows. I do not think it is happening on Indian television talk shows where you are shouted down and you do not see others' views being respected or the person at that end being respected. More people, more frequent participation on issues which divide us and where we have not only the representations of the governments but representations of the civil society, people who can stand out and express themselves freely and they are not attached or affiliated with any political party and speak with a spirit of harmony and goodness and proper understanding of others.

Second important thing is that this is a very unique kind of workshop or seminar or a conference. On a subject such as media promoting peace and harmony and understanding or regional stability, we need to have workshops that are attended and participated by and organized by media outlets, by media organizations. If you look here, there are of course journalists but I think such kind of workshops we need to hold across South Asian countries and there can be a major project. I think there will be a lot of donors from within the region and outside the region and with a focus of five years or ten years. At least in three to five years we are going to create a fraternity of journalists who are trained and who are oriented towards understanding other societies rather than saying things without knowing anything about that country. You are not a superficial expert but you generally understand that society and then you talk about that society and things happening in that society with some knowledge and with some understanding and understanding also means that you take other's point of view. You are sympathetic and you also look at their situation that how they feel about it.

Last thing that I would like to say is how to promote understanding, how not to promote misunderstanding. That is extremely important. I think first we have to prevent this negativity and I see a lot of negativity. I must say that the perception in Pakistan about Indian electronic media is that it is overly anti-Pakistan, it demonizes Pakistan and then it generates a debate amongst Pakistanis and the media that how jingoistic and how anti-Pakistan Indian media is and how you are so soft on India. You also get into that kind of fist fighting. So, I think how not to promote misunderstanding is quite important. It comes with professional integrity and responsibility and I assume that journalists in India and in Pakistan have that. I cannot doubt anybody's integrity or honesty. But with kind of conventional humanism and a spirit for humanity and for society and with responsibility that what we are saying does not hurt others but rather helps others. But it will take time to cultivate that culture in the media.

Syed Badrul Ahsan:I think over the last couple of days, yesterday and today, we have discussed a whole lot of issues relating to South Asia and as a beginning to my talk today, a small speech you might call it, the first thing I would like to say, I wish 1947 had not happened and another point I raised a few years ago, I came to Calcutta because I happen to have my in-laws there. So I asked this immigration official at Calcutta airport why I have to have a visa? You are a Bengali, I am a Bengali why do I have to get a visa to come to Calcutta and he also gave me a wonderful little smile. He says, *Dada*(in Bengali), in 1947 a little something happened and we left it at that. It is unfortunate that we happen to be part of a world which has got divided. When I come to Delhi I see the focus is always on India and Pakistan, naturally, because you have Punjab, Western Punjab and Eastern Punjab. When you go to Calcutta, the focus is on West Bengal and Bangladesh. So it is very uplifting when people talk about their commonalities. At the same time, it is very tragic when you remember what happened, the Great Calcutta killings in 1946, 1947, etc. But right now, at this point in time, the wonderful thing is in South Asia all of these countries represented here today have democracies. We do not have a single state, in Myanmar, Bangladesh, Pakistan these three states particularly, we do not have military rule. We have democracy. In Bangladesh, we have an elected government. India you had a wonderful election recently. In Bangladesh, we were very worried that Nawaz Sharif might be toppled by Imran Khan and Tahir-ul-Qadri. That has not happened. We are very happy. Whatever our political differences, ideological differences we would like to see democracy stay on in Pakistan, everywhere in fact. Having said that, about the role of the media, what can the media do? The media is not a state player. The media can only suggest, but on its own the media can come to terms with certain realities on the basis of pragmatism. Despite our political differences, our philosophical differences in all these three countries—in Pakistan you have a Muslim League government, in India you have a BJP government, and in Bangladesh we have putatively secular Awami League government. So apart from all that, in the media we need to be liberal, pragmatic and without prejudice as far as links among these countries in the region are concerned.

First of all, we have to come out of our narrow prejudices because the media in all these three countries must understand certain realities and country perspectives. When I write in Bangladesh for my newspaper about the Teesta waters issue as a journalist it should also be my job to understand the other point of view and similar is the case for a journalist in India particularly on bilateral issues. We have been using the term "jingoism" frequently. That keeps happening. I have friends in the Bangladesh media who will tell you that the Indians are taking away our water. They would not give us any water and then again these days, of course, the focus has shifted from a perceived hostility to Bangladesh's interests in Delhi to very clear hostilities in Calcutta because people thought Mamata Banerjee had come to power, she is a Bengali, she is a woman, we have a woman prime minister, we have all women in positions of power or out of power in Bangladesh. For us journalists, we should focus on these issues in a way that convinces you that we understand the other side of the issue too. I will not write about my interests only but let us have the other point of view also and it is very important that the media in our countries, our eight SAARC countries they should not be seen to be the voice of the establishment or the tool of government. That is a very dangerous thing to do. In Bangladesh, since I come from there, one of the cornerstone of our foreign policy which again, (personally to me and to a whole lot of other people) is pretty unrealistic. In the beginning it was given out that Bangladesh's foreign policy is based on the principle of friendship for all and malice towards none. The friendship for all, that is fine. You cannot be friendly with everybody but then you have to be pragmatic and malice, no malice at all. But foreign policy should be based on the questions of enlightened national self-interest. Beyond that, also look at the interests of the other country. Then there are certain areas within the region we have to be very clear about what the media can do. The state is there, the state will always be there. It is very often an obstructive factor. But then take the case of ULFA (United Liberation Front of Asom) leader Anoop Chetia. He has been in a Bangladeshi jail for years and he should have been handed over to India a long time ago. That has not been done. Why it has not been done is for the government to say but in the media we should be focusing on it here as well as in Bangladesh. Then this morning one of the latest news items is about the anti-Bangladesh activities, JMB (Jamaat-ul Mujahideen Bangladesh) activities in West Bengal.

These are again issues that are being focused on, which is a very good thing. Indian newspapers are carrying it and we are also sometimes reproduce excerpts from these Indian reports. The point here is fanaticism in all aspects, in all forms throughout the sub-continent, throughout South Asia must be confronted and we should call a spade a spade. Whenever I have visited India over the last three years, at seminars like this, I was asked a question. No one asked me this question here yesterday or today. But the question is: why is the Hindu population declining in Bangladesh, which is true. At the time of partition we were 35 per cent of the population in Bangladesh, then East Bengal or East Pakistan. It was 35 per cent. By the time 1971, the War of Liberation came around it had gone down to 29 per cent and today in independent Bangladesh where we were supposed to have a secular democracy, a country for all people, for all Bengalis we do not call ourselves a Muslim country, although, western ambassadors are sometimes very condescending. They try to portray us, they even tell us that we are happy that you are a moderate Muslim nation. No, we are not a moderate Muslim nation. We are not a Muslim nation at all. We are a Bengali nation. After that we are Muslims, Hindus, whatever. Today, the Hindu population has come down to less than 10 per cent. We need to talk about that. You talk about, you raised this question. Back home in Bangladesh we need to talk about this. But very few journalists have written about it. I do not know why? Whether they are kowtowing to the establishment? That is for them to deal with. Then the question of the influx of Bengalis into Assam. That is one area, one issue we have denied over the years. You cannot go on denying facts all your life. But thankfully the media, sections of the media in Bangladesh have picked up the subject and are actually acknowledging the fact that there has been an influx of Bengalis into Assam and problems are being created there.

Again, I have been talking about India-Pakistan. About Pakistan and Bangladesh obviously there are sensitivities involved here because of 1971. We were one country, same country. But then again you will notice that everywhere, anywhere you go, whenever a Bengali, a Bangladeshi and a Pakistani meet it is with a kind of weariness. They are very polite towards each other but that terrible legacy of 1971 is there. This is also an area where we could talk about things. For example, few years ago in 2010 if I remember, there was a discussion on Pakistani Geo Television channel. They called in Urdu *Sakuthe Dhaka* (the fall of Dhaka) and there were articles in Bangladesh's newspapers on how Bangladesh came into being, emerged in December, 1971. In Pakistani newspapers, it is exactly the opposite. So we need to talk about so that we can understand. Their sensitivities are there. I am not denying them. Our sensitivities are there. So all these things should be discussed openly by the media because the state will not discuss it. You may have diplomatic relations. We have our High Commissioner in Islamabad. Pakistan has its High Commissioner in Dhaka. But then the interaction is not there because of these sensitivities involved. So, we need to face the issues and the only way these issues can be faced is to talk about them openly in the media. And then again, the media in South Asia should also be focusing on another area which we seem to have missed out, the growing Chinese influence in the area. There are people in my country—in fact, one intellectual, he calls himself a leftist, but then last year he was on the side as a rightist who tried to topple the government. Farhab Majhar is his name. He once wrote an article that the only way for Bangladesh to confront India is to develop friendship with China. That sounded more like a throwback to the 1960s when during the war (1965 and 1971) Zulfikar Ali Bhutto went to China and sought Chinese help. They thought the Chinese would come and prevent the rise of Bangladesh.

Finally, we need to, as one of my friends pointed out here (Professor Rasul Bakhsh Rais), we need to have articles, we need to have comments from each other's country published in newspapers so that you have a country perspective of what is happening. Indian journalists do not know what is happening and last year at JNU I was asked to deliver a talk on Bangladesh's history since 1971 and I did and I was quite surprised. At at the end of the session, a lot of these young people and even their teachers said we did not know what has happened. We know what happened till 1971 or maybe up to 1975 when Sheikh Mujibur Rahman was assassinated but beyond that we do not know. So these media exchanges/articles/news items/other forms of communication specially steered by the media should be there so that these country perspectives are there. The last thing is, in journalism, let us have good cooperative journalism. We will promote our own interests, country interests but at the same time we refuse to be jingoistic, we will not have what we call adversarial journalism. So, cooperative enterprise is what we need at this point.

Amrullah Saleh:I borrow a quote from the presentation of Mr. Kunda Dixit yesterday. But I change it a little bit. He said, when and if the mainstream media lies, the social media comes to our rescue. That is very true and applicable to the situation in Afghanistan where monopoly of news has ended with the entry of Facebook, Twitter and other social media tools in Afghanistan and also monopoly of lie has ended because if they do lie, the social media tools will enable the population to break the news in their own way. Afghanistan, today has, with a population of in and around 25 million people, a Ministry of Communication of Afghanistan and they say they have sold about 16 million SIM cards and a big part of our population has access to means of communication.

Also, I borrow another quote from Lakshman Gunasekara from Sri Lanka who said there is mass communication and also there is segmentation and fragmentation of the communication and I call it community communication. So again, that applies very much to Afghanistan where national news is no longer the only news. We have sub-national news, we have provincial news, we have district news and if the national news does not appeal and or have relevance to the lives of communities at sub-national level, they ignore it. So, media in today's life in Afghanistan plays a very, very vital role and I do not want to repeat what I said yesterday. But in two areas the national news in Afghanistan is the most dominating—on the issue of security and foreign policy. So, Afghans across the country stick to the national narrative when it comes to foreign policy and when it comes to security and within those two themes—Taliban and Pakistan dominate our debate. Terrorism and Taliban and insurgency and sanctuaries across the border, they dominate our themes and roundtable discussions and talk shows, etc. As our distinguished Pakistani friends said yesterday, they have their own narrative and we have our own narrative. Since 1965, Kabul and Islamabad have many times issued joint communiques, statements. They have even signed memorandums of agreements trying to calm down the anti-this, anti-that propaganda or cool down the media against each other but it has not worked because media by itself is not a force to perpetuate either friendship or animosity. There has to be triggers. There has to be people at the decision making level to use the media as a tool to foster either friendship or other agenda. Despite the massive interaction between the two peoples, I totally echo what Pakistani participant Professor Rais said, we have tens of thousands of Afghans crossing the border, going to Pakistan but it does not change the perception. The perception is yes we do need Pakistan, yes, Pakistan needs us but the security problem remains the same.

Coming to India and this particular conference, what I observed since yesterday is India has gained a centrality in the perceptions and in reality in South Asia by virtue of its wealth, by virtue of its military power, by virtue of its need for energy. India cannot remain a status quo power. They have to have quest for friendship, they have to have quest for alliance and Afghanistan has signed a strategic partnership with India which envisions close cooperation in the area of defence, economy, energy, etc. India's entertainment industry in my country is very attractive. It is very popular (Indian cinema names and even people, in Afghanistan). But India's media is not parallel with India's entertainment industry in Afghanistan. We hardly hear deep analysis or news from Indian outlets about our country or the situation as a whole. As far as I remember, in the past several years there are a couple of NDTV documentaries on situation in Afghanistan, a few in-depth interviews with Afghan decision makers and policymakers. With all the knowledge that is in India we are not seeing that knowledge reflected in India's media about Afghanistan. We find Indian columnists, we find Indian writers and authors to be very, very well-informed. They have access to tens of thousands of Afghans who travel to India and many thousand Afghans study here today in Indian universities. But we hardly see a lot coming out in the print media or in TV. So that does not suit, it is not compatible with centrality of India's role in South Asia. While India is leading in so many other areas, when it comes to media and its focus on Afghanistan, it is lagging behind.

At the end I want to outline our expectation. What is our expectation? The expectation is if misunderstanding is a problem, if terrorism is a problem, if injustice of history is a problem and if we have other problems in terms of border crime and other things, we do not have a common counter narrative. Thus, there is need for such exchanges to take place more frequently and more regularly at strategic level. The aim should be, if possible, over the years, maybe in a decade time, the region should have a common strategic community who will have the same perspective, who will have shared the same views on challenges, on problems that we all face as people of this region—chiefly today, terrorism, militancy, sectarianism and exclusion. Some people call it rights of minorities, etc. We lack that type of, at least when it comes to the media, a visible and solid common narrative. Media is helping us in a lot of other ways in Afghanistan too. A month or so ago the Taliban spokesperson posted the Eid greeting of his leader Mullah Omar on his Twitter and he had forgotten to disable the location feature and it said Karachi which became a good news for all of us. They are using it. The other side is also using it. We are also using it and it has, as I said, for Afghanistan, our parliamentarians and our commentators they love to repeat a phrase. They say media is the fourth pillar of our state. It is so strong in Afghanistan that it is media a lot of times which brings accountability, which brings the truth to the surface. It has reached a threshold as far as the society is concerned that any type of political fluctuation in Afghanistan will find it extremely, extremely difficult to reverse the achievement that we have in the area of free media and private media.

Chandan Mitra: There are few small things that we tend to ignore and it is very right that the Indian media has not really made the kind of effort that it can and should be doing with regard to Afghanistan despite our long association, despite the fact that so many Afghan people are living in India or studying in India I think our lack of knowledge about modern Afghanistan is truly appalling and I thank you for reminding us of the importance of this.

S.D. Muni: I am not a media man. I do not know the intricacies of the industry or instrument, whatever you call it. But I will have some comments based largely on my impression of this conference and largely also on the broad subject, not very specific, not very nuanced. To begin with, the question of this session I think Nitin has beautifully answered—media can play a role, media must play a role, but media has not played a role—and I find that even in our conference there were absolutely fascinating presentations on media in South Asian countries, how they are doing, what their dynamics is. There were some peripheral comments on regional relations—India-Pakistan, India-Afghanistan, India-Bangladesh, India-Nepal—not on the region. We need not have anywhere a kind of a composite view of it. Why it happened I cannot say though the theme was very loud and clear as to media's role on regional understanding. I am a bit surprised by the absence of one name, by and large. It was uttered by one or two persons, the name is called SAFMA (South Asian Free Media Association) and Mr. Imtiaz Ahmed played a magnificent role along with many of the Indians to build in the media a huge constituency of South Asian regionalists. He held conferences. Even today, he has an excellent web page. SAFMA has an excellent president. These days Vinod I think. Even earlier, Mr. Katiyal was very deeply involved and nobody mentioned to this as to what is the role which SAFMA has played in promoting, not promoting, defining, and deciphering the regional perspective from media's point of view. Therefore, I was thinking for two days where does the problem lie, and to my mind, and I may be wrong, the problem lies in do we really have regional understanding as a theme in our priorities in terms of foreign policies, in terms of corporate interests, in terms of social sector whether we have a priority? I would say and I talk about India, let me not go into other countries, but I will have some reflection on that. India's policy did not evolve in a regional context. It evolved country to country. We had relations for a very, very long time. But India is changing and India started changing with the beginning of this century, certainly by 2004 even at the official level it was announced that India wants neighbours to share into its growth, its prosperity, and its dynamism, whatever else it is. So the policy has been changing and now the Indian policymakers and the best evidence was Prime Minister Modi's invite to his inauguration to all the South Asian countries and that India cannot do in the world without taking neighbours along. Therefore, the message now is loud and clear that India will have to be regional in the sense of taking the neighbours along while doing various other things individually. Do all other countries have the same feeling? Do they really want to relate, associate, integrate with India and we had this question in the previous session. Deepak

Adhikari very articulately talked about the anti-Indian nationalism in Nepal. If the countries have identified themselves as being distanced from India the question of promoting a push towards India faces lot of hurdles and problems at almost every level. Therefore, this is one of the major problems. Even when nationalism is not defined in Indian terms in the neighbourhood, I find that the political polarization in all the neighbouring countries is such where India is a major dividing factor. Some parties, some stakeholders would stand up and say we are with India, others would say no, no, and we are not with India because media functions on all these. That is why I am trying to identify that this is what it is there.

Look at the stakeholders. I said states are the principal stakeholders even in driving and moving media like on LoC (Line of Control) we have had debates or on Nepal whenever there is a controversy, we have a debate. Bangladesh we have a controversy we have a debate. One telephone call either from MEA or PMO to the Indian television channels, to the Indian media will do a lot, stir them up on that issue. Therefore, state is a major stakeholder in what policy has to be projected. The question arises that when a state is promoting regionalism, media will play a positive role. But in circumstances where state is not quite committed to it, will media stand up, and that is a major problem. I want to see media courage in such instances where the stakeholders are taking a line which is not in conformity with regional understanding, not in conformity with promoting or building regional understanding and this could be states, this could be corporate and business circles. I will give you an example how business circles are also interested when their interests converge with the regional understanding. Modi Xerox, in 1987, said please write an article on SAARC and see how it can be done. I said, how the hell you are interested and they said we want to sell Modi Xerox in China via Pakistan. So we want to see this trade relationship building up. So you have corporate interest, you have security establishments which have interests in building regional security at times and in not building regional security at times. So the question I am posing before media is how much courage we have to stand up at a time when the stakeholders, be it state, be it corporate sector, be it religious groups, be it other social constituencies when they said that look this is not the time or this is the time to abuse the neighbour or this is the time to ignore the regional constituencies. How much of this has been done?

My last point, very briefly, is that I find there is, yes, lot of corporatization of media has taken place and we have talked about it. But earlier, at least in India, there were editors—Giri Lal Jain, Nikhil Chakravarty, H.K. Dua, George Verghese, Inder Malhotra and others whom I know, Marvin de Silva, Khaled Ahmed (now in Pakistan), there may be many others– who had a certain emotional, certain ideological commitment to building regional understanding of various types. They worked individually with the countries, they worked at the regional context, after corporatization I do not see such blend of editors who are committed to this idea or who are inclined to this idea and who push. We had some of the observations on the commentaries to be written. Today, you write a commentary on the SAARC or regional understanding which is more positive and not very sensational nobody would carry it perhaps. They used to telephone people and ask them to write. This is how this whole thing was... This commercialization has done some positive things, no doubt. *Aman ki Asha* we talked about yesterday, or in case of Bangladesh the initiative which has been started. Not only that, I do not find why this phenomenon is not spreading like some of the Indians have invested in media in the neighbouring countries. *The Himalayan Times* which you have in Nepal. Why not more of this is taking place? Why not more of this is taking place from neighbours into India? We were only talking about stationing of the correspondents. Is it not amazing that India does not have media correspondents from all the neighbouring countries? Is it not amazing that India does not have correspondents in all the neighbouring countries? But this is a fact of life and unless people are moved into this direction we probably will have six other seminars on regional understanding, unless the stakeholders in regional understanding are stirred up, mobilized, if not pressurized, persuaded I do not think we will reach much of it and there is no point in further debating. Yes, we have found the limitations and faults of media but there are red lines beyond which media, with all kinds of commitment and dedication, would not be able to cross those red lines unless there are stakeholders pushing them.

Chandan Mitra: Professor Muni, as expected you have given a very down to earth assessment of what is wrong at the moment and what are the things actually perhaps we have slipped back over time in this matter. But I just wanted to bring to you one point that talking about correspondents in other countries, even in the region, there are so many restrictions on journalists, in their movements. So even if you post a correspondent how and where does he or she go? Therefore, ultimately what happens is that the temptation here of those who are footing the bill is that what is the point of sending a person permanently to a neighbouring country, paying in dollars and then hardly getting any news that is different from what the agencies have already filed? Hence, I think there is something we editors should apply their minds a little more and this is something which will have to happen from all sides of picture. If I think about correspondents from India to other SAARC countries and from other SAARC countries to India, actually in India there are hardly any restrictions on this. But in many of our neighbouring countries, unfortunately, there are restrictions. In India, yes, there are restrictions in one or two places but otherwise it is fairly free. We need to see how these restrictions can be eased so that we get the news from our own people rather than depending on western sources who are allowed fairly unfettered travel and we ultimately take those copies or those reports on television.

Ibrahim Waheed: I am just here on a learning curve. So let me share with you some of the things that I have learnt during this conference and thank you IDSA for the opportunity and as Brig. Rumel Dahiya said, sometimes commercial considerations cannot come in the way of peace in the region and I totally and wholeheartedly agree with you, sir, on that one. As our chief guest, the Hon'ble Minister did say the poor class now has aspirations and talking on that issue, all of us I think we watched the opening address on video, there was mention of newspapers turning into views papers and I am going to take that away with me because I think that opened up the door for perhaps looking at media from the side-lines, perhaps even from the bottom-up. As my honourable friend Pakistan, Rasul Bakhsh Rais, mentioned that Pakistani journalists often viewed the West as serving democracy when it serves its interests. The question that immediately rose up in my brain was this, but do we not all do that? All of us do that. Do we all not talk about democracy only when it suitably suits our needs? Could we ask ourselves this question when we write about something and that goes to this place where I would hesitate to go, but I think I should. Do we sometimes need to consider the quality of the journalists that we get and I will quote my friend Syed Badrul Ahsan, with your permission. Anyone who cannot get into diplomatic service, government service or academia, find themselves in journalism. That I believe is the truth and straight from a practitioner's mouth. Perhaps this is something we should take into consideration. Perhaps we are the *gurus* of everything. My friend Kunda Dixit from Nepal, I am not going to misquote you here, are journalists guilty of this, fear of inadvertently telling the truth. This is us speaking, if we are media people, about ourselves. Seriously, I do not consider myself a media person. I have delved in it. I still have my TV programme on Television Maldives. But that is another story. Lakshman Gunasekara, my friend, when he said that the product is the audience and it is sold to the advertisers—is that the truth, is that a home truth that we have to face? Let us assume for a moment that we are the readership. We are being sold to a bunch of capitalists out there to buy the media. Is that a home truth we have got to face, and then we have had this thing, throughout these two days we talked bilateral issues and very often we were talking about how we view each other and again I think I owe this one to Kaberi Gayen from Bangladesh who pointed this out. Our school kids, those in secondary school and up there, how do they see the rest of the world? How do the Bangladesh kids see India? How do they see the Maldives? Apparently, in Bangladesh they see the Maldives as a country with climate change problems and nothing else despite the fact that at any given point in time the Bangladesh expatriate labour population in the Maldives would sometimes equate the population of the country itself. Despite that the perception there is this, this is a country undergoing climate change. So is every other country, believe me. You see we come from a very, very small country. But what we have to realize at the end of the day here and this is a message going out to some of the bigger countries in this region, it just happens that the Maldives is also very strategically located right in the middle of the Indian Ocean and with the China equation coming up, I think it is time we sat up and paid more attention. Having said that, we also still say this, we play this card. Hey, we have got one vote in the UN and we can still play that card as well which also brings up this issue, have you heard of this that a little butterfly flapping its wing somewhere out there in the Amazonian jungle actually can set off chain of events which will eventually lead up to some sort of hurricane or something right up somewhere near Hong Kong. You have heard of that one, we have all heard of that. But my point here is this when we talk about role of media in promoting regional understanding in South Asia should we not address some of these questions that I have just told you about. Should we first look at ourselves, find out where we are coming from, who owns us, who drives us, who has got the yokes on us. Are we qualified to do this? Do we know everything about everywhere as we sometimes pretend to? Do we need to look at ourselves first or we kind of like some kind of aircraft where when passengers board they have no idea where they are going, they have no idea what the captain is up to. They do not even know if he is up there or is it more like commercial aircraft where you know where you are going, you get on board but you know the captain is sitting out there but most of the time the guy is not flying it, he is doing it autopilot. When you are landing at something like Male International Airport, short runway on its own little island you do not even touch the controls when you are landing. It is all instrument landing. Are we that? On autopilot all the time, subservient to the powers up there whom we do not even know who owns the aircraft or the airlines? Are we that or do we owe it to some sort of audience, hey, wait a minute, let us all sit up and look at this. Perhaps just like they said that someday the pen would go out of fashion. Just like they said that illuminated text written with quilt pens would go out of fashion when print media came out. Perhaps, it is time we sat up and thought. Media houses, all newspapers, TV channels, radio channels when are we going to face up to the reality that this thing called the internet has now put the ability for even the smallest man out there to set up his own blog and, believe me, there is a saying in the Maldives the fish go where the water is. Therefore, if we serve up the truth on a platter perhaps your customers will come to you. Please do sit up and listen—this is a huge guy from a small country talking. But maybe IDSA has got it right when you put the Maldivian flag up there on the top of the heap. So much for that when it came to your logo because at the end of the day the reality is this and this is where India got it right when it put it up on its insignia these words and this is the truth you will have to face it because sooner or later truth will have to prevail—*Satyamev Jayate*. Thank you very much.

Chandan Mitra: Sharp and incisive critique of the media and the need to turn the mirror inwards from time to time, to ask ourselves what we are doing, whether what we are doing is right, whether we are compelled to do certain things we ought not to be doing and so on. Of course, these are perennial questions which we have been debated and will continue to be debated I fear for a long, long time.

Myo Lwin: Actually, I do not have much to add to what has already been said. The media in Myanmar is still very young and we have the capacity problems and we have the new information access from the government and the stakeholders. So I would say that the media in Myanmar is still young and then talking about the regional understanding is, in my opinion it is a little more than what we can actually do. It is my own opinion for the media in Myanmar because we have been even trying to make our coverage's more and more professional. So, the media in Myanmar is still young and then the capacity building for the young journalists is an urgent requirement. What I would like to mention about the media owners is that they also need to run the business professionally, properly, in a profitable way. They have to make better judgment between the editorial policy and the commercial concerns and then they can do a better job. These are dual requirements if we could achieve in Myanmar, the role of media in fostering better understanding or promoting regional understanding in South Asia will be enhanced. Thank you very much.

Chandan Mitra: For the media that has only just emerged really in many senses in Myanmar and I am sure that neighbouring countries, including India which has a fairly developed media, would be able to welcome you in this capacity building effort.

Kunda Dixit: I am going to go ahead and completely contradict myself from what I said yesterday at my panel. I think we have been whining a lot about the media and we journalists have been whining a lot. We are complaining we do not have the attention span, we have the superficiality, and we are sensational. But that is the nature of the beast. We knew it when we joined the profession and we just have to work within those rules, try to change them if we can. We have to infiltrate the system. But it is not going to change on its own. So, coverage will be politically top heavy. It will be concentrated on the perimeter of the national interest. It will be governed by national interest. You cannot force a media in a country to go and be interested in some other part of the world where there is no strategic or economic interest.

That is the nature of the media. We smaller countries surrounding India should not be really complaining that India does not give us enough coverage. Of course, it would not. India is obsessed with its own domestic concerns and it is a huge country. South Asia is like a solar system I keep saying. India is the sun and we are the planets orbiting it. We are pulled by its gravitational tug, but we have our own little gravitational pulls as well. So why would Nepal get more coverage than it is already getting in the Indian media? It would if, as it is happening now, four or five large mega hydro projects that are funded or with Indian investment being built in Nepal come online in the next five years there is a lot of economic activity and trade and investment going on between India and Nepal then Nepal will be covered in the Indian media. It will happen automatically. But as things stand now, when things are so politically, economically stagnant, it is futile to complain that the Indian does not write about us.

And of course we also forget about our own domestic media's role in poisoning or worsening relations. I think if you read the Nepali language press, especially the political ones, you would have the impression that India and Nepal are actually at war or something, or that India is micro managing to such an extent Nepali politics that we have absolutely no say in it and this is not just detrimental to India-Nepal relations, it is detrimental to our own self-esteem. And I think a lesson learnt from all this is how Prime Minister Modi's visit to Nepal earlier this year managed to completely reboot the hard disk on India-Nepal relations and in just one speech or one visit how was this possible? I think it is a very interesting case study and some researchers maybe you should do it and maybe it can be replicated with other neighbours as well, is how you plan your interventions, your speeches to parliament, your spontaneous street walkabouts so that there is a perception that the prime minister of a neighbouring country is being overwhelmingly and spontaneously received. It may not be the truth. But that is the perception, and if TV, live TV can get this message out, both in the host country as well as in the country of the visitor then you create the perceptions. Someone in the earlier session talked about shaping the narrative. Well, Prime Minister Modi shaped the narrative proactively and not for us. He did it obviously for India's national interest. But we stand to benefit from it. So, as they say in public relations, perception matters more than reality and the perception is that India-Nepal relations is now back on an even keel, it is stable and it has got to the point where public opinion is so favourable to India at the moment that is politically untenable now for our leaders to succumb to the temptation of bashing India. So, India has turned from a bullying big brother to this benevolent *daju*, benevolent elder brother and the joke in Nepal after the visit was that if Modi ever stood for elections in Nepal we would probably vote for him. We have been discussing actually that the theme here in this session is how does media impact foreign policy? Actually, I think we should be asking how do foreign policymakers shape the media agenda? I think it is the other way round. For example, Professor Muni just said that he writes Op-eds. Lots of your ex-Generals and ex-diplomats write opinions in the papers and it is now social media, your political leaders Tweeting and Facebooking all the time. So it is not just us journalists who drive the content of media. We have to understand that. It is you. You are all part of media. You are all citizen journalists as well and you are shaping the agenda as well. It is not just us and so there is an equally important role for you to steer it towards a direction that is constructive and not warmongering and making thing worse.

In the end, I think it is all about what should be our priority. I think it is regional cooperation so we all benefit. Our country has development and economic parameters that are at sub-Saharan levels and there is absolutely no reason why we should be a locked into this politics that keeps us poor and unequal and unjust as societies. So regional cooperation is not just this goody-goody thing that you talk about at SAARC summits. It is actually an economic and political imperative and that is what it should be all about lifting the living standards of our peoples.

Suhasini Haidar: I have an apology to make which is that I am sorry I missed the last two days of your session. I really wish I had heard much more of the kind of views I have heard today and the other apology I want to make is in advance, because when many of us meet again for the SAARC summit in Kathmandu we are going to let you down once again. We are going to let down South Asia as an idea because it is going to be over-run by the immediate problems between India and Pakistan as several SAARC summits in the past have done. My apology is not going to change the situation there. I think the only thing that will change that situation is if leaders decide to actually take their roles of leadership a little more seriously and stop blaming the media for promoting or not promoting regional understanding because I as a member of the media do not really think it is my job. I do not think that I have a role either in trying to build peace or to go to war. That is not my role. My role is to take on my government, to ask questions about my region, to perhaps educate my readers and viewers about just what they are missing out by not being a part of perhaps a larger idea. But it is not my job to make peace, it is not my job to make love or war and that is something that we can always debate about. On the issue that the media does not take the government on when it comes to decision that do not promote regional understanding—I think every media house did take on Prime Minister Manmohan Singh when it came to his decision not to go to the Commonwealth last year in Sri Lanka. I think it made absolutely no difference to the powers that be and to the government what they said at that particular time and I think we have to understand the limitations of the media. What is the media's role? The media's role is to build those windows. We are not opening any doors. We are building windows for our readers and our viewers to understand the region we live in better. Yes, South Asia as a concept is only common sense. If you are talking about a market and you have a choice between a market of one billion people and a choice between a market of 1.5 billion people, it is common sense to say which one you would prefer. If you want to draw a pool of scientists and engineers is it better to draw from a pool of 5 million or is it better to draw from a pool of 8 million of the engineers that are known worldwide. You go to any university worldwide and the likelihood of a South Asian engineer, not just an Indian engineer being at the top of their class is quite high. It is common sense. If you want to manage a river is it better to cut up that river into a lot of little bits and behave as if rivers can actually be broken up and used upstream, downstream and measured by the litre or whatever, or is it better to actually try and jointly manage these resources to the best use for all your populations? I can go on with this list. The basic summation is that South Asia makes common sense. But it is not necessarily just the media's role or in fact the media's role at all to be able to in a way promote those better relations. What we can do is promote a greater understanding and I think we fail at that duty quite often. Why do we fail at that duty, and I am going to try and keep it short because I was actually hoping that we get a few questions in the session. To begin with, the fact on the ground is that linkages within South Asian are abysmal. Why did our Pakistani guests have to leave right now because there is only one flight between India and Pakistan actually? Delhi and Lahore, it is the PIA flight that goes twice a week and there is no Indian flight that flies to Pakistan at all, to any part of Pakistan. Delhi and Dhaka have got connected in the last few years but how many flights do we have to Myanmar, despite all the promises of the last few years? We still fly via Thailand to get into Nay Pyi Taw, as many of the journalists next month when they go for the East Asian Summit will. I can go on about the actual linkages. How many of us, we are privileged in a sense in South Asia because we have actually seen more than one South Asian country. But to most of the outside world you will not actually meet a lot of people who have been to Bangladesh, Indians who have been to Bangladesh or have been to Pakistan or been to Afghanistan or been to any of these other places. Perhaps, Sri Lanka and Nepal a little more because of tourism, but certainly not of the kind of numbers who might go to Singapore or Dubai or any of those other countries. The linkages are poor on the ground. The visas are always going to be an issue. They are more of an issue for South Asians than they are for other countries which again seems to defy common sense as far as I see.

I am very glad that Mr. Ahsan brought up the issue of history. We are all brought up with different histories. How is this possible? How is it possible that history has become so subjective that no two South Asian countries really have the same idea of their own histories when they look back? How far back do we go? Do we go to 1947, do we go to 1200? Do we go to the year B.C.? Is there a point at which we understand that there is a commonality and a shared history in South Asia that somehow we are missing out on because none of our history books seem to add up or match up if you were to put all of them into one room. And then, there are the internal pressures on the media which a lot of our participants have spoken about already, the pressure of the TRP, the pressure of the government, the pressure of a different form of government, sometimes a democracy which does not run as a democracy, sometimes it is a form of self-censorship. All of these are issues that we are all well aware of and each of us South Asian countries suffers from one or the other of them. But I think the largest problem is still the mind-set. We do not see ourselves as South Asians and we do not necessarily see better regional understanding as a given. It is all very well to say more Indian journalists should be read in Pakistan or Pakistani journalists should be read in India in times of peace. But where do they all disappear when things are not so peaceful? Why is it that for the past month very few Pakistani channels and very few Indian channels bother to bring on what we call the peaceniks, i.e. the non-warists or the anti-hawks. We do not. All channels run basically various shades of the same point of view which is that somehow or the other the sub-continent that has not solved one problem with war is somehow going to find that elusive solution in war. The problem is that we had a major national daily that actually is the country's leader put on its front page a story that began thus: *even as the guns were blazing at the LOC members of India and Pakistan's journalism and retired army personnel were actually meeting at a Track II summit in Dubai.* That was horror. My question to that and a member of your party once asked me that on a television chat was when do you expect us to speak. When the governments are speaking to each other! It is basically the mind-set and I do not want to make this about India and Pakistan because as I said we have already committed that we are going to disappoint you when we go to Kathmandu next month. But the truth is that we do not, we do not have that mind-set that will take us towards a South Asian destiny just yet.

Nitin I think, was speaking about the fact not just of attention span but the fact that we do not follow a story and I completely agree with Mr. Dixit when he says that Prime Minister Modi's speech in Kathmandu changed the entire atmosphere. It moved the temperature from minus something to a really warm point. But are we going to take that same amount of understanding a year down the line when those roads that have been promised to be built are not actually built, when the joint understanding between the two countries has not been taken. Are we going to ask our government are they going to go through by listing in parliament the understanding with Bangladesh when it comes to the land boundary agreement? The problem is that mind-set that we are still really thinking about our own countries. We are not thinking about a South Asian destiny, and finally, there is a sense that the media somehow should not just have a role as your subject suggests, in perhaps promoting regional understanding, but the media somehow should be actually the government of the countries. We are, each of us identified by the most establishment or extremist point of view in our countries. Years ago, I had this ridiculous situation in Pakistan when I went over to speak to some college students and we finished this and there was a Q&A session and the session seemed to be overrun completely by the story of a parrot and every one of those students over there wanted to ask me but *woh bechare tote ne kya kiya tha* in Hindi. They said what did that poor parrot do? I was completely flummoxed. I had no idea what they were talking about. It turned out, what they were talking about was a story they had seen on some Indian channel that had been picked up by all Pakistani channels and was running as a headline which essentially was about how a parrot which was the Indian equivalent of that octopus had picked Pakistan to win in the World Cup cricket that was being played between India and Pakistan. Pakistan lost but the parrot had its neck round and this somehow was the big story in Pakistan about India. I just said is this how you really think we are. But the truth is, yes. We judge each other by our most extremist and our most establishment positions and I think this idea of conflating the media constantly is what leads to what Mr. Dixit called this whining or self-flagellation because I think we have in South Asia a lot of media that we really should be very proud of. But we should not mistake that to mean that they can take on a role that frankly media should not be expected to take on. There is just so much that we should do.

Finally, I just want to end by saying, in this past few months we have been taken to the heights of optimism and the depths of despair when it comes to South Asia. We started this new government's rein with a wonderful South Asian moment. I am not sure how much of that we can salvage by the time we get to the actual SAARC summit in Kathmandu. But the truth is, it has to be beyond that. When India and Pakistan have issues at the LoC between each other, when they trade charges between each other, it does not behove the media of either country to ignore civilian deaths on the other side. It means that we have not moved in all these years of SAARC summits and all these years of conferences such as these to actually be able to see each other as humans and I will leave you with that last thought was given to me by a journalist I respect when he said that in times of conflict more than in other times we have to remember who we are and journalists have to remember that they are humans first, journalists next and citizens only last. Thanks a lot.

Dawa Penjor: I will be very short because a lot of what I would like to speak has been spoken by my predecessors and it makes my work much easy. But nevertheless, I would like to delve on some of the points that I have said earlier. One thing is how actually media can be responsible especially when we are talking about understanding South Asia. We have diverse perspective here on the forum as well where some feel that the media is not the sole agent or responsible agent that can bring change. But at the same time, there have been different thoughts where actually media can play such a role that if it is used in a negative way it can poison the minds of the society. So,how do we create that balance?

I believe we have a lot in commonality in South Asia. We have lot to harvest. History is what we are all bickering about, our past. We are still in the past, going on and again and again. I think the media has a role to shape the history that you want to handover to our future generations and I think that is very important. What is also important, is the present. Past, we learn from it, the mistakes that we have committed. That is why we know about history. We learn about history. That is the reason what we have to do. But the present is very important. At the same time, the present will determine our future. Therefore, I think the media plays a very crucial role in actually charting that discourse. It is the responsibility of our individual governments to give those policies, make those frameworks, build strategies but more importantly, to implement those actions where we can have better interactions, where our journalists from our neighbouring countries can come without visas, travel around freely so that we create more understanding on the region. I think that should begin from the government itself.

Secondly, I would like to share this with Professor Muni that actually I did talk a bit about SAFMA, the role of SAFMA in this regional understanding and actually how it can be harvested further. SAFMA has functioned well so far. But it has been modest. What it has done, tried to do in the past, with all the shortcomings, it has done its best. But this is not the point where it has to retire. If you look at the local chapters everywhere, the SAFMA is almost at a low key rate now because of financial constraints, because of individuals. Now how do we reinvent that? How do we give the re-emphasis on that regional body so that we do not have to create another one? We do not have to invent a new wheel. We have to just invest on the same wheel. I think it should be not just the government but individuals starting from the media houses, journalists who have to come together and further build that regional body. It also is the responsibility of the media—as media houses and as professionals how do you deliver and assure that at the end of the day it is not the story of the journalist or your face on the television or your picture on the newspapers that is important. It is the story of the people that is more important than anything else. If you want a society, an enlightened society who would work towards contributing peace and harmony, it is important that you reflect this story. It is not important as a journalist to show your face. Now with the innovation of technology and internet you want to showcase yourself more than the real stories and that has been what is happening.

Lastly, I would like to say, with internet and technology, we have immense potential where we can harvest. There have been initiatives like *Aman ki Asha*, *Maitri Bandhan* and *Romancing the Borders* on social media. Such activities should be harvested. We should encourage more of those projects, more of those prototypes so that we can increase our interaction, increase our understanding and see a better South Asian society. I would like to end by saying that it is not the responsibility of one individual or the media alone. It is a collective responsibility. So, today, can we pledge that when we go back as a journalist, as a policymaker, as someone, as a family member, as a father, as a mother that you in a way share to you near and dear ones, at the same time, share through your channels, through your print media, a better understanding of South Asia. And also the fact, I believe change begins with oneself and only then you can see the change in others.

Chandan Mitra: It is a very important element in the discussion today, the element of sensitivity and emotion. Without sensitivity and emotion, a complex problem of this kind that we are discussing cannot be resolved. We cannot really move forward unless we have a commitment and passion towards it.

Dilrukshi Handunnetti: There was a mention of corporate enterprise—media being a corporate enterprise. Clearly, there is no magic formula. If not, we would not have had this discussion for one and a half days and still come up with conclusions that might even help us move forward perhaps. What I want to do is just give, in three bullet points, what I may want to suggest and I speak as someone who has worked in the region, across the region for the past 20 years and I think it has been an absolute privilege to be working in South Asia. So, primarily though I work in a national context, I consider myself a South Asian journalist. I have even worked in Myanmar. Hence, it is a privilege position to be in. Three things I would like to mention would be a couple of ideas for the region, the regional bodies some of which has already been mentioned and the state itself and two other ideas for the industry in our respective countries because individual practitioners work within those parameters within our countries, within our regions, within the industry.

The first idea is about SAARC. Already the role of SAFMA has been mentioned whether it has delivered, whether it has been effective enough, etc., SAFMA being associated to some extent with SAARC. But whether SAARC has been an enabling body to the extent that media has been used? I do not like the word "tool" and "instrument" which was discussed extensively in the morning, not to call media a tool or an instrument but I would like convey some ideas on how to build regional understanding? So can that be an idea that we want to take home, a role that SAARC can play to promote regional understanding using media as a vehicle. Of course, about regional connectivity, lot of us who are here had to go because there are flight issues and then the visa regimes. I am coming back to India within these two weeks. I will be here thrice. So then my multiple visas are not granted because my passport says I am a journalist. So issues like that. There was supposed to be something for SAARC journalists and there was a limitation on the number of visas that they were issuing to SAARC journalists. Things like that can facilitate us because there is nothing like going to a place, trying to work from there. If I sit here and try to write a story on Myanmar my understanding is going to be completely skewed. But it is very different when I work there, sit there and work with local journalists and it enhances my understanding and I do not think that anything can replace the experience of working in a place.

Some of the regional bodies, SAFMA is only one thing that I want to mention. But beyond that, there are different things because we are fortunately living in this age where there is lot of technology and we are using the new media in a big way. Also, there are platforms which are virtual. Dawa Penjor just touched upon it. I just want to elaborate a little more because there are platforms which are South Asian, which are online, and necessarily there are no physical infrastructure per se. All of us can look at the nexus approach than the silo approach of looking at other countries. Our country specific issues are very important and country specific reporting analysis is very important. But beyond that, there is that nexus how would I report on India and Nepal and what things would connect me to those countries and the commonalities. There is a lot that we can do better and I speak as someone who has done this to some extent, modestly, because there are portals that are for South Asia. There are publications, there are online platforms which promote this kind of content generation and I know some of you contribute to that. I am talking of a simple journalistic practice that can help us move forward. That will also help us go beyond that portrayal of South Asia as diverse, volatile place and a troubled area. Of course, we are. We have our multiple issues but beyond that, there are lots of things that can help us go beyond the biases, go beyond the narrow politics and reach a level of understanding and the good news is that it is actually happening. Yesterday, I think there was somebody, I think Smruti Pattanaik mentioned, that okay we have this great South Asian dialogue but then we also have to put our own content out. There is an issue about the industry practitioners and do we look at all this information, this knowledge that is available. Do we look at it and do we try to seek and absorb something from it?

The last one I want to mention is about, again, the industry and the market. Believe me, South Asia is a huge market, not just India and Pakistan—content that can be sold to Al Jazeera. But there are lots of other stories from climate change to industry to economics that you can actually practically share and there is a little bit of trans-boundary reporting that is happening. So there are reporters, journalists, analysts working in different countries, working on the same issue. Can we practically share that, have an exchange where those ideas, what we produce, our content can be shared and published across those countries so that we understand, that I will understand Bhutan better and someone will understand Sri Lanka better instead of just giving out that very contentious story—the political stories tend to be very skewed and contentious but there is life beyond that too. There are issues. For example, we are affected by climate change in different ways. No matter what our politics would be, we are affected and that is something that we need to deal with and the last one is for the journalists, the practitioners because I spoke about the region and the state as well as the industry. There is a market and we need to understand that market dynamics and cater to that because, as everyone has been saying since morning, if we do not understand the market you cannot put your content out and there is a problem. The individual practitioners can actually influence in-house policies and practices and this again I speak as someone who has done it because I work for a newspaper that has a South Asia page and probably the only one in Sri Lanka that has a South Asia page—and the market understanding is that particular content is read better, people respond to it which means people like those stories and that means there is hope.

Chandan Mitra: I must thank all the participants and speakers because there was a danger that we would slip into lot of the usual homilies and the same points would get repeated over and over again. But I am very glad that every participant has made an attempt to give something new in his or her presentation and I think when this is compiled, you will find a lot of points emerging from this which deserve to be taken up in much greater detail as we go along. The problem of being chairman is that by the time the chairman's time comes to sum up or say something, the time is up. I will not take up or use my prerogative to say anything except one issue which I want to flag and this is going to actually, I fear, stay with us for many, many years to come. We have, today and generally, whenever we talk all tend to praise the role of the social media and the new channels of communication. I myself also mentioned that it has made journalists of all of us and it is a good thing. But there is a downside to it. The downside is the misuse of the social media to foment discord and spread disinformation. South Asia, we all know, is a very complex society with lot of strife that goes on in almost all countries. Barring one or two, South Asia is, as somebody said, dangerous place. But more than dangerous place, it is a place of great deal of struggles and contention that are going on here and are likely to go on for few more decades. In this context, when there is spread of disinformation, as was done two years ago with regard to false photos being put up in a communally surcharged situation, they were put up from one country, flowed into another country, created ethnic situation in India, and this can be replicated. Examples can be replicated. I do not want to cite, I am sure you all know what I am talking about and this may happen again. As journalists, it is our responsibility to counter this kind of disinformation and the misuse of social media. We must be proactive as and when it happens. It has not happened too many times, but we have to always keep that caveat in mind. The social media is helping us, it is creating greater understanding, but there is a danger that it may also create very deep-rooted misunderstandings or promote further misunderstanding. As journalists, we should all be aware of that. I think that is one issue to be flagged. All that remains is to thank you all. I personally enjoyed this discussion. Thank you.

Index